TRUE BOO

TRUE BOO

Gator Catchin', Orangutan Boxin',
and My Wild Ride to the PGA Tour

BOO WEEKLEY

with

PAUL BROWN

St. Martin's Press ⋈ New York

www.stmartins.com

Library of Congress Cataloging-in-Publication Data

Weekley, Boo.
    True boo : gator catchin', orangutan boxin', and my wild ride to the
PGA tour / Boo Weekley with Paul Brown.—1st ed.
        p. cm.
    ISBN 978-0-312-61729-5
    1. Weekley, Boo.   2. Golfers—United States—Biography.
3. Golfers—United States—Anecdotes.   4. PGA Tour (Association)—
Anecdotes.   I. Brown, Paul T.   II. Title.
    GV964.W44A3 2011
    796.352092—dc22
    [B]
                                                          2010042631

First Edition: March 2011

10   9   8   7   6   5   4   3   2   1

This book is dedicated to my grandparents, the Weekleys and the Kirbys. To my mom, Patsy, and dad, Tom, and my sister, Ali. To my wife, Karyn, and my two sons, Parker and Aiden. To all of my friends. And of course, to my devoted fans.

CONTENTS

FOREWORD

When Boo called asking if I would be interested in being his teammate for the 2007 World Cup in China, I was thrilled. Of course my answer was yes. The chance of a lifetime, I reasoned. To go to China with Boo—my dear, close (and crazy) friend—well, I knew anything could happen. I mean, here were two guys from Milton, Florida, meeting up in China to take on the world in a little game called golf. What were the odds of that happening? Then again, what were the odds of Team U.S.A. winning the Ryder Cup in 2008? Or of Boo Weekley writing a book and getting it published? If there is one thing you should know about Boo, it is that when he is up against the odds, the odds do not stand a chance. Neither did China.

Not only was that trip to China a blast, but it helped me gain a whole new respect for Boo. I knew he was a good golfer, because I had seen him play all my life—from the ninth grade on, I watched him play and develop. The whole experience of the minitours, the Nationwide Tour, and his PGA career—well, it all reached its pinnacle at the 2007 World Cup.

As close as I have been to Boo for years, I did not know how good he really was until then. I had taken his talent for granted. Honestly, Boo carried my butt for three straight days in China. He played the most amazing golf I had ever seen up close. I left that tournament with a renewed appreciation for his talents and abilities. I had never seen any golfer, not one, play as well as Boo played during those three days.

I have been paired with and have played with the best players in the world for the past eight to nine years. I have played with Tiger, Phil, Ernie, you name them. Still, I have never seen better golf played than the golf Boo played right there in front of me during the World Cup.

Let me give you an example. In the alternate shot play—I think it was hole 12—Boo had the second shot, an iron shot. I looked at it from my point of view—thinking what I would do with the shot—and figured I would lay it up left of the pin at about 30 feet, with an outside chance at a birdie, and be happy to make par. Well, Boo took dead aim at the pin and let it fly. We could not see it when it hit the green, but the Chinese crowd around the hole went crazy, doing their version of "Boooooo." Boo holed it! He took the shot, and he holed it. Like I said, I would not even have taken a crack at the pin.

Here is another one. On the last hole of the tournament, we had to make birdie to force a playoff. I actually hit a pretty good drive. Then Boo took his 8-iron and hit the most beautiful shot I had ever seen, right in there at 8 feet, which allowed me to make the putt and push it to a playoff. Then, in the playoff, he did it again, this time leaving me about 10 feet to the hole. Boo made so many amazing shots during that tournament that I looked at myself and thought, *I just do not have that.* He was simply incredible, and he made it look so easy. It really opened my eyes to how good he really is. Also, it was ironic that it was happening in China, which is often called a sleeping giant, because I could tell a true sleeping giant had awakened and that Boo was going to be hell on the golf course for a long time to come.

On the lighter side, I was with Boo later in the media room, too. Now, historically the British media are the harshest critics, but let me tell you, the British journalists there that day absolutely fell in love with Boo. It was the ol' Boo charm—Boo just being Boo as only Boo can be. To watch members of the media cracking up as Boo told of his experiences in China was a rare treat, and a memory I will always cherish. There was a smile on my face the whole time, as I tried not to burst into laughter. It was hilarious watching our Chinese interpreter struggling to translate Boo's lingo. It was better than any movie I had ever seen, that is for sure.

As good and as comical as Boo was at the 2007 World Cup, he was really just warming up for another Cup . . . During the 2008 Ryder Cup, I was playing in the Viking Classic in Madison, Mississippi. I have lots of family close by, in Louisiana, so my mom, grandparents, and an aunt and uncle were there to watch me compete. Still, they soon turned into part of the "Boo Crew." And Boo was not even there.

We had all been watching Boo play lights-out in the Ryder Cup on TV. I finished my round early on Sunday and had just sat down in the family dining area with my face right in front of the TV when Boo teed off on the 1st hole and— what did we see? We saw a guy straddle his driver and ride it down the fairway, whipping it back and forth like a big kid having fun playing Cowboys & Indians. We all looked at each other in disbelief, then started laughing in unison. None of us had seen that one coming, but soon we all had expressions that said, "Well, that is about right."

Not only was Boo riding his club like a horse—in the Ryder Cup, no less—but he was doing it wearing white socks with black pants. Only Boo could have pulled that off. His clowning around could not have been scripted any better, and really, I think that is because it was not scripted at all. It was just Boo being himself. I think that is why, for the bunch of us who know him intimately and love him to death, it was a special moment. Boo had brought a sense of levity to golf that no one else could have. He truly is one of a kind.

He is not just a funny guy, though, and that is the best part. Yes, he made us all laugh that day, but then to sit there and watch him play some of the best golf I had ever seen anybody play . . . man, it took me back to my time as his teammate in China. Boo has the ability to play with anybody in the world when he wants to. As I said, I have seen him up close and personal, so I know.

As good as Boo is at golf, though, he is equally adept at hunting and fishing. I recall a time when I went deer hunting with him. He walked me to a stand, a place I had never been, and I asked him, "Boo, what are you going to do?" He said, "I'm just gonna walk." Then he took off, and I sat in that stand for four hours and did not see a single deer. I did hear a shot, about an hour before Boo came back to show me the way out. He asked if I had seen anything, and I reported, as I always seem to do when hunting with Boo, that not a single deer had come near my stand. I asked if he had seen anything, and of course, he had killed a nice buck. It is the same when we go fishing. I will catch one little something, and Boo will reel in fish after fish. That is just Boo.

Boo was always really, really talented. I mean, really talented. Back on the minitours, when Boo got comfortable with himself, he went from missing cuts to winning almost every single week. I was privileged to have a front-row seat for that progression, but sometimes I think it was not a progression at all. It was just Boo finally being unleashed. As I said, a sleeping giant.

When Boo regained his PGA card in 2007, he was a completely different player. It was not as if he had just learned how to play golf, however. I think we were all just finally seeing the true Boo. I was lucky enough to be paired with him when he made his only hole in one on tour, at the Viking in 2007.

He had the belief again at that point. His mind matched up with his talent, and that makes a guy like Boo very dangerous. He shocked many people, but I was not one of them. I already knew what Boo could do.

At the 2007 Verizon Heritage, which Boo won, I had finished my round and was in the locker room watching him on TV. I badly wanted to go out to the 18th green and watch, but I was too nervous to go see it in person. I was more nervous watching the end of that tournament, pulling for Boo to win, than I have ever been during any of my own wins. Then, when he chipped it in, then chipped it in again, it was all I could do to contain myself in that locker room full of grown men and not jump right out of my skin. When Boo wraps his brain around the fact that he is just plain good, he is hard to beat.

It is difficult for some people who know both of us to understand how Boo and I can be such close friends, because we are so different. I cannot speak for Boo, but let me say that I have remained his close friend because when we are together, he adds life to me. A little like oil and vinegar, I suppose, but we share a passion for many things, too. We grew up as brothers, and to this day he is as close as I have to a brother. I am a much more fulfilled person knowing Boo and having spent so much time with him.

This book is your chance to spend a little time with Boo, too. I am very happy for you that you get to experience *True Boo*. I know exactly what you are getting into. If you get from this book even a fraction of what I have gotten from Boo, then you will have gotten far more than your money's worth.

—HEATH SLOCUM

PREFACE

Like most golf fans and sports enthusiasts, I was captivated by the story line of Team U.S.A. soundly hammering the European team in the 2008 Ryder Cup at Valhalla Golf Club in Louisville, Kentucky. While I was watching accounts of the event on TV, video footage of an American player riding his driver, whipping it like a Thoroughbred racehorse and galloping down the fairway, played repeatedly. I was awestruck by what was taking place. I couldn't get enough. The huge throng of fans cheered wildly as this guy dumped typical golf decorum and held nothing back—just having fun and being himself. Enter Boo Weekley, the newest icon in American golf.

"I felt like I just had to do it to loosen it up a little bit," Boo said about his antics during the Ryder Cup. ". . . It's just my nature to be a little goofy anyway."

That was it for me. I became a Boo fan right then and there. *Now, that's what golf needs!* I thought. Well, that's exactly what golf got.

After Boo Weekley and Team U.S.A. beat the odds and won the Ryder Cup, I watched on TV as a celebration unfolded unlike any this country had seen in years. Not one related to golf, anyway. Then I learned just how big a role Boo had played in this great victory for the United States.

The Ryder Cup propelled Boo to new heights in his golfing career. His cheerleading to get the crowd involved led to "Booing" from the gallery, which firmly placed his name forevermore in the history of the Ryder Cup and U.S. golf. Besides all the great memories of fun, victory, and celebration, Boo generously gave us a new word during that tournament to add to the English language: "compatibate." (It means to "gel" with teammates.) Fans also got a glimpse of the unusually expressive side of Boo, such as when he compared his fellow rookie teammates to a pack of hunting dogs, "It's like getting a new pack of hounds when we were growing up and going deer hunting. You don't know what kind of dogs you've got until you run 'em, so let's run 'em, and we'll see."

Few would question that Boo's one of the most interesting and charismatic figures on the PGA Tour. Many consider him second in popularity only to Tiger Woods (and perhaps even that gap is closing). He's undoubtedly one of the Tour's biggest draws, attracting huge galleries that boisterously "Boooooo" at every opportunity. His eccentric, down-home country humor, fun-loving attitude, and Yogi Berra–like quips set him apart from other fan favorites on the Tour. In fact, Boo's been called "Gomer Pyle with a dip" and "golf's answer to Forrest Gump." Media attempts to describe his unpretentious and quirky personality aside, Boo Weekley can really play the game of golf. He proved this to everyone with his breakout performance at the 2008 Ryder Cup—going

2-0-1 in his three matches—and his back-to-back Verizon Heritage wins.

Boo and I didn't meet on a golf course, at a clubhouse, or in a media room. Fittingly, we met at a deer camp outside Pittsfield, Illinois, in the heart of Pike County, arguably the hottest whitetail deer hunting area in the country. It was 2008, and I'd already agreed to collaborate with Boo on this book chronicling his ride to the PGA Tour, although I'd not met the man himself. A mutual friend, Ronnie "Cuz" Strickland, senior vice president of Haas Outdoors/Mossy Oak, hooked us up. Cuz twisted Boo's arm— it didn't take much—and got Boo to fly to Illinois for a primitive-weapons deer hunt. Cuz and his crew were there to tape hunts for future airing on Mossy Oak's many television programs.

One of Cuz's cameramen had come down with strep throat and couldn't make the trip. Cuz asked if I'd run the camera for Boo's hunt the next morning, suggesting that this would be a great way for me to get to know Boo. I jumped at the chance.

I'd seen Boo on *The Tonight Show with Jay Leno* and had gotten a hint of his mischievous side and wonderful sense of humor, but it wasn't until I met him in person that I fully appreciated his character. Flashing his megawatt smile, addressing me as Mr. Paul, and answering questions with "yes sir" and "no sir," Boo made an immediate and indelible impression on this fellow southerner.

As we talked, I discovered that Boo's quick wit and his love of life, people, and country harmonized with his behavior. The man is as country as cornbread, and there's absolutely no pretense about him. Literally, what you see is what you get—and let me assure you, what I saw then is exactly the same Boo you're getting in this book.

At 5:30 A.M. Boo and I headed out for our hunt and were dropped off at a shooting tower reaching some 30 feet into the sky. With the ladder swaying and wobbling with each step, we slowly climbed the rickety stand and crammed ourselves, our guns, camera, and tripod into the tiny 4-foot-square homemade enclosure.

Cuz had been right. Four hours later, I had a deeper sense of the true Boo. His straight-shooting country charisma and philosophy of life just didn't fit the stereotypical image of a pro golfer. Boo's no country-clubber. Up there in those trees that day, I found a humble person who refuses to wear the "celebrity" moniker, no matter how much others think he deserves it. No, in Boo I discovered a simple, people-loving man who tries to find the good in everyone. He's as tough as a Tennessee mule, yet as soft as Mississippi Delta cotton. Oh, and let me tell you, he can dress a deer better than most butchers and has as many ways to cook venison as Forrest Gump's friend Bubba had to prepare shrimp.

As with Gump's box-of-chocolates philosophy, I wasn't sure what I'd get from Boo when the time came to sit down with a tape recorder and start asking him questions. Would I pull out an ooey-gooey-chewy piece, a plain milk chocolate, a molasses-coated hard heart, or a dark-chocolate nut cluster? Well, I got all of that and more. During thirtysomething hours of interviews, held in four different states, Boo recounted his story with refreshing candor, exposing his emotions and addressing his fears. Just as he was at the Ryder Cup, Boo was himself during our interviews: holding nothing back.

I was so enthralled by his stories of misadventures I hardly noticed how much he butchered the King's English. Or that he used way too many double and triple negatives. It's just part of who he is, and it doesn't take long to get used to. Besides, he's really no different from the poet Chaucer ("He never yet no vileynye ne sayde"), the Rolling Stones ("I can't get no satisfaction"), or Pink Floyd ("We don't need no education / we don't need no thought control"). It matters less how a man talks and more how many people are listening to him—and let's be honest, Boo isn't short on listeners.

Thanks to his solid play, Boo has plenty of company on the golf course, attracting quite a following of devoted fans. It's his life outside of golf, however, that has captured the hearts and minds of most fans. He's passionate about the outdoors, specifically hunting and fishing. Those who share that passion see him as "just one of the guys," and they understand what he means when he says, "If it was up to me, I'd rather hunt and fish, but golf is where I make my living." As much as he cuts up, Boo takes his God-given talent seriously and gives his all on the course. He fully realizes that God has blessed him with the ability to play golf.

Above all, though, he's a family man through and through. With Boo, it's not all about Boo; "selfishness" is not in his lexicon. He knows he has responsibilities as a husband and a father, and that's the most important thing to him. One of my rewards in this joint effort was the opportunity to get to know Boo's close-knit, loving family. I quickly understood his devotion to his kin. They took me in right away as a member of the "Boo Crew," allowed me to walk 72 holes with them several times, and fed me more Boo stories than could possibility be included in these limited pages. I can honestly say that getting to know Boo, his family, friends, and fans; following him on tour; and going hunting and fishing with him in the process of helping with this book has enhanced my life immeasurably.

Boo Weekley is colorful, energetic, and obsessed with his loves: golf, hunting, fishing, and family. His cavalier approach to golf etiquette and his unshaven, slapdash appearance have brought criticism from some golf purists. To Boo, however, the arm waving, fist pumping, and snuff dipping are all part of his game. Moreover, his outfit of sneakers and camouflage rain pants is his trademark. Boo is Boo, bottom line. As I said, what you see is what you get.

You'd have to go back nearly fifty years to find a personality that matches Boo's. Not since the sensible insight of World Golf Hall of Famer Slammin' Sammy Snead has there been a character of Boo Weekley's stature. Slammer once said, "The only reason I played golf was so that I could afford to go hunting and fishing." Doesn't that sound familiar? He took the words right out of Boo's mouth. Or maybe it was the other way around. Either way, talk about kindred spirits!

Boo's perspective on life in general is refreshing, and his straightforward insights into professional golf are inspirational. He's a living testament to the power of the human spirit and the strength that comes through a trusting faith. In short, Boo's the man.

Let's face it, not even Walt Disney or Hanna-Barbera could've drawn a character as colorful as Boo Weekley. I'm sure you'll agree after getting to know him a little better in the pages of this book. Just one warning: Buckle up!

—PAUL BROWN

TRUE BOO

1 I AM WHAT I AM

Hey, thanks for picking up this book. You know, it could've been titled *True Thomas Brent,* written by Thomas Brent Weekley. That's my real name. If it were, though, you probably wouldn't have picked it up, 'cause you know me as Boo. I've been going by Boo for so long that it almost doesn't seem like a nickname anymore. They've been calling me that since back in the day in Jay, Florida, population 687, give or take a few, depending on the day. You'll have to keep reading to find out how I started going by Boo, but let me just say it's been a good name for me as a professional golfer. It's sorta nice 'cause it doesn't really matter if I flub a chip shot or sink a 30-foot putt—the crowd always has the same reaction. They "Boooooo" me.

Seriously, though, there must be something in the water down there in the panhandle of Florida, where I come from, and I ain't talking about no oil. That's a whole different story, and I probably shouldn't get started on that. Nah, I'm talking about something else in the water. Some sort of magic golf potion or something, 'cause little East Milton High School down there produced three pro golfers who currently play on the PGA Tour. Heath Slocum, Bubba Watson, and I all come from that little school. Oh, and all of us have won at least one championship on the Tour. Like I said, magic golf potion.

Pro golfer or not, though, I sometimes have trouble finding my place in the world of PGA golf. I'll get into all of that more in the pages ahead, but let's just say now that I've been called things like "a nobody from nowhere" and the "Crocodile Dundee of Golf." Maybe they call me that because they think I act like or live like the *Crocodile Dundee* character, or maybe it's because they think I'm out of my element in the world of golf (like Crocodile Dundee was out of his element in the big city). Either way, it's pretty clear I don't fit the mold of a PGA star. In deer-huntin' terms, I reckon you could say I'm a "nontypical."

Listen, I'm a redneck who'd rather watch a NASCAR race than a golf tournament, okay? I just happen to be pretty good at golf. Plus, though a lot of folks know me 'cause of what I do on the course, I'd say most know me best for what I do off it. I have a reputation for rasslin' alligators, fighting primates, and playing practical jokes using snakes as the punch line. Well, okay, fightin' primates and playing pranks with snakes . . . yes, sir. Guilty as charged. I just ain't never rassled no gator. I've roped a few, for sure, but no down-in-the-mud rasslin'. Not that I'm opposed to the idea. Just never done it. Only caught them suckers—cowboy style.

When I was younger, we'd lasso them gators because they'd get after my granddaddy's cows, especially the calves. Once we'd get 'em caught up, we'd duct-tape their mouths so they couldn't bite (you know, they really ought to list "gator mouth taping" as a use for that stuff), and we'd put 'em in the back of the truck and execute "Operation Gator Relocation." We'd just relocate those bad boys to a safer place. I guess you could call it our own little version of "Gator Aid."

Anyway, all this is to say you never know what you're gonna get with me. The media can attest to that. In fact, they did just that when I received one of the greatest compliments I've ever gotten from a reporter. I'd just signed my scorecard after a tournament and had stopped at the water cooler on the way to the clubhouse to get a sip, when I overheard one of the media guys talkin' about me. He said, "You know what? Out of all the golfers I talk with, Boo Weekley's got to be the best interview day in and day out. You never know what's going to come out of his mouth. He's always going to tell you something funny, or he's going to make a joke about it. By far, Boo's one of the greatest at giving interviews." I really felt good when I overheard that.

Of course, I wouldn't say I always give the greatest interviews, and I've got some stories I'll share later on along those lines. Let's just say there are probably some reporters who think I'm a tad rude at times. Well, I blame that on the fact that I treat everyone the same depending on my mood, so when I'm not in a good one, that's what you get. I guess I treat everybody the same because of who I am and where I'm from. Like they say, a nobody from nowhere.

I grew up in a working-class family. I learned what it meant to work a hard job (and you're going to learn about that, too, if you keep readin'). We went to church on Sunday, said grace before meals, kissed one another, said "yes, sir" and "yes, ma'am," removed our hats indoors, and did all the polite southern things for the ladies. Probably most importantly, though, as kids, we played outdoors.

Maybe I took it for granted or just didn't know no better, but I lived in the outdoors growing up. I was free to go to my grandparents' place on the river to swim, fish, and hunt whenever I wanted. Nowadays, it seems, kids just want to sit inside and look at screens of some sort all day. Not me. I played outdoors all day, every day and, in my opinion, that's the only way to play. Shoot, that's the only way to live.

I also played every sport there was. Soccer, baseball, football, basketball—everything. Oh wait; there is one sport I didn't play: golf. At least not until I was fourteen years old, and I really only took it up then because I kept getting hurt playing all them other sports. I'll fill you in on all of that here in a bit, but let me just say golf wasn't exactly a breeze for me (even though I didn't get hurt much playing it). Despite what people might think, it seems nothing comes easy for me. I have to work hard at whatever I do, and golf was no different. I toiled on the minitours for five years before getting my PGA Tour card, and I was living out of my truck most of that time. I might've driven ten to twelve hours or something just to play in one minitour event, hoping to win $2,000. Yet it'd cost me $200 for the chance to win that money, and if I didn't win it . . . Well, you do the math. Even with a number of good wins, it was often barely enough to get by.

So I had to work hard. Had to keep at it. Had to keep improving my game. It wasn't easy to stay on track though, 'cause I'd get so dang aggravated when I wasn't playing well. Still do. The most frustrating part of golf for me is when I'm not hitting the ball right. Putting is always going to be a weakness for me, and I know that, so I'm not too bent out of shape about it. I ain't never gonna be the Brad Faxon of the PGA Tour—he's the best putter ever to play the game, in my opinion—or a Zach Johnson, or Heath Slocum. Nah, I'm a ball striker, so when I'm not hitting the ball, it's annoying as all get-out. Sometimes I'll tee the shot, I'll visualize the shot, and then I'll stand over it and I still can't hit it. That's when I get aggravated. Of course, sometimes things happen that put me right up there in the clouds, too.

The most amazing shot I've ever made was when I was an amateur. I was on the Pensacola team, and we were playing against the Mobile, Alabama, team. My partner and I teed it up on a par 4. The other team hit first. I asked my partner, "Whatcha think?"

It was 289 yards to the hole. "Why don't you go ahead and hit your driver?" he suggested. "See if you can hit it up on the green, because I can lay it up on the fairway."

I got up there, hit my driver like my partner suggested, and the ball looked like it was going to make the green. "Get down, get down," I said. Then, all of a sudden, *bam!* It dropped in the hole. I'm talkin' string music, baby. Nothin' but net. Swish! Hole in one. Straight into the hole, and the hole exploded, like a bomb had gone off. Like a meteor hitting the earth. A 6-inch cup blew up into a 10-inch cup. That ball blew the grass away from the hole. That was the greatest shot I've ever hit in golf.

It's a rare enough thing to have a hole in one anyway, so my greatest shot ever really had to be one. I've had only nine in my lifetime, and only one on tour, at the Viking Classic in Madison, Mississippi, in 2007. It was the 12th hole during the 2nd round; I hit an 8-iron. I was playing with my buddy Heath Slocum, with his daddy, Jack, caddying. The funny

5

thing about that was when I got paired with Heath, I walked up to Jack at the first tee box for some friendly trash talkin'. I was like, "Get ready for an ass whoopin' today, 'cause I'm fixin' to give ya'll one." Jack said, "Well, bring it, son. We're ready for you." That was just us having some fun, and fun is what it's all about.

When I made the Tour again in 2007, my agenda was to have fun instead of looking at golf as a job—and boy, did I ever have some serious fun, starting then and on through to today. The Ryder Cup in 2008, for example, was the most fun I've ever had in a tournament. I still get chills just thinking about it or seeing a replay of it on TV. What a thrill and an honor to play on Team U.S.A. in such a phenomenal event. You can read all about it in the next chapter, but let me say that what I've learned most since 2007 is that it isn't golf that makes golf fun. It's people who make it fun.

My caddy, Joe Pyland, is also my teammate (and a close friend). We go way back. Joe and I were high school classmates. He's my right-hand man, and boy, does he like to work. Many times he'll go around the course without me. He'll laser different elevations, look at grass thicknesses and grains, and on and on. I'll bet Joe walks 5-12 miles a day, and on five of those days he's totin' a bag that'll weigh 30-40 pounds easy. Joe believes in what he's doing, and I trust him. Oh, and I pay him (base plus percentage of winnings), so he has a financial interest, too. Bottom line: The man works hard for the money. So hard for it, honey. He works hard for the money, so (I guess he figures) he'd better get it right.

Joe's been through a lot more than golf, and he's been under a whole lot more pressure in his life than I have. He served two tours with the army in Iraq. Sometimes I get uptight out there on the course about a lie or a shot, and then I'll look over at Joe and think, *That man's been through hell on a mule, and here I am worried about a dang golf shot. Ain't nobody gonna die over this shot, so just calm down and hit the dang thing.*

Now, Joe is cool and all, but the love of my life is my wife. I don't want to give away too much, so I won't say a lot about that here, but I'm madly in love with that woman. Then there are my two boys, Parker and Aiden. They can't grow up fast enough for me so I can take 'em out on the water and into the woods with me to teach them the immeasurable glories of huntin' and fishin'. Now, I'll play golf with my boys, too, of course, but if they want to pursue it like I have— well, that's their choice. I ain't gonna push it on 'em. That's not what life's about. I just want to give them what my father gave me, and that's a love of the outdoors. Everything else will take care of itself.

There are two things I really love about golf: First, it's played outdoors, and second, it's played in front of a bunch of fans. Well, okay, I guess I can't say I love playing in front of *all* of them fans. I have to be honest and say I'd rather some fans stayed home. Some of them will say the darnedest things. If I could trade places with those fans and put them inside the ropes, maybe then they'd see just how dim-witted they sound. It's one thing if I'm playing good and I make a birdie and get encouragement from the fans, but it's another thing if I'm sitting there at 4 over and there's a guy behind me yellin', "Boo, you gotta make this one. I got money on you!" Man, I don't want to hear that when I'm out there! I almost want to miss it on purpose just to shut that guy up.

Oh, but there's something worse. You probably wouldn't

think it, but there is one "southern" phrase I just don't like hearin' from fans. I was playing at the TPC Sawgrass in 2009 and getting ready to tee off when a guy shouted out, "Git 'er done, Boo!" Okay, now, I appreciate the sentiment and all, but that expression is kind of like nails on a chalkboard for me. I mean, Larry the Cable Guy hung out with us and entertained us at my annual charity event in 2010, and he's a funny man, for sure. I like him a lot—but I hate that line. I guess everyone thinks they should shout that out at me since I'm the country boy. Man oh man, how I hate that line.

Anyway, all that aside, most of the time I love my fans. The fans at the 2008 Ryder Cup were the best. They were definitely the thirteenth man out there. Even when I'd hit a bad shot, they'd yell out stuff like "It's okay, Boo. You've got it, man." They really lit a fire under me, and got me wanting to give them all a good show. Which I did, I think.

You just gotta love the kids on the golf courses, too. They don't care if you're shooting 100 or you're shootin' the fur off that thing. "Go get 'em, Boo!" they'll yell. "You're my favorite!" Hearing stuff like that from them kids makes it all worthwhile. It ain't just me they're yelling for, of course. Those kids all have their favorites, like Tiger, and they say the same things to him. Sometimes I just want to go into the stands and hug those kids, and hang out with all the cool fans supporting me out there. It's a shame that the Tour's gotten away from how it used to be, when players like Fuzzy Zeller and Lee Trevino played. Trevino would hit a shot, walk over to a fan, and ask, "What did you think about that shot?" That can make someone's day, and I ain't just talkin' about the fans. I'm talkin' about the players, too.

So I try to include the fans when I can. I ain't supposed to do this, but I walk outside the ropes with my family and friends and speak to the fans to let 'em know I'm one of them. I thank them for their support, too, because it really does mean the world to me. The Tour doesn't want me to walk outside the ropes, but I do it anyway. I like being with the people.

I hope someday the Tour stops trying to pull us players away from the fans. It's almost like they want us to act like robots or something. They don't let us be who we are. They fine us for things like hitting our bags. I just don't get that. It's my bag, isn't it? Why can't I beat the darn thing? They're my golf clubs, right? If I want to break them or throw them down, why can't I? I mean, I can understand that if there are thousands of people lined up along the fairway, you can't go tomahawkin' your club. Yeah, I get that. If you do it then, you ought to be fined (maybe even go to jail if you hurt someone). However, if you toss your club on the ground a few yards in front of you 'cause you're human and you get aggravated, you shouldn't be fined for that. We pro golfers aren't perfect. We're people. We do things people do. So I wish the Tour would just let us show some blasted emotion!

Anyway, enough of that. You go on ahead and read about my adventures during the Ryder Cup. I'm gonna go get ready to pay the fine I'm about to get hit with for writing that last paragraph.

2 BUCK UP AND WEAR A RYDER CUP

I never thought much about how or if I'd become famous. It never crossed my mind as a golfer. What crossed my mind, in 2008, was that the United States had lost its swagger and hadn't won the Ryder Cup since squeaking by in 1999 with a 14½–13½ victory (the closest score possible without tying) over the Europeans. After that, Europe won the next three. In 2004 and 2006, they beat us up pretty good. It was like we just couldn't get fully focused on golf after the tragic events of September 11, 2001. I wasn't on the team in 2002, 2004, or 2006, but I know how I felt on 9/11. I sure as heck wasn't thinking about golf for a while. The year 2008 was different, though. We were in the South, in Louisville, Kentucky, home to the greatest horse race in the world. We were the underdogs in this, the 37th Ryder Cup, and that seems to be when America is at her best. I don't think golf fans expected what was coming—I know the Europeans didn't—but it was high time we got our swagger back.

The Ryder Cup is a trophy. An American team and a European team play each other for that trophy in biannual "matches." In 2001, the years went from odd (1999) to even (2002), because they skipped 2001 because of the 9/11 attacks.

I was on the bubble of making the Ryder Cup team for 2008, but I really wasn't keeping up with the standings much. When it comes to tournaments and such, I've always taken the attitude that if I make it, I make it; and if not, I'll just go fishing with my friends. Either way, I'll be happy. Turns out, though, there's no way fishing would've compared to what was waiting for me at the 2008 Ryder Cup.

The qualifying period for the 2008 Ryder Cup team ended after the final round of the 2008 PGA Championship at Oakland Hills Country Club, in Bloomfield Township, Michigan, on Sunday, August 10. It felt good to be among the top 150 or so players in the world and participating in the PGA Championship. I was living the dream and lovin' life. To keep lovin' life, however, I had to play good golf. I teed up in Michigan knowing I had to finish in the top twenty to make the Ryder Cup team, so I was focused on the tournament at hand and nothing else. I just wanted to play well enough to stay in contention for winning the match.

After the first two rounds, I was in 15th place and playing solid golf, shooting 72 and 71 on the par-70 course. I was 2 under in the third round of play when rain suspended play and forced me to finish the next morning. That meant I'd have to fit in the end of my third round on Sunday, the day of a full round four. Maybe that bit of pressure got to me. I shot myself in the foot by finishing my third round with a 79, which knocked me back to 40-something in the standings.

Beginning the final round, I felt I had to shoot 4 under to make some noise in the event and finish strong. I started play hitting well, making some birdies, making some putts. Suddenly I found myself 5 under, which meant I was really gaining ground. That course is tough, too. There weren't but three players who finished under par for the tournament.

Oakland Hills Country Club's 17th hole is one of the most challenging tee shots in championship golf: a par 3, about 230 yards long, with the pin cupped on the right-hand side. I hit a 3-iron just as pretty as could be, and I was saying, "Get up, get up just a little," when I stuck it about 4 feet from the hole. My caddy, Joe Pyland, said, "Alright, let's just go make that putt. It's an important putt. Let's concentrate on this one putt." I was in a listening mood, I guess, because I got a good read and poured it right in.

I parred 18 and finished the final round with a 66 (4 under) then headed to the clubhouse. I signed my scorecard, headed out of the locker room, and stopped to do a few media interviews. One of the reporters asked, "How does it feel to be on the Ryder Cup team?"

"I don't know. I reckon you should ask the guys who made it." Maybe he had me confused with another player—or maybe I was confused. "I didn't make it, did I?"

"Well, you had to finish in the top twenty to make it."

I looked at him like *Yeah, and?*

"You finished twentieth right on the number."

"No kidding? Are you sure?" I asked, but I already knew he was sure.

This country boy? Going to the Ryder Cup matches? Wait until I tell the folks back home in Jay, Florida.

I called my wife, Karyn, to tell her the news, but she'd

already heard. I called Dad, but he knew, too. News always travels fast in small towns, but nowadays, with satellite TV, text messaging, and the Internet, there's a whole lot more news to be told. We're way beyond the good ol' over-the-fence network from back in the day. Technology done stole my thunder.

Paul Azinger, the 2008 U.S. Ryder Cup captain, called and said, "Congratulations, Boo, you're on the Ryder Cup team."

"That's what everyone's been telling me, but I believe it now, coming from you."

"Well, you've earned it. You worked your butt off for two years to be here."

Azinger had, in fact, played a big role in my making the team. He'd persuaded the PGA of America to overhaul the Ryder Cup qualification structure to base it solely on money winnings, with more weight given to the majors: the Masters, U.S. Open, British Open, and PGA Championship. The top eight players for 2008 were determined through the newly devised system that began on August 27, 2006, and concluded on August 11, 2008, with the PGA Championship at Oakland Hills.

Let me break the point system down for you. For every $1,000 of prize money you earned during the 2007 major championships (the Masters, U.S. Open, British Open, and PGA Championship), you got one point. The same was true for every $1,000 earned in "official events" (excluding the major championships and events played opposite both major championships and World Golf Championships) from January 1 through August 11, 2008. For every $1,000 earned in the 2008 major championships (the Masters, U.S. Open, British Open,

PGA Championship), you got two points. For every $1,000 earned in 2008 events played opposite the major champion-ships and World Golf Championship events between January 1 and August 11, you got one half point. With the 2006 point system in effect prior to the 2008 point system being an-nounced, it was determined that all U.S. players who finished in the top 10 in all official events from August 27 through No-vember 5, 2006, were awarded another quarter point for every $1,000 earned. In addition to the point system, Azinger was granted four "captain's picks," which he used to select Chad Campbell, J. B. Holmes, Hunter Mahan, and Steve Stricker.

When all the qualifying dust had settled, our 2008 Ryder Cup team was stacked with guys like Phil Mickelson (who had won eleven events in the past four years and finished in the top 10 thirty-two times) of Rancho Santa Fe, California; Stewart Cink of Duluth, Georgia; Kenny Perry of Franklin, Kentucky; Jim Furyk of Ponte Vedra Beach, Florida; Anthony Kim (a Ryder Cup rookie) of Dallas, Texas; Justin Leonard of Dallas, Texas; Ben Curtis (a Ryder Cup rookie) of Stow, Ohio; Steve Stricker (a captain's pick and a Ryder Cup rookie) of Madison, Wisconsin; Hunter Mahan (a captain's pick and a Ryder Cup rookie) of Plano, Texas; hometown hero J. B. Holmes (a captain's pick and a Ryder Cup rookie) of Camp-bellsville, Kentucky; and Chad Campbell (a captain's pick) of Colleyville, Texas.

I mean, these are some serious golfers. Real powerhouse names in the sport. Then there was little ol' me: Boo Weekley, a Ryder Cup rookie from Jay, Florida.

The media asked what I thought about the Ryder Cup play, and all I could tell them was, "Heck if I know. I'm a Ry-der Cup rookie." The closest I'd ever gotten to something like the Ryder Cup was in '94, '95, and '96, when I was on the minitour and the Mobile, Alabama, team played the Pensacola, Florida, team under the Ryder Cup format.

Another reporter asked me, "What about all the rookies on your team?"

"What about the rookies?" I asked back.

"What do you think about having six rookies out there?"

"We're just like a pack of dogs," I said. "It's like getting a new pack of hounds when we were growing up and going deer hunting. You don't know what kind of dogs you've got until you run 'em, so let's run 'em and we'll see."

I had a lot to learn, and I needed some advice. The week before the Ryder Cup, I played in a tournament with Jim Furyk, who'd played in five previous Ryder Cups and had also made the 2008 team. I asked him about his experience in Ryder Cup play and for any tips he might throw my way.

"When are you getting there?" Jim asked.

"I thought I'd get there two days ahead so I can get in some practice rounds."

"Don't waste your time; you'll have plenty of time to practice. Just get there when everybody else does."

I took Jim's advice and arrived at the Valhalla Golf Club in Louisville, Kentucky, with everyone else. Our team stayed on the sixteenth floor of the Brown, a historic, four-diamond, triple-A hotel in downtown Louisville. We had a large meeting room complete with a foosball table, video games, big-screen TVs, and so forth. The Euros were three floors below, on the thirteenth floor. Lucky thirteen. Still, I've chugged a Lucky 13 lure across lots of still water and caught many a largemouth bass, so I thought, *Maybe we can fillet us some Euros over the next few days.*

Joe and I made our way to the locker room. I looked at my locker and thought, *That's it. I'm on the team. Whether I play a match or not, I'm on the Ryder Cup team.* I shook my head, thinking of past U.S. players like Jack Nicklaus, Arnold Palmer, Sam Snead, Payne Stewart, Lee Trevino, and Tiger Woods. Then I thought about our European opponents, Nick Faldo, the European team captain, and Lee Westwood, who owns an incredible record in Ryder Cup play. Westwood had been on four victorious Ryder Cup teams. Faldo, too. Shoot, he'd played in eleven Ryder Cup matches. Talk about experience!

I picked up my "uniform" and tried on the expensive pants. They were poles apart from my usual camo pants. Those new britches felt more like a pair of silk long johns I might wear on a cold day of hunting.

By the time the 2008 Ryder Cup rolled around, Paul Azinger had been there and done that, playing in four previous Ryder Cups (1989, 1991, 1993, and 2002). So he knew what to do with the team. On the first day, in the team's first meeting, he broke the twelve of us down into three groups based on our personality traits, pace of play, performance, and how we meshed. Some doctor type helped him organize our three units. He put outgoing personalities like J. B. Holmes, Jim Furyk, Kenny Perry, and me together. Of the guys in my foursome, I showed the most emotion. In Anthony Kim's foursome, Kim was the emotional leader. In the other foursome, Steve Stricker was the emotional go-to guy. Each of us brought a positive energy to our respective foursome. I wanted to motivate my group to play at an emotional high, and the way I'd do it would be to show my true emotions. Azinger had a good concept and an excellent game plan. At the end of each day, he paired us for the next day's play.

We practiced for two days. Azinger talked to us every day about what it'd take to win the event. "Be yourself, relax, and have fun," he said. "Show passion." We stayed within our groups in practice rounds, and he told each of us to take ownership of our group, to embrace it.

Azinger was the emotional leader of the team as a whole, and we took our cues from him. There were times I thought he'd bust a blood vessel getting us fired up. His enthusiasm was contagious.

On Wednesday, two days before the tournament started, Azinger arranged for former Notre Dame head football coach Lou Holtz to speak to our team. I'm a huge college football fan, so I knew Coach Holtz's reputation as a legendary leader, and his ability to motivate individuals and teams really stuck out in my mind. He'd made a name for himself pulling off big upsets and knocking off highly ranked opponents. On more than one occasion he was David taking down Goliath, and in the late 1980s, he took a downtrodden Notre Dame team, built them into a powerhouse, and helped them win the 1988 National Championship.

That day, Holtz talked to us specifically about embracing team values, working as a team, and holding ourselves accountable. He challenged us to work hard, think positively, and to get our slingshots ready.

I left that pep talk pumped up. After Coach Holtz's speech I could've played middle linebacker for the Fighting Irish. He had me hoping we'd all get to slap a PLAY LIKE A CHAMPION sign for luck when we finally took to the course. Though I was ready to settle for slapping me a Euro.

I didn't think the first day of play would ever arrive, but on Friday morning the battle began. The weather was gorgeous, and the course in peak condition. The temperature was in the low 80s with light winds. It was the perfect day for golf.

J.B. and I were paired against Lee Westwood from England and Søren Hansen from Denmark in a fourballs match on Friday afternoon. Fourballs is a match pitting two teams of two players each (with four balls being played, hence the name) against one another using better-ball scoring. All four players play their own balls; at the end of each hole, the low score of the two partners on each team is that team's score.

I'd known Westwood for some time. He's an experienced Ryder Cup player, and I respect his play. I didn't know much about Hansen, other than that he was a rookie, like me. I also knew he was European, so we weren't going to be buddies on that day.

Azinger never told me up front to act one way or another with respect to the Euros. All he said was, "Be yourself, and have fun; show emotion." My personal goal, though, was to disrupt the Euros' play. I wanted to get in their heads.

I did just that. After every good shot, I'd throw my arms up at the gallery. I wanted to get the crowd fired up from the start and keep them involved. I wanted them to be as pumped up as I was. This definitely affected the Euros, even though they had plenty of time to get their shots off. They'd wait for the crowd noise to die down, but there's no way it didn't disrupt their concentration. They had done the same thing to us two years earlier. Heck, Sergio Garcia had pumped up his teammates on the Euro home turf in the 2006 Ryder Cup by doing backflips and cartwheels.

I suppose Westwood forgot about it being a two-way street, because he got really pissed off. He said we were disrespectful, rude, and unprofessional. Faldo agreed with him and let everyone know it. During the tournament when the media asked me what I thought about their opinions, I said, "I don't give a shit! We're here to play golf. They have enough time to get their shot. They can wait. Their fans can do the same thing. Let's go. Let's play golf. Bring what you got."

That night, Azinger said I was at level ten in terms of showmanship—that is, I was being too much of a showman— and he needed me at about a five. I appreciated his thoughts and all, but I was enjoying level ten way too much. I don't think I could've brought it down even if I'd wanted to. My emotions overtook me, and I let it rip. It was a dream come true for me to be there at all, and I was going to give everything I had to win. I was representing my country, and when I hit a good shot, I wanted to share my excitement with the crowd. I felt like I owed it to them. After all, there hadn't been much for them to get excited about with regard to golf since 1999.

I've never been big on holding back, and I've never understood why emotional celebrations are generally thought of as unprofessional in golf. Why is it we can't show emotion? I mean, sure, we don't have to do the Lambeau Leap into the crowd after chipping it in from the bunker, but let's holler and whoop it up once in a while, let our hair down a little bit. Some of the folks at the PGA Tour frown on our expressing too much emotion. I guess I have a rebel streak in me or something. I mean, what good is an emotional leader who doesn't show emotion?

We played first-class golf that day, but it was an up-and-down battle all the way. They'd go up on us, and we'd go up on them. It was a good clean knockdown, drag-out fight, Ali-Frazier style.

We jumped on them right out of the chute and went 1 up after the 1st hole. They pulled even on the 2nd hole and held on until hole 4. J.B. hit his tee shot into the crowd. I drove short of the green. Westwood and Hansen both drove it solid. Hansen chipped to within a foot and had a birdie conceded. I chipped 15 feet short on my second shot. J.B. chipped to 8 feet. I barely missed my putt, and J.B.'s rimmed out of the cup. The Euros went 1 up.

Westwood's approach shot landed 15 feet from the flag, and J.B.'s landed 3 feet behind Westwood's. J.B. missed his 18-footer, but Westwood holed his putt to put the Euros 2 up. The match stayed even through 8 holes.

J.B. drove 60 yards past everybody else, and his second shot spun back to about 5 feet. J.B. holed his birdie putt to win it for the United States and make it Euros 1 up.

We played even until the 12th hole, when I chipped in from 40 feet on the edge of the green for birdie, putting us 1 up for the first time since the 1st hole. We maintained the lead through 17 holes.

On the last hole, I drove it right where I was looking, but it went into the water. So J.B. aimed at the bunker. J.B. can hit the ball a country mile, say, 360–370 yards pretty much on command, but this time he followed my lead and hit it in the water, too, about 30 yards past my ball. I was too far back to do any good. My lie was bad; my stance wasn't good enough for me to make birdie. J.B. had a chance, but he didn't make it, either: His long putt from off the front apron of the green shaved the hole. I don't know exactly how he felt, but I felt like I'd let my team down. We had the Euros beat, but we let them come back on the last hole to halve the match. We were the better team; we just didn't close it out. Our putts were rimming out, just not dropping. We were hot down the stretch, but we didn't put them away on 18.

After everybody left I was sitting in the locker room and Azinger came in. I wanted a do-over. I told him, "If I can get that same chance, I want it. I want to play those guys again."

"Do you feel that confident?" he asked.

"J.B. and I can win our match. No doubt."

So Azinger paired J.B. and me again, for Saturday afternoon's fourballs match, and the Euros threw Westwood and Hansen at us again, betting on a repeat of Friday's match.

On Friday night, Karyn and I were hanging out in the meeting room on the sixteenth floor of the hotel, visiting with one of the security guards, when we started talking about the movie *Happy Gilmore*. In the 1996 comedy hit, actor Adam Sandler rides his golf club cowboy-style down the fairway. A lot of people call me a real-life Happy Gilmore, so I looked at the security guard and said, "I tell you what. Tomorrow I'm going to run out there and ride the pony, just like in the movie." Karyn started laughing and joined the security guard in saying that I wouldn't have the guts to do it. The more they dared me, the more I insisted I would. I'm really not sure even today if I was serious; I think I was just kidding around.

The next day (Saturday), as J.B. and I got ready to face Westwood and Hansen in our fourballs rematch, I told J.B., "Anytime you feel like you want to hit first, you step up there and take it. If not, I'm going to take us to victory today. I'm fixin' to go out there and make me some birdies today and skin me some Euros."

I thought I'd try pumping up the crowd by throwing my hands up and waving my arms, hoping they would get excited and make some noise. It worked, too. The crowd responded with roaring cheers. As J.B. and I made shot after shot, we started high-fiving, which was like pouring gasoline on the fire. We just kept pouring it on, applying as much pressure to the Euros as we could. Every time they got into trouble, we were right there on top of them with a good shot and a bucket of high-five gasoline.

We took our first lead of the match after hole 6 and went 1 up. After the 7th hole, we were 2 up, and we increased our lead to 3 up after the 10th hole.

Hansen was playing badly, missing two birdie shots that would've won holes for the Euros, basically taking himself out of the match. It then became a two-on-one matchup: J.B. and me versus Westwood. We took advantage of that. On hole 17, J.B. and I both put the ball on the green 5 and 7 feet from the hole respectively. Westwood hit it about 9 feet away and then missed the putt. I told J.B. to go ahead and putt first. He drained it. Then I made mine to secure the victory on the 17th hole.

This marked the first time Lee Westwood had ever lost in the Ryder Cup. I can't speak for J.B., but it sure felt good to be part of the team that brought the hammer down on the mighty Euro. You should have seen the look of shock on Faldo's face. It still brings a smile to mine.

After the round, a reporter asked me about the adrenaline surge during the competition, and I answered, "I feel like a dog that somebody done stuck a needle to, and it juiced me up like I've been running around a greyhound track chasing one of them bunnies."

J.B. and I continued the celebration in the locker room, high-fiving, huggin', and enjoying our first victory together. To be able to do it and celebrate with him, Kenny, and Jim was special for me. All of our other teammates were yelling, "Keep rockin' 'em. They'll fold. Keep pouring the coals to 'em. Let's go! They can't stop us!"

After Saturday's play, I ran into that security guard from Friday night, the one who'd dared me to ride the pony like Happy Gilmore. She said, "I watched you tee off, and you didn't ride the pony. What's up with that?"

"You really can't do that in golf," I said. "I was just joshing y'all."

She looked at me with mild disappointment, kind of as if I were a wimp. I didn't like that at all, but I just didn't think I could get away with it. Riding the pony would've been way beyond level ten. I'd rather have let the security guard think I was a wimp than embarrass my captain. So that was that.

Every time I play a big match, I make sure to eat a big breakfast. I'm talking a good ol' southern-style breakfast, with eggs, bacon, potatoes, grits, maybe even a muffin or two. That particular Sunday, however, brought with it the biggest match of my life, and I wasn't really in an eatin' mood. I managed to eat only a couple of pieces of toast with a little jam.

When I went out to loosen up and get ready to play, the crowd was already some forty thousand strong, standing shoulder to shoulder at the first tee. They were right on top of us. It was an amazing, once-in-a-pro-golf-career kind of moment . . . unless you're Tiger Woods. Those fans were the "thirteenth man" on our team. Even when we'd hit a bad shot, they'd yell out, "It's okay, Boo. You've got it, man," or "It's only one hole. You've got him, dawg." They gave us way more than the typical PGA "golf clap." Maybe it was because we were in the South, and it was mostly southerners in the gallery. They were pretty rowdy. It was as loud as an Alabama-Auburn football game.

Sunday was my first singles match, and my opponent was Oliver Wilson, one of four rookies on the European team. He'd been a consistent player on the European Tour in 2008, with four second-place finishes. Wilson picked up most of his Ryder Cup qualifying points by virtue of those second-place finishes.

Wilson was up fifth, and I followed him. He teed off and hit it perfectly, right down the middle. I paid no mind and teed my ball up before his landed. As soon as my name was announced, the crowd howled, "Boooooo!" Good thing my name is Boo, or that wouldn't have sounded so nice.

I took my first practice swing, looked down the fairway, and then a thought entered my head. I'm not sure if I tried to stop it, but there it was, right in the middle of my mind: *I could probably get away with riding this club like a pony if I hit over that tree down there.* I then thought about Karyn and the security guard, and I started to grin a little. I got in my tee box, and I sent it. As soon as I saw it was clearing the tree, I said to myself, *That's it, I'm doing it. The security guard'd better be watchin'!* Then I straddled my driver and galloped down the fairway like Adam Sandler in *Happy Gilmore.* I did the ride-the-pony trot, whipping the club like a Kentucky Derby thoroughbred. How do you like me now, Miss Security Guard? Karyn, I know how *you* like me.

I heard shouts all around me. "Boo's the man!" "Ride it to the house!" "I can't believe he's doing that!" "He's my favorite!" "Hey, look at all those weird tattoos!" (Wait. That last one was from a past tournament.)

I'd just made history by being an idiot: wearing black

pants with white socks and riding my club. I never meant to become the team comedian; I was just being myself, trying to loosen things up a little bit. Whatever works, ya know?

Wilson and I both parred the 1st hole. He birdied the next, and I parred it, so he went up by 1. The 3rd hole, I birdied and he parred. The 4th hole, we both birdied. So we had a pretty good dogfight going. Every time I birdied, I'd rev up the crowd again. When we approached the 5th hole, I told my caddy, Joe, "This is where we can turn the tide and make something happen. This is the perfect yardage for me." I birdied the hole, and Wilson parred it. We both parred the 6th hole.

Then, on the 7th hole (which was a par 5), Wilson hit his second shot way right, and I knew he was done. I told Joe, "We've got it now. He ain't about to make as many birdies as we're fixin' to make."

As we approached the green, the crowd encircling it started doing the wave and cheered, "Booooooooo," yet again, but even louder this time.

"Let's see what you've got," Joe said, trying to keep me at an emotional high.

Wilson's third shot fell short of the bunker.

"Doesn't this break a little to the left?" I hollered back at Joe with Wilson standing within earshot.

"Yeah, it breaks slightly to the left," Joe quickly responded.

"How fast do you think it breaks?"

"I think if you can land it right in this little area here," he said as he pointed toward the cup, "then you'll get it close enough to make birdie." He made sure Wilson could hear every word he was saying.

I chipped it in from the green-side bunker for eagle. I two-fisted the crowd, and they went nuts. They started the wave again and cheered like a bunch of maniacs. Wilson birdied the hole, but I was still up 2 strokes after hole 7.

Valhalla's 8th hole, called "Thor's Hammer," is 180 yards, a short par 3. I stuck my tee shot 2 feet from the hole, and then tapped it in for another birdie. Wilson left his tee shot about 40 feet left of the hole. He 2-putted for par.

Heading to the 9th hole, I was up 3. The 9th was probably the most crucial hole for me. Wilson teed off and drove it perfectly. I drove it up into the brush and had to declare the ball unplayable. Bummer. I took a one-stroke penalty, dropped it, and hit it up onto the green. The crowd was eerily silent. I got up to the green and had a 20-footer. Wilson had a pretty easy 10-foot putt, just left of the hole. I had a swinger—a big break to the hole—that was going to break about 2 feet.

"Where do we need to strike this?" I asked Joe.

"Start it right here." He motioned.

"You know, Joe, if we make this one right here, this place is going to erupt."

"Well, what're you waiting on? I'm ready to hear it."

I putted it as if I were pouring it into a thimble. I turned to Joe, and we knuckled up [fist bumped].

"Damn, you hurt my hand!" Joe complained, but with a smile on his face.

I pumped my fist to the crowd as if I were giving upper-cuts to Mike Tyson. They roared with approval.

Wilson still had to putt. He missed.

"This is over with, dawg!" I yelled to Joe.

"You haven't done nothin' yet! Finish this off."

I had so much adrenaline flowing that I hit my longest drive of the tournament on the 10th hole: a 330-yard shot.

"Let's birdie here," Joe said. "Let's not get ahead of ourselves. Let's just birdie here."

I started talking to myself. *He won't beat me here, not in my home. Not now.*

Wilson hit his shot in the bunker, and I put mine 10 feet from the pin. I had an eagle putt; he had a birdie. He missed his birdie, and I rolled my putt just short of the hole. He conceded the hole.

I was ready to close the deal, but Wilson decided to match me shot for shot on 11, 12, and 13. I knew if I allowed him to stick around he'd be tough to put away. I could've closed him out on hole 14, but I misread an 8-foot putt. Still, I was up 4. The crowd backed me up, chanting my name and yelling words of encouragement.

On hole 15 we both hit it right down the middle, and he hit a great shot to the green. My approach shot stopped 15 feet behind the flag. Wilson holed a long shot for birdie. I misjudged my putt, missed, and lost the hole. Wilson cut my lead to 3.

We went to hole 16 and both sent it down the fairway. His shot rolled off into a shallow valley, and I smelled blood. This was bad for Wilson 'cause I was playing out of my mind. I was hitting my shots 7 to 8 yards farther than I normally do. I'd hit an 8-iron when I would normally have used a 7-iron.

"Pick a spot where you want it to go," Joe advised. "Hit it high and let it float in there. He's got a tough up-and-down. All you have to do is get it on the green, two-putt it, and we're outta here."

My approach shot with a 6-iron settled about 12 feet from the pin. The crowd began to shout, "Boo-S-A, Boo-S-A, Boo-S-A!" [A word play on U.S.A.] Others chanted, "Boo-lé-Boo-lé-Boo-lé-Boo-lé!" [An adaptation of the Euros' "Olé" mantra.] I looked at Joe and grinned. "This is it, isn't it?"

"Yeah, this is it," Joe agreed. "This is the end, cuz."

"What's going on behind us?" I asked.

"I don't know, but we've won the Ryder Cup. You and I have won the Ryder Cup."

"Dude, what do you mean we've won the Ryder Cup?"

"We've won all our matches. We've won our side of this tournament. Now, let's hope the others pull through on their side. You've played the best golf you've ever played. I'm impressed, Boo Weekley!" Then he quickly brought us both back to earth. "Now, when we get up here, don't let that shit get in your head. Let's focus, go out, finish, and putt this ball in the hole."

Wilson chipped a beautiful shot 2 feet from the hole.

"Do we concede the hole, Joe?" I asked.

"Hell, no! It's a pretty tough putt. You gotta go up a little ridge, and it flattens out."

"Alright, how do you like it?"

"I like it about a ball and a half out."

"Okay, a ball and a half. Are you sure?"

"If you miss it, I want you to miss on the low side, and then I'll know you hit it a little too soft. Then you'll have a tap-in for par, and he'll still have to make his."

My putt centered over the cup. It was over! I tipped my hat and bowed to the crowd. Joe and I high-fived and hugged. Karyn ran out crying. Azinger ran out, giving me more high fives. Adam Sandler looked at me and said, "Niiiiiice!" Okay, that last part didn't happen, but I won the match 4 and 2.

"I can't believe what you did at the first tee," Azinger said, screaming it to be heard over the deafening crowd. "You're an idiot! I can't believe you're such an idiot! You *are* an idiot! You're the man, but you're such an idiot! It's unreal what you have done to this crowd. You've electrified this crowd and this country. You're the man this year. You are the man!"

"No! It's all of us. It's you, it's everybody."

I guess that brought Azinger's focus back to the team. He knew it wasn't over for us as a unit, and he wanted me to do one more thing.

"Boo, I need you to go back and talk to J.B.," he said in a suddenly serious tone. "He's breathing heavy. His nerves are getting to him. Go back and talk to him. Pump him up, calm him down—whatever it takes."

Joe and I got in the golf cart and took off looking for J.B. We found him waiting to tee it up on the 16th hole.

"Is everything all right, J.B.?" I asked, making him look me in the eye.

"Yeah, everything's okay," J.B. said with a heavy sigh. I could tell everything was, in fact, not okay.

"I just finished it up. Now it's your turn," I said, trying to push him through his nervousness. "What's all this heavy breathing about, man? Are you going to fold like a cheap suit when you're wearing them expensive golf pants? Get a hold of yourself. Ain't this your house? This is your house! Ain't you from Kentucky? This is Kentucky, dawg. You're a Hilltopper. Come on!"

J.B. heard me loud and clear. He closed it out on hole 17.

We'd just done what nobody thought we could do. We'd beaten the Euros. Team U.S.A. had won the Ryder Cup, and we'd done it with a resounding 16½–11½ victory. Now that's what I call getting your swagger back.

I've never hugged so many people in my life. We were smack-dab in the middle of the crowd, high-fiving and even drinking beer with them. The celebration went on all night. We stood on the balcony of the clubhouse while the crowd cheered nonstop. Champagne, beer, hugs, kisses, mingling with the crowd—not your typical golf decorum, but this is how it went down at the 2008 Ryder Cup. Late into the night, the crowd was still chanting, "U-S-A, U-S-A, U-S-A!"

When the whooping and hollering finally died down, we had a private dinner at the hotel for the players and our families. We were presented with the Ryder Cup trophy, which we promptly filled with champagne. That's probably against a rule in some handbook, but this tournament was all about breaking those kinds of rules.

We each had to stand on our chair and recount our greatest moment of the Ryder Cup. Before we gave our accounts, though, we each had to take a drink from the cup. When my turn came to share my most treasured experience, I thought for several seconds, took a chug, and began, "I don't have just one great moment. I have a whole week of 'em. I got to meet and know every one of y'all. To hang out and talk to you was an honor, and it was an honor to be representing this great country. It's an honor to be holding this cup and saying we're the champions. That's all I have to say about that, but before I get down, I reckon I'll have another swig."

Then the calls came for me to tell the infamous orangutan story. If it hadn't been for that second swig, I might not have told it. Well, here's how it went . . .

One Friday night in 1989, my freshman year in high school, a bunch of us boys were driving outside of my hometown of Milton, Florida. I was only sixteen and had just started driving. The county fair was about to get under way and was setting up down a country road that veered off toward the river. There was a sandbar close by, where we set up our tents and began partying. I was drinking underage, trying to keep up with the older boys and not doing a very good job of it. We had gathered firewood, brought fishing gear and other camping stuff, and were all piled into my buddy's red-and-white Ford Ranger pickup truck, complete with a spare tire in the back. We were hanging around the truck, next to the fence of the county fair, drinking, talking, and watching the carnies set up their rides and sideshows, when at around 8:00 P.M., a flatbed truck pulled up close to our spot and a man, probably in his fifties, got out. The man began putting together a cage of some sort. When he was done, he had a 20-by-20-foot pen. All of a sudden, he hollered out a name, and this big orangutan got out of the cab of his truck, walked up, and got in the cage.

The man then set up a table and put a big box on it. He opened the box and took out several pairs of boxing gloves. The man called out the orangutan's name again, and it walked toward him, its hands pressing the floor of the cage as it pulled its body forward. The man then put a pair of boxing gloves on the orangutan.

I'm telling you if you've ever seen an orangutan's hands, they're about as big as Shaquille O'Neal's, or that motivational speaker guy's, Tony Robbins. They are huge. The carnie then started yelling, "Five for fifty. Five to win fifty! Who can hit the orangutan?" So for $5 you got a chance to hit the orangutan, and if you could connect, you'd win $50.

Well, my buddies, who were all older than me, wanted that $50 for party money. We'd watched a couple of guys get in there and get knocked down, and a couple of my boys said they were going to try it. One of them said, "Let's shotgun a beer, and whoever the low man is will have to fight the orangutan."

"Guys, I ain't into this shotgunning beer thing," I said.

"Oooooh, yes you are. If you don't, then you're a little punk." Well, the peer pressure got the best of me, as it usually does, so I said, "Okay, let's do it." We keyed holes in the sides of some cans, shot it up, and guess who was last? Me. So we got $5 up between us, and I jumped the fence. The Ferris wheel was 50 to 70 yards away, and I could hear kids screaming. People started leaving the Ferris wheel and running over to the orangutan cage. I'd soon become the main attraction.

The man was still yelling, "Five to win fifty! You pay five dollars and if you hit the orangutan, you get fifty." He pulled out a bullhorn and kicked up the volume, "Five to win fifty! Step right up! Try your luck."

I threw down my $5. The man handed me this legal-looking piece of paper and said, "Here, sign this."

"'What's all this say?' I asked. "I'm not reading all of this."

"It just says if my monkey hurts you, you ain't gonna sue me."

"Sign me up, buddy!" I said, and I signed the darn thing.

The man fitted me with an amateur boxer's helmet that covered my head, ears, and chin. If you've ever been in a real fight, you know you don't have anything covering your chin. Then he gave me the boxing gloves. Usually you're fighting someone who has his hands right in front of you, not below you. So I was standing in the ring waiting to get started, and I'm acting like a drunk Muhammad Ali, dancing around the cage. Then I turned to my boys and said, "Watch me, boys, I'm fixing to skin this monkey's ass." I was bouncing around like I was as tough as Rocky Balboa. "Watch this, I'm gonna fake him with a right shot and hit him with a left." Like any good boxer, I didn't know when to shut up. I was talking some kind of trash. Steady trash talking.

The fight started and I thought I had that orangutan at a perfect angle. My buddies were going wild. "Get him, Boo. Kick his ass!" I knew I could get to him, and I started to fake right. Next thing I remember, I was coming to in the back of my truck with my head resting on the spare tire. I just lay there in a daze, thinking, *What in the hell just happened? Damn, I'm bleeding. What hand did he hit me with?* My friends told me that the son-of-a-gun orangutan had hit me with a right. I never saw it coming. "He hit you with an upper cut," one buddy said.

"I never saw it!"

"We know. It's a good thing, too, because it was nasty. Wahoo!"

"How did it look?"

"He hit you and you looked stunned for a few seconds, and then you started wiggling all over. Then you just fell over, and everyone in the crowd was laughing."

"No way!" I said. "Dawg, did he hit me with one that came over my helmet or over the top of my glove?"

"Neither. He just came right off the ground and straight

up." After thinking about it a long time I realized that the helmet had acted like blinders on a horse. I couldn't see below, and that's where the punch came from—way down south! I lay there for a while, until the guys poured beer on me.

"Get up. You can't lie here all night. Let's go have some fun. We've got partying to do. You done cost us five bucks. I can't believe you."

As I told the story at the Ryder Cup dinner, I couldn't tell if my teammates were laughing with me or at me. Probably at me, just like the crowd at that county fair. It didn't matter much, though.

Just as I was finishing the story, the Euros walked into the room. They went around congratulating all of us. You could tell they were biting their tongues, but they were pretty darn cordial.

Later, at around 2:00 A.M., when the partying was at its peak, Karyn came over and said that Lee Westwood and some other Euros were writing stuff on our posters. I walked over to see. They'd already written on mine, but I couldn't have cared less what they did to it. We'd just skinned their asses, and they were acting the fool. Steve Stricker wasn't there to protect his poster, so that's the one I felt like defending.

By the time I stepped in, though, Westwood had already written across Steve's poster, "You are one of the biggest pricks I have ever met." I tapped Westwood on the shoulder and said, "Lee, look man, don't write anymore on that poster. Got it?"

"We're just having a giggle."

"Did you just say 'giggle'? Look, it ain't funny, Lee, and I ain't telling you again." About that time, Padraig Harrington came up behind me with a silver marker and said, "What if I sign it?" and he commenced to sign his name on the poster, right over my shoulder.

"Padraig, you really don't want to mess with me, man, 'cause the next son of a bitch I see writing on these posters, I swear I'm kicking all of y'all's asses." I knew they'd be a lot easier than that orangutan, so I was feeling pretty confident. Westwood acted as if he were going to write on another poster, so I started getting mad and loud. I grabbed him by his shirt and said, "Lee Westwood, we are friends. We know each other, but I promise I will skin every European's ass up here in this room. Now, y'all have disrespected us, so get the hell out of here right now."

Then the cavalry showed up. Big Stewart Cink rolled into the room. "What's going on over here?" he asked. Then Jim Furyk showed up, and Justin Leonard, and both wanted to know what was happening.

"I can tell you what's going on, boys. They're getting the hell out of here. They don't need to be in here. They're signing our posters, writing shit all over them."

"Who's doing that?" Cink asked.

"Lee just wrote on Stricker's poster, and Stricker ain't even here."

"Look, y'all, leave. This isn't good," Jim barked out to the Euros.

"Yeah, y'all need to leave. I feel like skinning someone up," I said as I started to lose it a bit. Jim and Justin pulled me to the side. "Y'all get the hell out," I yelled over my shoulder as my teammates held me back. "Come on, let's go. Anybody want some of this?" I'd had a little too much juice, I guess. I was talking pretty good trash.

We'd already skinned them up one time, on the golf

course (where it really counted), but I was ready to do it again there in that room with my fists. The Euros finally wised up and left. Then, out of the blue, Jim Furyk said, "Let's go downstairs and crash *their* party."

"Man, I don't know," I said. "I'm telling you, if I go down there and someone smarts off to me, I'm fixing to whip some ass—no ifs, ands, or buts about it."

"If that's what you have to do, Boo, then do it," Furyk said, "but I'm telling you, they're way drunk, pissed off, and aggravated. If that's what you feel like you need to do, though, then do it."

"You got my back?" I asked.

"Not if you start it, I don't, but if they start it, I'm with you."

That was good enough for me, so Karyn followed my drunk ass as we eased on down to the thirteenth floor, where the Euros were. I was pretty deep in the booze by then. We walked into their big meeting room, and they started cheering us, "Here you go! Here's to the U.S. team. We got Boo, Cink, Leonard, Furyk—here's to all of you! Congratulations!"

It was nice and surprising to be welcomed like that, but it didn't take long for one of the Euros to start smarting off. I don't know who said what, but it didn't matter.

"Let me over there, I'll tell them a thing or two," I said as I headed to the source of the wisecracks.

Karyn stopped me. "No, no, no, you don't want to do that," she said, and a couple of the Euro caddies joined her and lobbied for her cooler head to prevail over my hot one. "It's all good. We're just having a chant," one caddy said.

"It doesn't matter. They're asking for some birdshot, and

I'm gonna give it to 'em. You're barking in the wrong direction," I said. I couldn't believe what happened next.

Totally out of character, Furyk made the infamous World Wrestling Federation "suck it" sign in the direction of the Euros. You know, the gesture pro wrestlers use as a taunt, by crossing their arms and their hands over their crotches.

"You can chant all you want," Furyk said, "but if you watch wrestling, then you know what this means, and if you don't watch wrestling, then let me just tell you, Suck it!"

I didn't expect this at all, and I figured it was time to leave, before things got out of hand. As much as I might've wanted it, I was starting to think that an international brawl would place a pretty dark cloud over our glorious victory. Ending things with Furyk's "suck it" was going to have to be good enough. Looking back, I see it definitely was.

Though we all got very little sleep that night (the night before we headed home), I still couldn't sleep on the plane. I was just too jazzed, I guess, from whipping up on all them Euros. As soon as we got home, I made my way to the bed and collapsed. As I lay there, I started reliving the past few days, thinking, *Holy cow! I can't believe everything that went down and what has happened to me.* Then I started to feel it. That "uh-oh, here comes Niagara Falls" feeling. All of my emotions exploded at once, and I just started crying. That's not something I usually do. The only other time I remember crying like that is when I was a kid and I lost my favorite dog. As I cried that evening, though, I heard all the cheers in my head. "Boo-S-A, Boo-S-A, Boo-S-A!" and "Red, White, and Boo!" and "Boo's the man!" and "Boooooooo!" Pretty sweet.

I cried and cried until I cried myself to sleep. Boy, did I sleep. The next thing I knew, my little boy Parker was shaking me, asking, "Are you going to sleep all day or are you going to sword fight with me?" I decided that since we'd sort of left things unresolved with the Euros, I could use a good sword fight.

After my son vanquished his old man as usual, I checked my cell phone and saw that I had over a hundred text messages and over two hundred voice mails of congratulations. Some of the people who'd left messages said I'd made their dreams come true. *Their* dreams? I knew my dreams came true during the Ryder Cup, but I had made *others'* dreams come true, too?

I received the ultimate accolade from one of my closest friends, Heath Slocum. Murray Rutledge, my golf coach in high school, told me that he and Heath were talking and Murray asked Heath what he thought about the way I'd played in the Ryder Cup. Heath said, "I've played so much golf with Boo, but I learned something about him this week. He only plays as good as he wants to play, but when you put him in an element where he *has* to play, he can take his game to the next level, a level no one has seen. And he got to that level during the Ryder Cup. I've never seen the look on his face or the stare in his eyes that I saw that week. It's scary to know that at any moment, in any tournament, the Boo we saw this week might show up. He can win as many events as he wants to win if he can get to that level and hold it. There's nobody who can stop him. I'd like to have seen Boo matched up with Tiger that day, with Tiger at his best and Boo on top of his game."

To hear this from a close friend meant the world to me. Maybe I'll give him that dream matchup someday. For now, though, he'll have to settle for knowing that my play during the Ryder Cup put me on the cover of *Sports Illustrated,* got me on *The Tonight Show with Jay Leno,* and even sent me to the White House to meet the president.

Now, I ain't one to brag, and I ain't one to be impressed by all that stuff, but everyone else sure seems to be. So I guess you can say it was my Ryder Cup performance that sort of made me famous. I just want to be clear, even if it made me famous, it ain't what *made* me. What made me is where I'm from, and where I'm from is what I know. Fame or no fame, golf glory or no golf glory, I'm Boo Weekley, and that's that.

3 WELCOME TO MY TURFGRASS

It was kind of by accident, I suppose, how I started playing golf. Growing up, I was an athlete, but I never really considered golfing to be all that athletic. I played baseball, football, soccer, and basketball. I thought those were the "real" sports. According to my parents, kinfolk, and all the other kids around town, I was good at whatever sport I tried. I'd have to agree with them, for sure. It's just that golf didn't really ever ring my bell.

I was ambidextrous as a kid (still am, for the most part), but I fancied myself more of a southpaw. That always seemed cool to me. I liked calling myself a southpaw, and I guess I tended toward that simply out of pure desire. In truth, though, I was and am a "bothpaw." (Does that make me amphibious?) I believe I was born that way. It certainly wasn't learned.

As far as sports go, soccer and baseball were my favorites growing up. I was stronger with my left foot, but I could control the soccer ball almost equally well with my right. When I played baseball it felt natural to bat right-handed, but I always felt perfectly fine swinging from either side. To prove I could hit both ways, I worked on my left-handed swing using a tennis racket as a bat, hitting a tennis ball off the garage door. I loved the way switch-hitting Pete Rose played the game, and I wanted to be like him. Once my confidence grew, I began switch-hitting all the time, and felt I could park one equally well from either side. Boo Rose, baby!

I pitched the same way. Once, during a game, I pitched several innings and got a bit tuckered. It must've been showin' in my throwin', because my coach came out to the mound and asked, "Are you worn out, son?"

Even though I wanted to finish and thought my team needed me in there, I had to be honest. "Yes, sir," I said, looking at the ground. "My shoulder is hurting."

I could hear some guys saying, "Take him out." Others were saying, "Leave him in." Pretty soon it was just a constant buzz of, "Take him out, leave him in, take him out, leave him in . . ." To this day, I'm not sure which guys from which bench were saying what.

Turned out not to matter all that much, because the coach already knew what he was going to do. He called for a pitching change. I looked to the bull pen to see who was coming in for me, but no one moved. Coach just told me to use the arm that didn't hurt. Made sense to me, so I simply switched the glove from my right hand to my left and finished the game pitching right-handed. I guess you could say I was my own closer that day. Probably the only guy ever on that team to pick up a win *and* a save in the same game. Even Pete Rose never did that.

These days, I swing my golf club right-handed, throw

anything I'm throwing with my left hand, eat right-handed (unless I'm sitting to the left of a true southpaw; then I eat left-handed), shoot guns and bows left-handed, cast a fishing rod and reel with my left, and when I plumb-bob in golf, I look with my left eye, even though I look through a camera right-eyed.

In the past, when I was up against a tree while golfing and a right-handed swing would have been difficult, I'd pull a left-handed club from my bag and punch it out left-handed. I haven't carried a lefty club in my bag since I turned pro, but I have turned a righty club around more than a few times to strike it left-handed. Is it right-brained, left-handed and left-brained, right-handed? I don't have a clue. All I know is I'm one screwed-up dude. As I said, I was born that way.

In the beginning, there was me and Santa Rosa Christian School. I went there for kindergarten. Then I went to East Milton Elementary for grades one through four, and then back to Santa Rosa to repeat fourth grade (which you'll read about in a minute) and all the way through until high school.

One of my uncles was married to a teacher at East Milton. She really didn't care for some of her nephews, including (some might say *especially*) me. One day, I was horsing around as usual on the playground and my teacher/aunt got onto me about it. She threatened to report me to the principal, and I said something smart under my breath. I can't remember exactly what it was, but I do remember what it made her say: "That's it. You're in trouble now, young man."

For some reason, that phrase had a little more punch than normal on that day, so I freaked out a little. I ran straight toward one of the portable buildings close by and crawled under it. Just felt like the right thing to do. I found a good hidey-hole under there and hunkered down as if World War III had been declared on little ol' me.

Ten to fifteen minutes passed, and I thought they'd forgotten me and that I was home free. Then I saw the light at the end of the tunnel—literally. Someone was shining a flashlight at me that seemed all but blinding. Turns out that "someone" was a group of three full-grown men doing an army crawl toward me. World War III didn't seem too far off at that point. I froze, and the next thing I knew, one of them "soldiers" was dragging me out, facedown, by my heels. All I could think about was that now there was no way to keep my daddy from finding out—and let me tell you, World War III had nothing on my daddy.

I got into trouble at school like that more times than I can count. That's just what kids did where I'm from, but I took it to a whole new level at times. I was talented like that. Mr. Jarvis, the principal, was pretty talented, too—with the paddle. He wore my butt out with that thing, I'm ashamed to say.

I see Mr. "Paddle-Happy" Jarvis frequently these days. He's a friend now. We talk about the good ol' days every time we run into each other. I have to listen each time as he reminds me of when I crawled under that building. "You remember that time . . ." is all he needs to say. Oh yeah, I remember. I'll always remember, Mr. Jarvis.

I also remember the time, when I was about ten years old, somebody gave my daddy a set of golf clubs. When I first saw 'em, I seriously thought they were meant for beating snakes or some other wicked creature. Like most things back then, those clubs seemed like implements for destruction, certainly not tools of a "sport" used for lofting a little white dimpled ball.

Before I figured out exactly how they were supposed to be used, I found something else to do with those peculiar looking clubs: Rock whacking seemed the perfect application. I'd often smash rocks with a powerful over-the-head downward swing. I really enjoyed taking a baseball-like upper swing, too, which would drive rocks a pretty far piece. The greater the distance, the better. The more movement, the better. Seemed I never quit moving back then.

I was a very hyperactive kid—extremely hyper. I'm slowing down (at least a little) as I get older, but as a kid I was pretty much a spaz. In fact, I was so hyper back then that it's truly amazing I can even say I'm getting older. You see, I could've died many, many times. Take your standard chair, for example. Normal kids would sit on a chair. Seems logical enough, but that just didn't work for me. For me, a chair was something to climb up on and jump off of, and that's all. If I looked at a chair long enough back then, I'd seriously consider putting it on a table and jumping off from there. Who knows what could come next, but you get the idea.

Ritalin was somewhat new when I was coming up, and I never took it or any other "smart" pill, which was my parents' decision. I don't know, maybe had I taken Ritalin or something else, things might've turned out differently, but I'm not complaining. I survived my childhood, and looking back, that's good enough for me. I wouldn't change a thing about it for that very reason.

I've always had a short attention span, and that's something that's definitely followed me into adulthood. It's on level ten when my wife speaks (kidding, Karyn!). Maybe my short attention span saved my behind on occasion without my even knowing it.

In addition to my bouncing off walls and bouncing from thing to thing, it always seemed that learning bounced right off of me. I've always struggled with SLD (Slow Learning Disability). As a kid, I had a lot of trouble reading, writing, and spelling. I did well enough in math, geography, and history, but I just couldn't sit down and spell much of innie-thang. Or is it *anything*? (Thanks, Mr. Editor.) Listen, school was tough. I was like a lost ball in tall grass, and it seemed no one would find me out there, or even bother looking.

Sitting in class, I'd find my mind slowly but surely drifting to the outdoors, which is where my spirit always was and where I usually thought my body should be. Fishing, hunting, exploring, even playing baseball—all that stuff's what grabbed me. I wasn't too fond of discussing verbs, equations, or Shakespeare. Anything having to do with the outdoors always seemed to be in perfect order for me, but words and whatnot just got jumbled.

You see, in addition to being hyperactive, having a short attention span, and struggling with SLD, I'm also dyslexic. It's like I get in a hurry when I read and get going too fast. I can't keep up. I don't know what's supposed to lead. My eyes? My mind? The words? All of a sudden, I start reading backward, and then I have to start all over. I still can't comprehend what I read. I hope you're able to enjoy reading this book, because I won't be able to.

Hey, hold on a second. I'm going outside to get some fresh air.

Okay, I'm back. I thought about something while I was out there: I can really understand why kids who are like I was want to give up. It's very frustrating, and you feel hopeless, like there's no way you can ever get it. The problem is, a lot of the "tests" and teachers tell you the same thing. I was tested sometime during the fourth grade, and it was decided that I should be held back in fourth grade, because I just couldn't do it. The test said I was too stupid.

That's why I went back to Santa Rosa Christian School to repeat fourth grade. When that happened, the tests and teachers became the least of my worries. Since everyone now "knew" I was stupid, I had to worry more about the other kids. I hated facing them, but I didn't take any crap from the bullies. You can believe that.

There was one time, over the course of several days, when two older boys were picking on and bullying my cousin Brett and me. They gave me a pretty hard time about the special-ed class and even called me a retard at one point.

"Step back, everyone. Boo is thinking!"

"When you're as stupid as you are, do you even know you're stupid?"

"Boo knows . . . *not*!"

I don't remember exactly what they said (it's all sort of mushed together in my head), but it could've been any or all of those taunts. They were trying to turn school into a place of fear. I don't think they succeeded in doing that, but it sure wasn't fun for me anymore. One day those guys just pushed the wrong buttons, and Brett and I decided to take matters into our own hands. Those bullies didn't know it, but I always had a can of whoop-ass in my back pocket just in case. Brett and I opened it but good on that day, tearing into those guys as if they'd just cussed out our mammas. We turned those two "intimidators" into two yella-bellied chickens! Bawk, bawk! Brings a smile to my face even now.

What didn't bring a smile to my face back then was the

"award" I got from the school for that fight, which came in the form of a note to my parents. Of course, the note didn't explain the *why* of the fight; they left that part up to me. Fortunately, I had a daddy who understood the way things ought to be. He understood that bullies just sometimes need a hearty helping of what they were always dishin'.

Anyway, those guys stopped picking on me after that, but I still had to go to a special-ed class every day in addition to my regular classes. I hated going to that class, because of the stigma, of course, but looking back now, I'm mighty glad I went. That's where I met the best teacher I've ever had, Mrs. Carla Schopp. She seemed to get me and, more importantly, she seemed to really care about me. I wasn't a nobody to her. I was somebody. I was Boo Weekley. She believed in me and made me believe in myself. Those bullies had made me feel stupid and bad about myself. Mrs. Schopp made me feel smart and good about myself. She made me feel I could do anything.

For Christmas, my mother gave me the idea of making a wreath from grapevines for Mrs. Schopp. It was always hard for me to concentrate long enough to do something like that, but once I got started on it, I really wanted it to please Mrs. Schopp. That's what got me through it. I finished it off with a shiny blue ribbon and presented it, with a great deal of pride, to my favorite teacher.

Mrs. Schopp liked the wreath so much (even if she didn't really like it) that she hung it in her classroom. She later told my mother, in a parent-teacher conference, that I was the only student who'd acknowledge her outside of class. I'm not sure why the other kids wouldn't have wanted to treat her like a queen, but I just couldn't help it. Every time our paths crossed,

I'd blow her a kiss, wave, or wink at her. She took an interest in me, and because of her, I was never the same. Because of her, I knew I could be somebody. Of course, I had no idea I'd end up a professional golfer. A pro baseball player maybe, but not a golfer.

When I wasn't being the cutest and best little kid in town by waving to Mrs. Schopp outside of class, I was daydreaming about what I might become. I was watching Daddy swing a golf club once, and I remember thinking, *Wow! That's pretty neat!* Still, I didn't think there was any way I could take golf seriously. I preferred baseball and other sports, but mainly baseball. I never thought golf could hold my attention—not enough action. My attitude about baseball was, *I know I can do it in baseball.* Thanks to how Mrs. Schopp made me feel about myself, I knew I could go somewhere in baseball if I just stayed healthy. My fastball had excellent movement, with good velocity for my age, and my self-confidence was growing.

Still, I didn't have many teachers like Mrs. Schopp, so I still found myself always wanting to get out of class. About my eighth-grade year, when I was fourteen, I decided to come up with new ways of skipping class. I hurt my shoulder playing baseball, broke my arm playing basketball, and messed my knee up playing football. So I got to thinking, *If I'm just gonna keep getting hurt playing all these rough sports, I really need to find a sport that won't hurt and that will, if nothing else, get me out of study hall.*

That's how golf and I got to know each other.

No joke. That was my whole motivation: to participate in a sport where I could hang out with my buddies and get out of class. All I had to do was tell the teacher I was going to meet with a coach, and she would hand me a get-out-of-jail-free card. Of course, I'd stay gone the whole period. Most teachers weren't Mrs. Schopp, so most teachers didn't care how long I was gone. I think it's pretty funny that I was never questioned about those meetings or why they took so long.

Golf was finally getting its chance to woo Boo. I started practicing it and playing it with my friends, you know, just to learn the game. We all cut our teeth at Tanglewood, a 9-hole golf course we kids affectionately called Tangleweed, because you couldn't tell the difference between the fairway and the rough. There was a period in that course's life, in fact, where it went from some rough to all rough. If you hit the ball out into the fairway, you were likely to hit some dirt or a piece of crabgrass. To Boo the PGA golfer, it was a mess, but to Boo the kid (I sometimes really miss him), it was the ultimate.

Those days with my buddies out there on Tanglewood made for the time of my life. We'd play 9 holes, go swim for a while, get something to eat, then go play another 9 holes. Sunup to sundown. Every day. We were just messing around and having fun, though. We weren't really learning to play golf the right way. That wasn't really the point out there. Never really was. Until this one day . . .

My friend Michael Dee's dad managed a golf course called Whiting Field. It's called that because it's part of the Whiting Field Naval Air Station. I guess Tanglewood got old to us at some point because Michael and I started playing Whiting Field a lot. Whiting is a very open course, so I could hit the ball with everything I had. It was love at first stroke (okay, get your mind out of the gutter now; I ain't talking about bowling).

While playing one day, I lifted a shot that took off wildly.

That was my favorite kind of shot. It zoomed through some trees and then some bushes. Then *bam*! It hit some poor guy on the leg.

He hollered like a shot pig. I was shocked and thoroughly amused at the same time. I'm pretty sure I laughed a little before getting it together and working on my apology. I rehearsed it a few times in my head as we grabbed our bags and walked to the ball. I soon realized the man I'd hit was none other than Gene Howard, the golf coach at Milton High School. He was there at Whiting with his golf team. Man, oh man. I'd just hit Coach Howard in the leg. Only I could've managed something like that.

"Hey, what's going on?" Coach Howard said before I could say a word.

"Sir, I'm so sorry, I just . . ."

"You're a Weekley, aren't you?" he asked.

"Yes, sir, I'm a Weekley," I answered, thinking I was in a heap of trouble when it got back to my daddy that I'd hit Coach Howard in the leg with a golf ball.

"Who's your daddy?"

"Tom Weekley. He owns Weekley Pharmacy."

"That's what I figured," Coach said. "What are you doing out here? I thought you played baseball."

"Well, you know, I hurt my shoulder . . ."

"Are you serious about golf?"

"Honestly, I don't really know nothing about it, sir. I just hit and stuff for fun."

"Well, let me see you swing a couple of times." The apology I'd rehearsed in my head was long gone and seemed no longer needed. I got to swinging.

"Let me see you swing from the other side," Coach said

as he handed me a right-handed club. I swung from that side a dozen times or so.

"Okay, that's enough," he said. "I'll talk to you later." He turned around and got back to his team.

I thought, *Alright, whatever.*

I forgot about that encounter and didn't expect to hear anything from Coach Howard. I thought he was either just being nice or wasn't impressed with what he saw out there. So I was surprised when, a few days later, Daddy got a call. "Coach Gene Howard called, and he wants to take you golfing," he said.

"Really?" I said, waiting for the punch line (which usually lands in the gut if it's coming from my daddy). "Why does he want to take me?"

"Not sure. I didn't even know you liked golf. What's going on?"

"He saw me playing out at Whiting Field," I answered, and then went on to tell the story of our meeting. I left out the part about hitting Coach in the leg with a wild ball. Just didn't seem all that important, ya know? I mean, with it being my daddy and all.

"Well, he's serious. You want to go?"

"Yes, sir, I'll go."

I rented a set of left-handed clubs for the day and headed to the course not knowing what to expect. I started off just playing around, goofing off as usual. I was having a lot of fun out there. In fact, it was the most fun I'd had playing golf up until that point. I got to thinking, *Wow; I might be able to do something with this.* This was a thought I normally reserved for baseball at the time, so I guess you could say that was the day golf started feeling more like an actual sport for me.

Coach Howard had found a set of right-handed clubs hidden in some dark closet and brought them along for me. "Save your rent money, son, and let's see what you can do with these bad boys," he said.

As you know from my going on and on earlier about being bothpawed, changing from left-handed to right-handed wasn't a big deal for me. I made the switch without fussin' at all. Coach Howard liked the lack of fuss, I could tell, and he decided to start working with me regularly.

Every weekend during my final year of junior high, we'd get after it. During that summer before high school, it was every day. I never played an actual round of golf, mind you—just hit golf balls. But boy, did I hit 'em! I hit anywhere between a thousand and two thousand balls a day. Just on the driving range. Killin' those poor little guys. I'd go through all my irons and hit and hit and hit some more. I'd let my imagination run wild as I clobbered the heck out of those balls and sent them off to a new zip code.

Now, even though Coach Howard was working with me, our arrangement wasn't exclusive. I wanted to think I was a young stud full of potential and worthy of his undivided attention, but remember, he was also the high school coach. He was still giving lessons at Whiting Field. So, while I was hitting balls off to one side, he'd be giving a lesson on the other. Realizing I wasn't Coach Howard's top priority made me want to be. That's when I got hungry and really wanted to do something with golf.

I labored in obscurity, though, for at least two months, without even playing a round of golf. It really got to me. I wondered why I couldn't just take full lessons like the others. I felt that I was as coach-up-able as the next guy. But I just kept it to myself as the fire in my belly inferno-ized. I did as Coach told me and kept working hard at the driving range.

If only iPods had been around back then. Man, oh man, I could've really put one of those babies to use. Instead, I had to turn to the BooPod in my head. I guess for me, even today, an iPod is a BooPod since the "i" before the "Pod" is me, when you really think about it, and the "me" that is "i" is Boo. Anyway, as a kid I'd sing to myself out there. Tunes like "Gimme Back My Bullets," by Lynyrd Skynyrd, and "Ramblin' Man," by the Allman Brothers. My favorite out there on the driving range was "I'm So Lonesome I Could Cry," by Hank Williams.

At the end of summer, Coach and I walked out as usual, but he said something to me I didn't expect, and won't ever forget. He said, "Alright, I think now you can get it airborne, I can see that. You can really make it go. You can launch it from right to left or left to right. You can hit it low. You can hit it high. Now let's go see what we can do, okay? Let's go see what kind of ball striker you can become."

I knew I wasn't going to be lonesome no more.

Kudos to Coach Howard for teaching me how to hit the ball that summer. I couldn't see it back then, but it was sort of like the Karate Kid and that Mr. Miyagi guy. I was young and couldn't understand why he'd just have me out there hitting balls all day, every day. Left, right. Up, down. Side, side. Wax on, wax off. Well, I didn't get a new car out of the deal like Daniel-son, but I certainly learned how to hit a golf ball.

When high school came around, it was actually the first time in my life I was excited about starting the school year and I didn't really mind saying good-bye to the summer. Not only was it clear that I'd be on the golf team during my first year of high school, but I ended up starting. Only two other freshmen started along with me, and one of the guys was none other than fellow PGA golfer Heath Slocum.

Of course, Heath is awfully successful on the PGA Tour. You know that, or you should. Plus, he has a number of Nationwide Tour wins. Bubba Watson, another winning PGA player, attended the same high school a few years later. Bubba was a freshman on the team right after I graduated. Though we didn't get to play on the high school team together, Bubba did knock around with us during the summers. He was a great golfer as a kid and just plain fun to be around.

I went through the whole cycle of working my way up, starting out as the fifth man. Still, I was just thrilled to be on the team, having basically just picked up golf the summer before. I think Heath started as the third man, but he soon moved up to the first man. Heath was always the number one man in my eyes. No doubt. He was a very disciplined and seasoned player, even back then, having been taught the game at a young age by his father, Jack Slocum. I looked at Heath as sort of where I wanted to be as a golfer. Using him as someone to measure myself against truly helped me. I got better and better, and by my sophomore year, I was shooting in the upper 60s and low 70s all the time, every time.

Then I received a golfing wake-up call.

On June 1, 1988, during summer vacation, I began playing in some of the junior golf tournaments. My parents chose the ones within a reasonable traveling distance and that usually played on Tuesdays, Wednesdays, and Thursdays. Those tournaments took an ugly stick to my self-image and really magnified just how hard I'd have to work to be a great golfer. I was just never as good as most of the other kids.

All those kids were serious about golf and seriously good at it. It was like a freakin' mini–PGA Tour. That summer of '88 was my first time, out playing against kids who'd been playing in competition all their lives, and it showed. I was a newbie playing against battle-hardened veterans. I saw right off that these kids took golf and competing as seriously as I took such things as climbing under portable buildings to hide—which is what I wanted to do at the time, because it felt like school all over again. Boo Weekley: always just a step or two behind the others. It was discouraging, for sure, and becoming more competitive (kickin' my level of care up a notch) was my biggest challenge.

That challenge reached its peak in the form of fifteen-year-old Stewart Cink (one of the PGA Tour's big money winners). I was paired with Stewart in one of the tournaments, and even as a fifteen-year-old kid, Stewart was fully awesome. I mean, some of you reading this book probably think you're pretty good at golf. You get out there with your friends, and you kill 'em every time. You smash the ball and talk all kinds of trash, and you go to bed thinking you might've missed your calling. Well, trust me when I say you wouldn't want to face little fifteen-year-old Stewart Cink. That kid would make you cry like a baby and have you giving up golf for something like . . . well, baseball. Yep, that was Stewart. Our skill levels back then were worlds apart, and I'm not sure we even belonged in the same galaxy. But being paired with him was something I needed. I didn't want it; I needed it. You see, playing alongside Stewart taught me that if I were going anywhere with golf, I'd have to practice my little bothpawed butt off.

I played all summer in 1988 and picked it back up the

next summer as a sixteen year old. My competitive spirit grew, and I just kept feeding it with plates full of golf balls. I could tell this was all really starting to matter. I was feeling the game, and the game made me feel alive like never before. The nerves of stepping up to a critical putt grabbed hold of me, and I grabbed back with all I had. By the time that second summer rolled along, my competitive spirit had grown into a wild beast, and all I needed was a little confidence to tame it. That confidence came when I finished second in one of the tournaments. I was on my way.

Of course, that was golf, and school was still school. During my senior year, my mother enrolled me at the Sylvan Learning Center. She'd drive me to the center, where I'd work as hard as I could on reading and comprehension. Golf had me feeling like I could do anything if I worked hard enough at it.

Nonetheless, it was still embarrassing that while my buddies were going to PE class, I was going to another school on the side to learn how to read. Dealing with the shame was pretty difficult at times. I was always hearing things like "Man, what's wrong with you?" Sometimes it wasn't even from the other kids. Sometimes it was from myself. My close friends were supportive and said only positive things to me, but all the negativity and sarcasm from others seemed to resonate the loudest.

I didn't respond well to it. There's no doubt it all got the better of me, and I felt the need to strut my stuff like a gobbler in the spring. If kids were going to throw words my way, they'd get a big fat helping of sticks and stones in return. I got into a lot of trouble as a kid, but in high school it was mostly for fighting. All the name-calling turned me into a pretty nasty little cuss. I was meaner than a one-eared alley cat and ready to rumble at the drop of a hat. Didn't take much. Sometimes I'd feel like punching a kid just because he was standing there.

I was never expelled from school, but I got enough detention slips to wallpaper my parents' house. Detention, detention, detention. I hate that word to this day. It felt like prison, prison, prison. At my school, they kept up with how many days each student spent in detention, and I think I still own the record for most detention days in one year. Now, that's really something, ain't it? Actually, I couldn't even manage to be the best at that. I finished second in detention for my four years of high school. Seems like I'm always fighting to finish at number two.

Anyway, the point is I was always in detention, and I hated it. I'd have much rather taken a beating any day of the week than go to detention. Before high school, I often found myself praying for a butt-whooping in place of detention. *Just whoop me. Just go on with it,* I'd think. Back then, I wasn't fighting as much, but I was getting into trouble just the same. I was mostly just being my hyper self. I'd be sitting there like a bump on a log, studying as best I could, and the next thing you knew, I'd be bouncing off the wall on the other side of the room. I know "bouncing off the wall" is just an expression, but I mean it here. Literally. Or I'd argue with the teachers about their teaching or whatever else was making me mad. Didn't matter. I'd do just enough to get detention but not quite enough to get expelled. It really became quite a skill.

I was probably also a tad bit disrespectful to my teachers. Okay, fine—I was a lot bit disrespectful. A teacher might've said something simple, like "What are you doing, Boo?" and I might've responded by saying something downright mean, like "Just wondering how you got to be so ugly."

I missed a lot of golf practice because I was sitting in detention all the time. Looking back, I don't know why I acted the way I did, and I can't believe I'd've risked golf like that. If *Parade* magazine had named an All-American detention team, I would've made first team for sure (maybe even MVP).

Though *Parade* magazine wasn't knocking down my door to bring attention to my mischief, my classmates made sure to shine a light on it. I was voted class clown my senior year, and I think it's still on my permanent record. You can look it up if you want to. When I told my mom about this honor (I was strangely proud of it at the time), she didn't share my joy. "Son, that's going to really do wonders for you in college and the world being the class clown and all. That's just great," she said with a thick layer of sarcasm. Well, she was so wrong. Being class clown prepared me very well for a serious role I was given the honor of fulfilling my senior year. You see, in addition to being voted class clown, my peers selected yours truly to be the football team's mascot, which was a black panther. You talk about doing some clowning. Some of the best times in my life were spent in that costume.

Seriously, though, my mamma was actually right. All of my clowning, though fun at the time, was really just stupid and almost got in the way of what would become my life. I'm fortunate to have realized the wisdom behind my mama's sarcasm before it was too late. It's simply amazing what you (and I say "you" because if I can do it, you definitely can do it) can accomplish once you take a hard look at yourself and realize, *Hey, I know I have a problem and this is how I have to deal with it. Period.*

Despite all the trouble and missing practice on occasion,

I still found time for golf—or maybe golf still found time for me. My game continued to improve all the way through high school, and I became a much, much better player. Honestly, playing against some future pro players while growing up and being driven by those guys really is what turned me into a pro. Of all those guys, I think I looked up to Heath Slocum the most. He was the first golfer I knew who actually made me want to follow his example.

Heath and I were such good friends, in fact, that we wanted to go to the University of South Alabama (USA) together. Unfortunately, my grade point average wasn't high enough, and they turned down my application. Heath had his heart set on going to USA, though, so he went on to Mobile without me. I couldn't blame him, and though I wanted to go, too, I was glad to see his dream fulfilled. My heart was broken, but it was my own dang fault for not working hard enough coming up.

So I headed to Tifton, Georgia, to attend Abraham Baldwin Agricultural College. Now, I ain't got nothing against that place, but I wouldn't be honest if I didn't say it was sad that Abraham Baldwin Agricultural College was my only possibility for attending college. I went there on a golf scholarship, so at least that was good. I majored in turfgrass and golf management. Yep, I said turfgrass. They have a turfgrass major. When I found that out, I was like, *Okay, that's it, then. Turfgrass it is!* My plan was to manage a golf course somewhere upon graduation. Seemed like a great idea to me, and it would've been a fine life, I'm sure. There was only one problem with my plan, and that was I flunked out of Abraham Baldwin Agricultural College after one year.

Looking back, it probably wasn't such a bad thing. The

school was having financial problems, and the golf team was part of the issue for them. They were taking a hard look at shutting the program down. Without golf, I would've had just turfgrass. Get my point?

So after flunking out and failing to get my valuable turf-grass degree, I packed everything up and drove it on back to my parents' house. I was starting to think I should've known: I should've known I wasn't college material in the first place. I should've known I was going to flunk out. I should've known I'd have to come back home. I should've known Heath would get out and move up, and I'd fail and move back. I should've known I was no good. I should've known all those mean, rude, and hateful kids were right about me.

The cold, hard truth is when I went back home I focused on all those should've-knowns. I turned into a worthless bum, lying around the house and playing a little golf here and there just for fun. I'd play with the guys who were still hanging around the area. We had a small group that played at Tangle-wood. We'd go beat around out there, just having a good time, as if we were kids again. But we weren't kids. We were grown men refusing to grow up.

Well, my daddy grew. Yep, he grew tired of seeing a perfectly healthy young man do nothing with his life, so he gave me an ultimatum, "Son, you can either stay here and go to school, or you can get your butt up and get a job."

I really didn't want to hear that. I was feeling sorry for myself and just wanted to stay home and do nothing. But my daddy is a full grown man, and I wasn't going to cross him. So I said, "Well, then, I'll go to PJC at the Milton campus." Pensacola Junior College seemed like a perfectly good way to maintain the status quo.

Well, none of the courses I passed in Georgia would transfer to Florida. On top of that, in the state of Florida, you have to have two years of a foreign language. I figured it could take me four to five years to get out of junior college. All of a sudden, I had a plan again, but it wasn't a very good one. I reckoned I could get by, spending four or five years living at home, going to school part-time, playing a little golf when I wanted, and making a little extra money on the side.

I gave PJC a shot, but after about three months of beating my head against the wall, I met with the dean. My grades were terrible, and the dean said I'd have to start over at the remedial level.

"But I passed math in Georgia," I told him. "That just don't make good sense. I spent a whole year over there and passed. Why can't it transfer over?"

I don't remember his answer. I was frustrated and aggravated. "Well, whatever," I said. "This just ain't going to pan out for me, then."

I went on back home with a head full of should've-knowns and feeling sorry for myself again. I'd stay out late drowning my sorrows in a whole lot of partying. I'd drag myself in at around two or three in the morning, and then sleep all day. Now, my daddy is a pretty cool and understanding man (remember, he understood why my cousin Brett and I had to beat up those bullies), but he couldn't take much of that mess. After calling some of his connections, he came to me and said, "Since the college thing didn't pan out, let's see if this job thing will," and he handed me a list of potential employers and told me to get on with it.

I applied at several plants around town. Namely, American

Cyanamid, Air Products Champion, and Monsanto. That's when I hit rock bottom.

My dream at one point had been to be a pro golfer. Then, a sort of sub-dream had come out of that: to get a turfgrass degree and manage a golf course. (Okay, maybe it's a stretch to call getting a turfgrass degree a dream, but I definitely wanted to manage a golf course.) Now, when it looked like I'd have to work at a local plant for the rest of my life, however, I was sunk.

I don't know if you've ever hit rock bottom or know someone who has, but you probably know it's not the worst place in the world to be. Seems like it is at the time, but it's often what someone needs when they just keep goofing off and messing up. Turns out my rock bottom was the best place I could've ended up.

My daddy could've just let me almost hit rock bottom. He could've just let me hang around and do nothing, feel sorry for myself and never get the motivation to overcome the should've-knowns. He didn't. He made me get out there. He made me see that time keeps on tickin', and I couldn't be a kid my whole life. There at my rock bottom, all of those should've-knowns were erased and replaced with all my golfing memories.

Picking up clubs and hitting rocks. Messing around at Tanglewood with my best buddies. Hitting Coach Howard in the leg with a golf ball. Swinging as hard as I could at balls all day long while learning how to hit for real under Coach Howard. Starting on Coach's team as a freshman. Looking up to and playing with some great high school golfers who'd become some of the great golfing pros. Befriending Heath Slocum, who'd become my inspiration and example coming up in golf. Competing at tournaments with skilled players who, unlike me, had been coached their whole lives. Having fun and just plain ol' dreaming.

That was it. I was ready. I remembered what I knew, and that is that golfing is what I did. It's what I was good at. I decided I was going to do it. At rock bottom, there's nowhere to go but up. When I looked up, I saw my good friend Heath as an example once again. Boo Weekley was going to be a pro golfer, and that's just the way it was going to be.

Before I knew it, it was 2009. I had a number of PGA Tour golfing accomplishments under my belt, most of which are described in this book. My clothing line was picked up that year by Bealls department store, and they had a "Boo Weekley Day" at the store in Milton, during which I signed autographs, apparel, and an occasional body part. When I arrived at the store around two o'clock that afternoon, I was amazed that the line to the signing table snaked through the store and went completely out of sight. I couldn't see the end of it. They said that folks had been there since one o'clock waiting to see me. What a humbling experience. I realized right then and there how far I'd come, and to be back in my hometown when realizing this made it extra special.

They had me sit up on a platform at a table. People would come by single file up to the table. The signing was supposed to end at 4:00, but I said, "No way." Not a chance. I told them I'd stay as long as there were people who wanted to see me.

At about 5:00, I was looking down, signing a cap, when a soft voice said, "Boo, my name is Carla Schopp. Do you remember me?"

How could I ever forget that woman? She had made me feel like I mattered. She knew me and cared about me. She made me feel smart and had convinced me that I could be somebody. She knew that one day I'd be Boo Weekley, the man, and that I'd do great things. I'd just gotten done giving autographs for everyone in town, and there at the end of the line was the one person out of all of them who believed in me before there was anything worth believing in. No way could I ever have forgotten her.

"Of course I remember you!" I said.

There she stood, holding that wreath I'd made for her over twenty-five years earlier. I jumped up, hustled around the table, and gave her a big Boo bear hug that lasted quite a while, but honestly, not long enough.

I couldn't believe it. She'd kept the wreath. I mean, she'd kept it! She'd really kept it all those years. She told me that wreath hung in her classroom until she retired. She said she used it as inspiration for troubled kids. She'd point to the wreath and tell them that the boy who made it was now a successful professional golfer. She would say, "He was in this class just like you, and it's okay to be here and have this kind of trouble, because you can still make something of yourself like he did."

Wow. I mean, just wow.

"It's so good to see you, Mrs. Schopp," I said as she handed me the wreath.

"Would you sign the ribbon, Boo?"

I signed that old faded, frayed ribbon with my Sharpie and handed it back to a smiling woman who'd made a real difference in my life. Still, I'm betting I'm not the only student touched by her care and compassion. Perhaps I'll get the chance to pay it forward and be a real difference maker for a kid or two saddled with a learning disability. Actually, I al-

ready know what I'm going to say when that chance comes
my way . . .

"Look, I struggled in school, too. All the tests said I was
stupid. I couldn't read, and I couldn't write. I wasn't supposed
to be able to do anything with my life, but that was then, and
this is now. I worked hard. I mean, I worked my tail off. And
lookey here: I wrote a freakin' book!"

4 WORK (AND OTHER FOUR-LETTER WORDS)

To say I worked hard coming up as a golfer isn't necessarily to say I've always enjoyed hard work. Lots of four-letter words have been known to fly around where I'm from, but the most common is probably "work." I'm not talkin' about a comfortable, cushy type of work. I'm talkin' good old-fashioned, back-breaking, hand-dirtyin', hard work. The kind of work that our great country was founded on (and that keeps her going). The kind of work that, well, like I said, qualifies as a four-letter word.

In early 1994, I got a hearty helping of that kind of work. After I flunked out of turfgrass school, my daddy made it clear that getting a job was my only option. I put in some applications, made a few phone calls, and was eventually hired on at Monsanto, the huge agricultural chemical company. On the application and during the interview, I told them I could run just about any type of equipment they could put me on. If it was a machine, I could operate it. Period. I could run it all back then (especially if it meant making some money), and probably still could if I had to. Bulldozer, backhoe, tractor. It didn't really matter what it was. If they needed someone to run it, I could do it. Even if they had some equipment I'd never run before, I'd just learn on the fly. I could do it for the green. Book learnin' may not have been for me, but buck earnin' sure was.

I must've been pretty good at selling myself during the interview process, because they hired me and put me to work immediately, under Floyd Daniels. Floyd was head of the maintenance crew, and he gave me some of that four-letter-word work right off the bat. My first job was to clean out a fence line that ran through a swamp. I was like, *Well, okay then. I guess they ain't messin' around here!*

The chainsaw crew went in first, for a sort of Swamp Tree Chainsaw Massacre. They cut the trees off the fence line, and then I came in behind them with my little D2 dozer. I scraped, pushed, and proved myself true as an equipment operator. In no time, I had that line clean as a gulf breeze (assuming there's been no oil spill in the gulf, of course). They were impressed enough with my dozer work that, once I was done, I was moved to the hydro-blasting unit.

Now, I've been around water all my life. I grew up on a river, and water's the lifeblood of Florida. Fishing is big business back home, and tourists come from everywhere to spend time in our waters. So I thought I knew everything about H_2O. Well, I never really knew water could *cut* you until I started running that hydro-blaster. I'm talkin' serious water pushin' here!

I mean, if I go to a carwash and spray the mud off my truck, the sprayer seems pretty powerful. If a buddy's with me while I'm washing off the mud, I'll probably turn the nozzle his way a time or two just for fun. He'll get soaked, but that's it. If I sprayed him with that hydro-blasting hose at Monsanto, though, he'd get ripped apart. Compared to that hydro-blasting rig, the carwash sprayer is a bit like a water pistol.

A guy we all called Mr. Ralph was the head crew chief of the maintenance/hydro-blasting crew. I'd work under him when running the hydro-blasting unit. When I started, he wanted to let me know just what I was dealing with. He said, "Let's get ol' Patrick to fire up the blasting rig."

Patrick, a fellow worker at the plant, quickly fired up the hydro-blaster to give me a demo. He changed the tip on the nozzle, and I'm telling you, it shot a tight stream no bigger than a pencil lead.

Patrick pointed his finger at a 6-by-6 wooden post and said, "Let that post down right there and I'll cut all the way through it."

A couple of guys rolled the post into place, and Patrick cut it as if he were using a buzz saw. He split it right in half, like one of those infomercial knives cutting through a tin can, smooth as a baby's butt. That thing could take a man's arm off in a flash, no doubt in my mind.

I started daydreaming about what might happen if I pulled up to a carwash with one of my buddies and one of those hydro-blasters was there. I'd turn it on, take a look out the corner of my eye at my buddy, and grin a little, thinking about what I was going to do. Then I might do it. I might turn it toward him and spray, tearing his leg clean off at the knee-cap. He'd then fall to the ground holding his bloody stump with both hands while smiling at me and saying, "Boo, look what you did, man!" I might just snicker a bit and come on over to lift him up into the truck. We'd probably then laugh all the way home about how I'd just cut his leg off at the car-wash. Good times.

Seriously, though, that wood-cutting demonstration showed me that water coming out of a spray gun can be a deadly weapon and should never get into the wrong hands. It certainly shouldn't get into the hands of someone day-dreaming about spraying it at one of his buddies. Yet those are exactly the hands it got into.

I knew the limits of the hydro-blaster, though, and I'd never actually point it at the leg of one of my buddies. I was at Monsanto to work, and that's exactly what I did. It was seri-ous work, and I took it seriously. That hyrdo-blaster was noth-ing to play around with. Playtime was over.

Soon after I was put on the hydro-blasting team, we had a maleic shutdown at the plant (maleic anhydride is an acid used to produce agricultural chemicals). Our hydro-blasting unit had 3,562 seals to clean inside a 1-million-gallon chemi-cal tank. For the job we wore our regular work clothes under a set of Kevlar coveralls. Over that garb, we dressed in our rubber rain suits.

Three of us handled the task of blast-cleaning those seals. One by one, each man would be lowered to the bottom of the tank, which was about 50–60 feet deep. One man in, one man watching, and one man drinking water and eating. Each man would be in the tank for an hour, maximum. That's all we could stand, really, because our feet would be on fire and we'd be sweating like an iced pitcher of sweet tea down there. I mean, we were already standing in a closed container that is 120 degrees Fahrenheit and blowing steam straight at us. By the time the water bounced by my way, it was hot, too. The tank took twelve hours to clean.

Hydro-blasting was four-letter-word work, for sure, but I enjoyed every bit of it. I didn't think I would, but I did. It was a very important part of my life and it helped shape who I am as a man, making it possible for me to do what I'm doing now. Really, working at Monsanto changed my whole outlook on life.

I look back now and think, *It's amazing that I used to do that kind of hard work and enjoyed it*. While at Monsanto, I began to develop a toughness and a never-quit attitude. I didn't know it at the time, but I'd end up needing heavy doses of both in the future to play pro golf. It just goes to show that everything you do in life's a stop along the road to where you're going, and you can't get there (or sometimes even know where "there" is) without making those stops.

Speaking of roads, I was initially hired on at Monsanto to keep the roads cleaned and patched up when needed. When a concrete or asphalt roadway needed tearing out, that dozer and I were ready to go. I just did the hydro-blasting off and on. I normally worked three eight-hour shifts, but when I wanted to make some extra money, I'd hook up with the hydro-blasting guys. So I guess you can say the extra hours were the hours I liked best. The best of the best hours, however, came when my boss announced one day we had to clean out some sewer lines. Now we're talking!

The first time I cleaned out a sewer line, my instructions were something like this, "Alright, run the hose down to here, and you're going to feel it hit the T. If you can take the hose, twist it, and roll it back to your right, it'll make a right turn. If you roll it to the left, it'll make a left turn."

He may as well have been speaking Canadian, because I zigged when I should've zagged, twisted wide of the mark or something, and made a wrong turn. A very wrong turn. You see, I shot that water up into the bathroom connected to the sewage line. We were just trying to clean the main pipes out, and I blasted it up into the dang bathroom. By "it," I mean *it* with an *sh* up front—and I mean a whole lot of it. It was all over the place, and it turned out to be the women's bathroom in the office. Boo strikes again.

Of course, I couldn't just crawl under a building and hide or go into detention for that mess. I had to pay. My boss was not happy, though I'm pretty sure he laughed about it when I wasn't around. When I *was* around, he made it clear that it was my bed of crap, and I was going to have to lie in it. He said, "We can reprimand you or you can go in and clean up all that shit yourself."

"Look, I'll clean it up, man," I said, a bit annoyed and embarrassed. "I'll put something over my face. I'll put some peppermints in that little mask. I don't want to get in no trouble here and lose my job."

So off I went.

Oh my, I can hardly even think back on it without wanting to puke. That bathroom was, let's just say, a complete mess! Have you ever walked into one of those Porta-John, looked down into the pit, and imagined how terrible it would be to fall in or drop something in that gunk (more about this later)? Well, I could smell peppermint for a while, but it wasn't long before I was overcome by the stench of raw sewage. It was downright nasty, but I knew I had caused it and had to take care of it, so I did. I don't even really remember actually cleaning it. I think I was sort of on autopilot, thinking happy thoughts and moving my arms in some sort of cleaning motion. Whatever I did, it worked. I cleaned that bathroom but good, and it sparkled when I was done. I felt there was nothing I couldn't do after that.

Good thing, too, because there was always more to do. Four-letter-word work isn't the kind of work that ever stops. It keeps coming right at you. One day, a year or so after that poop fest, my assignment was to clean some big fans in a warehouse. The outer edges of the blades were coated with dust, just like they get on the ceiling fans at home. Only thing is, these were huge fans mounted on exterior walls. The fans were in pairs, with a space in between. Well, it was time for them to be blast-cleaned, a task performed every six months or so, so this was nothing new. Of course, as you should know by now, I sometimes have a way of turning "nothing new" into "something new."

I installed the nozzle tip that sprays a wide, but strong mist (that's what you're supposed to do when cleaning fans), clutched the hose with its shotgun-like metal stock under my arm, and began spraying. I was standing in ankle-deep water, executing the same chore I'd done many times before.

Well, the fellas running the building were supposed to have killed the power to all of the fans before I started. They didn't. Yep, you guessed it. As soon as that water hit a frayed wire, ol' Boo here caught an electrified wallop. There isn't an orangutan alive that can pack a more powerful punch than I got that day working the water gun.

I don't know if I blacked out or what. I mean, if I blacked out, I was blacked out, so I don't know. All I know is that when I came to, I was on one knee. That shock knocked the fire out of me, that's for sure. It must've lit a fire under me, too, because I got up immediately and went looking for the men in charge.

"Look, y'all didn't cut the power off like you were supposed to," I said. I was pretty pissed and saying a whole lot of things (four-letter words that weren't "work," I'm sure) I probably shouldn't have said, especially to my boss and a couple of them around there. They understood, though, and cut me some slack. I mean, I'd just gone toe-to-toe with electricity because they'd failed to shut the power off, so I was entitled to raise a little Cain.

I could've died many times in my life, but that has to be near the top as the closest. As John Wayne might've said, "it just grazed me, pardner." I was really lucky, and that's all there is to it. It knocked me down, knocked me silly, but I lived.

I guess I wasn't satisfied with just getting up after being knocked down. Seems if something knocks me down, I might want to join it. In this case, that's exactly what I did. I applied for the position of "electrician's assistant." In reality, though, that meant I didn't fool with no electricity. I just helped transport everything the electrician needed to the jobsite. It was much easier than hydro-blasting, and ironically, I didn't get electrocuted as much.

It was a little hotter, though. The hottest place I've ever been in my life was the reboiler room at Monsanto. When I was an electrician's assistant, we installed sprinkler systems from time to time in there. You know, if a fire broke out, it would turn the whole place into a monsoon site. You couldn't stay in there but twenty minutes, though, because of the extreme heat.

We had to wear Kevlar sleeves on our arms, because if

you bumped into any of those hot pipes they'd melt your shirt. The heat would literally melt your shirt or your skin. I mean, you'd have but a second or so to respond if you rubbed up against one of those pipin' hot pipes. I often found myself thinking, *Oops, I almost touched that pipe. Gotta be careful!* You could imagine your skin sizzling like blackening redfish in a white-hot frying pan. Not a pretty picture if you're sitting on the noneatin' side of that pan.

I proudly wore the job title of electrician's helper for about a year and a half after that. I'd worked with the dozer and the hydro-blaster for a year and a half prior, so all told, I worked at Monsanto for three years. It seemed like a hundred years for a kid who'd never really had a four-letter-word kind of job before.

A lot of secondary good came from those three years, though. For example, I met my future wife's brother at the plant, and we became good friends. He and I lived close to each other, so we'd ride to work together. Two of my cousins worked there and joined the carpool, which made it more fun going to and from work. All three were electricians, and sometimes I'd get paired with one of them. Each day was different, because I was the assistant.

Soon after I'd been there three years, Monsanto started feeling the pain of a slow economy and experienced a bit of a lull in the agricultural and chemical industry. They started a series of personnel layoffs, and this is when my fun job at Monsanto became not so fun.

About the time I was transitioning from the maintenance crew to the electrical crew, a new guy came on with the company. When Monsanto started the layoffs, he'd been in the electrical department about as long as I had, though I'd been at Monsanto all in all about twice as long. I can't remember the guy's name now for nothing, but I'll never forget him.

I got wind that this guy was going to be one of the people being laid off. This bothered me deeply, because the man was married with three kids. He was a nice guy, a hard worker, and he needed that job. His family needed him to have a job. It just wasn't right that he was going to lose it, and I couldn't shake the way that made me feel. I'd clean up a thousand sewage-filled bathrooms before feeling like that again.

After a couple of restless nights, I went to the supervisor and said, "Hey, I understand we're hurting, and ya'll are going to lay off some people." Then I specifically mentioned the guy I'd heard was being laid off.

"That's the word," he said. "Just waiting on the orders."

"Look, I'd much rather you laid me off," I stated.

He looked at me with a bit of disbelief, maybe disappointment. "But Boo, you've got seniority," he said. "You've been out here for three years with the company."

"Well, I may have three years under my belt, but this guy here's got three kids. Kids trump years, so I think it's a little more important to him than it is to me. I can go find another job. And now that I've got a little experience under my belt by working here so long, I can go fill out another application. I can find a job. I'll be able to do something."

He smiled a sort of sad but understanding kind of smile. "I hate to lose you, Boo."

"I appreciate it, but I don't have nothing to worry about. He has a family to support."

"Are you sure this is what you want? Because once it's done, there's no reversing it."

"Yes, sir, I'm sure. This is what I want."

The guy kept his job, the family kept eating, and I could sleep again at night. I never told the guy what I did. I think the supervisor might've told him at some point, but that wasn't important. I wasn't looking for any praise from him or anything like that. It just plain and simply seemed like the right thing to do. Plain and simple's sometimes the only way to live, and I tell you what, it never fails that I'm happiest when I live that way.

I went home that day and told Daddy what I'd done. He understood, but couldn't help wondering what I was going to do for money. I said, "Well, I reckon I'm going to draw my unemployment pennies for a while. Just go down there to the "thang" and stand there for a little bit." "The thang" is what we called the unemployment office.

"Well, why is that?" he asked with the sort of "pick yourself up" tone that only a daddy can produce. "You're being lazy now, son. You can work. You can go find a job, you know, shoveling dirt or something."

"Yeah, I know I could," I said, not really knowing what I felt like doing, "but I don't know. Right now I just think I'm . . ."

He quickly cut me off to let me know he was having no part of what I was about to say, whatever it was I was about to say. "Well, you can't lie around the house like you did before getting on at Monsanto."

"Yes, sir, I know. I'll figure something out."

That must've been enough for the moment, because my daddy left it at that, and I started figuring.

During my three years at Monsanto, I was still playing a little bit of golf here and there. Certainly not enough to have a polished game or nothing; after all, I was a workin' man. During my time off, I'd travel to Atmore, Alabama. Birmingham.

Montgomery. You know, around. Just traveling, playing, gambling, hustling a little bit. Making a little money. And then the little bulb in my head started to light up. Gambling. Hustling. Making a little money . . .

Maybe it was time to give golf another shot . . . in a whole new way.

5 GAMBLIN' ON GOLF AND BETTIN' ON FAMILY

There's a movie from the early nineties about basketball starring Woody Harrelson and Wesley Snipes. That movie shows that even if white men can't jump, they can hustle (and I ain't just talkin' about trying really, really hard). Now, I can't speak to whether or not hustlin' and gamblin' actually take place on the basketball courts of America, but I know a thing or two about what happens on America's golf courses. Let's just say, things ain't always what they seem.

Golf might appear to be a laid-back, even lazy sort of sport to the common observer. It might not look like there's a whole lot of movement out there like in other sports. Saying something like "Come on, guys, hustle" during a golf game just wouldn't make sense. That doesn't mean, though, there isn't some hustlin' going on, if you know what I mean—and if you know what I mean, then you'll know what I mean when I say I wanted in on it. Shoot, I needed in.

You see, I wasn't making but about $350 a week when I

was at the Monsanto plant, doing all that dozing and hydro-blasting. Of course, if I worked a maintenance or repair shut-down and got all that overtime, then I'd make like $1,600 or $1,700 a week. Those weeks were a little like hitting the lottery for me, only with a lot more work than just scratchin' off a little ticket. In fact, looking back on my mishap cleaning that sewer line, I can honestly say that it was more like scratchin' and sniffin'. Anyway, when I gave up my job at Monsanto (along with all that income), you can imagine what it felt like to hit the unemployment line. I was drawing only $100 or so there, and that just wasn't cutting it.

Needing something more, I decided to see what kind of pocket change I could pick up on the courses. I understand more sophisticated folks might refer to this as "supplemental income," but there's nothing supplemental about it when you're unemployed. Whatever you want to call it, it's all "mo' money" where I'm from. That's what I needed, and that's exactly what I was going to get.

"Gambling" and "hustling" are sort of dirty words in sports, and they're illegal in most states when we're talking about pro sports. You can believe me, though, when I say that both take place on golf courses all across America every day by nonpros. You can believe me because, before I earned my Tour card, I was right in the middle of it, making a living playing golf without being a pro. It was sort of like what those characters in *White Men Can't Jump* were doing, only for golf—and a bit more complicated in terms of bankrolling and all that.

The money is out there, that's for sure. How much you get really depends on how serious you are about gambling and how ruthless you want to be with people. Where I am now as a person, there's no way I could do it, but when I needed money in a bad way before getting my Tour card, I thought nothing of it.

Gambling or hustling on golf in the way I was doing it is pretty easy, really. When I started out, I'd show up at a golf course alone in, say, Birmingham. I'd simply scout around for two or three guys who looked the part of local golfers and say (in my best southern twang), "Hey, ya'll got an afternoon game?"

"Well, yeah, we've got an afternoon game," the unsuspecting locals would say in their best unsuspecting twang.

I'd mosey on over and say, "I'm new in town. Can I play a little bit? You know, just learn the course?"

"Sure," they'd say, 95 percent of the time. Good ol' southern hospitality, right? I was banking on it.

A typical game like that'd cost $20 to get in, or some other small amount. Once in the game, I'd mostly focus on the other guys, studying how they were playing. I'd play with them for about a week or so. Basically, I'd lose as much money as I could afford. That was part of it to start. If I could afford to drop $500 or possibly something higher, like $3,000, I'd lose it to 'em. I'd walk away with an "aw shucks" demeanor, and they'd think they had my number. So it was all set for next time.

I'd go back, maybe a month later, only this time I'd bring a buddy with me, a guy who also knew how to play. My buddy and I'd play my "new" golf buddies. Now we'd win a couple of times here and there just so they wouldn't get suspicious, but we'd mostly lose to them throughout our time playing together. We'd hit the ball way right, into a pond, or top it at least once or twice. We'd just do crazy things that we normally wouldn't do if we were playing for real. It was as simple as that.

Timing was a huge part of it, and there always came a time to take them by surprise. That's when we'd finally play for real. We'd pour it on there at the end, and before they knew what had happened, we'd have won our money back and probably something like $10,000 to boot. It worked quite well, really, and it gave us a pretty good feeling, too. Then we'd ride that feeling (along with my truck) to Montgomery, Atlanta, or wherever else we wanted, and we'd do it all over again.

Though it was technically hustlin', I guess, the moniker "hustler" just seems a bit too much for me. It's a sexy title, though. I mean, hey, Paul Newman (*The Hustler*), Tom Cruise (*The Color of Money*) and, again, Woody Harrelson (*White Men Can't Jump*) didn't mind it, so I guess if you want to put me in that company, well, fine. Regardless of what you call me, there's no doubt I was hustlin', and my rationale was that I played only guys who could afford to lose.

Of course, within the groups of guys who could afford to lose money, there were always subgroups of guys who just liked to gamble. Period. I think those guys would've played whether they knew I was good or not. It's the same reason a young kid might lay his money down on a poker table when sitting across from a longtime player. It'd be a thrill for the kid just to play against the pro, but the real ride would come from the kid betting on the chance that he just might beat the pro. Anyway, those sorts of guys simply enjoy the adrenaline rush and the high that comes with the thrill of risking their money. I can tell you, when it comes to golf bettin', those guys live in Birmingham, Houston, Memphis, Philadelphia, and Tunica (Mississippi), to name a few—and no, I'm not naming any names.

Let me just say, it's hard to find many professional athletes who don't like to gamble. We all know about Pete Rose and Michael Jordan, of course. Heck, John Daly claims he's lost millions gambling in casinos. Now, don't get me wrong. I definitely don't belong in the company of those guys. I don't have their kind of money or their desire to risk it all. In reality, I never played for unusually large stakes when my own money was on the line. To a lot of the guys I played with, the money they lost to me was pocket change, but to a po' boy from the panhandle of Florida, it was a living.

Playing unsuspecting locals for money couldn't last forever, though, and the hustlin' sort of evolved over time into a kind of gamblin'. As I started playing more in public settings and began playing good golf in those settings, it was harder and harder to find "unsuspecting locals." That was the downside to playing well. The upside was that I drew the attention of some high rollers who were in it for more than the thrill of the game. These guys would bankroll good golfers who couldn't afford to gamble for big money on their own dime.

Though I'd never been a part of high-stakes gambling before those high rollers came high-rollin' along, I certainly wasn't a greenhorn by any means. I knew that kind of thing took place, and I knew what it was all about. I'd talked a lot with other golfers about their experiences with these "money-men," and it all seemed straightforward and safe for the golfer. You just had to go out there and play. And the best part was that it offered big rewards if you could win.

Once I started getting the attention of the high rollers, it didn't take long for me to connect with one. I agreed to a match with an unnamed twosome my first time out, and my backer was my partner. I was picked up in Pensacola by a private jet and flown to Houston for three days of golf at a very nice course. Honestly, it'd've been a nice deal even without my winning and without the money—but, of course, we won, and I made a nice payday and returned home. Easy breezy— and let me tell you, it's easy to get hooked on easy breezy.

That was my first experience with a high roller. It was no more complicated than that, and more opportunities came along from that first outing. I'd usually be picked up in Pensacola and flown to wherever we'd be playing, which wasn't up to me, and I'd always play three days of golf before they flew me back home. The bankrollers all lived in different areas, and I played for several of them, so I was all over the place at times. To me, I was just traveling and playing golf.

I wasn't any one bankroller's only player. They each had a bunch of different players lined up and would call on certain guys for certain situations and matchups. They were masters at setting it all up for the best fit and the maximum benefit. For them, it was kind of like playing chess with real-life golfers. Most of my "marks" were rich oil-type people, and even though they didn't need the money the way I did, make no mistake: That's all it was about. The green. The Benjamins. The loot. The money. And there was plenty of it out there to be made.

Now when I say money, I don't mean the kind I was used to making from hustlin' locals. I wasn't out there with these guys playing for $3,000 or nothing like that. I was playing for $50,000, $200,000, and sometimes $250,000. Of course, good ol' Boo didn't have that kind of cash to play with, so you can see why these bankrollers were necessary. It was sort of a secret society of moneymen. Golf 'n' Bones, if you will.

Of course, sometimes the bankrollers would want to play

as my partner. Sometimes they wouldn't want to be out there at all. Sometimes they'd pair me up, and sometimes they'd tell me I could bring whomever I wanted as a partner.

In a nutshell, you've got one guy bankrolling one side and another guy bankrolling the other side. Both sides are trying to win and are looking for the angle, the edge. Both sides are gambling on the golfers they put out there.

Whether the moneymen played or stayed behind the scenes, they weren't shy when it came to instructing the players. When a man is putting up that kind of cash, you'd better believe he's going to tell you how to play sometimes. My guy might come right up to me when we teed off, for example, and say something like, "I want you to play decent today, but you can knock a couple of birdies away, throw 'em off. I want you to try to shoot around an even par. You know, let this guy think he's getting the best of you."

Hey, it was his money, and I didn't care much. I was there to play golf, and I knew those guys wanted to win money, so I figured if I followed instructions, my payday would come. So I'd just say something like, "Oh, okay." Then I'd act like my opponent had just hammered me, as if there was nothing I could've done about it. The next thing you know, my guy's down $50,000 or so. With the other guy winning a bit, my moneyman would double the bet and set me loose. The other side would usually take the bet, thinking they were in full control, and then it was on. That's when things got serious, and I'd think, *Now let's go play golf! No holding back!*

Sounds a lot like hustlin', but there's definitely gamblin' going on there, too. With such high stakes, any hustlin' is really just finding the edge. That edge was always there when I played locals for chump change, but with high stakes, sometimes the edge just wasn't there.

You see, the problem was that I'm not Superman, and I don't always play good enough golf to beat other good golfers, even if I think, *Now let's go play golf!* Days when I'd be playing for big money were just like any other days. I could wake up with a massive headache, sinus issues, a sore back, a tweaked wrist, or any number of possible problems that'd get in the way of my playing good enough golf to win a game in which both sides were good enough to be bankrolled. You just never know if you'll wake up to an off day, just like you never know if you're going to wake up at all.

If you ask me, that's the fun part of getting into a high-stakes game and gambling at that level. It's the same reason folks watch (and bet on) the Super Bowl even if there's a clear favorite. One day you might be on top of your game, and the next day you can't hit it out of your shadow. Sometimes I couldn't even tell what in the world I was doing out there. There were days when it just didn't even feel like I was me, ya know? To me, that's real gambling. That's heart-racing gambling. That's high-stakes, high-dollar, high-rollin' gambling. When someone is betting $200,000 that you'll be on the top of your game that day, you can bet there's a whole lot of drama involved and adrenaline rushing.

I've never had that kind of money to throw around, and I ain't got it even today. I still won't gamble high stakes with my own dough, even though I have a bit to play with now. I might goof off with some buddies, playing some games and stuff, but I can't gamble high stakes with what I've got. The way I look at it, I've come too far and had to work too hard for my money just to put it out there and see what happens. No way.

Those moneymen didn't feel like I do. They'd put a lot of money out there, which meant I could make a nice chunk of change. So, even though I wouldn't have done it with my own money, I was perfectly fine with them doing it with their money and giving me a cut. I ain't stupid, but I also ain't stupid.

I've won as much as $400,000 on one match for some lucky moneyman before. My take was always 5 percent. And let me tell you, $15,000 to $20,000 was just fine by me. To play golf? Are you serious? Yep, I had no complaints about that part of it. I also wouldn't complain about flying on some dude's plane, being put up in a nice hotel, getting my food and drinks covered, and basically having everything I did taken care of for me. It was a pretty sweet deal.

If we went to Philadelphia or Tunica, Mississippi, I might want to go gamble a little in the casino, just for fun and whatnot. My moneyman might say, "Here's a grand. Go gamble. Go have fun." No joke; that was common. That kind of thing would never get out of hand, though, because I've never been a real big gambler. I'll go to a blackjack table for a while, but I'll bet no more than $50 or something. At the same time, I can sit at a 5 cent slot machine and have fun.

Whether playing for chump change or serious cash, you win some and you lose some. I've won a lot for the moneymen, but I've lost a lot, too. I've lost as much as $300,000 for some guys in the same way I've won it for others. Nothing intentional about losing, of course. It just happens when you're playing for high stakes. It's not normal to find yourself in a high-stakes game with golfers who are completely outmatched.

If you find yourself in one of those bankrolled money matches, it's safe to assume everyone can play, and sometimes you just lose.

Still, high rollers like the ones I was playing for don't lose even when they lose. If I lost money for my guy, he'd immediately demand a double-or-nothing game. If I lost $300,000, he'd be fixin' to get $600,000. They play to win, and they do what they need to do in order to win.

If you lose $300,000 for one of these guys, it doesn't ruin it for you. Losing $300,000 for one of them cats is like me writing a check for $300. But they don't like to lose and they won't tolerate losing again on the double-or-nothing bet. If you lose twice, your bankroller will roll next time with someone else he thinks is better.

I was fine taking my chances with all that and content to win just a few times for those bankrollers. Then I got a call that'd one day change everything.

During the time I was gallivanting across the South playing high-stakes matches, Heath and his dad, Jack, began kicking off a tour. They knew I'd been laid off from Monsanto. They knew I was beating the bushes for money and playing money matches to make ends meet. They knew there was something more for me, even if I didn't know it at the time. So, Heath simply called and said, "Hey, man, why don't you come play in our tour?"

I appreciated the gesture very much (and still do to this day). At the same time, though, I just wasn't sure if it was for me.

"Heath, I'm not a pro," I responded. "I don't know if I can really compete with ya'll, let alone beat anybody."

I thought I had my hands full at times with those money matches, so what did I need to be playing pros for?

"Listen," I continued, "I might go out there and make seven birdies, yeah, but I might also make three or four doubles. You know, 'cause it's a team thing I'm doing now. It's never a one-on-one. It's always just goofing off, ya know?"

Heath didn't even seem to hear me. "Boo, you are perfect for this tour," he said, steadily twisting my arm. "We've got a tournament coming up in Milton, at the Moors."

Okay, now that got my attention. There's no place like home, and the Moors is in my backyard.

"Really? The Moors? What's the tournament called?" I asked.

"It's called the Emerald Coast Tour and, yes, it's at the Moors," Heath said.

I love the Moors. It's a rare Scotland-style course that's very close to a true links course [links courses are natural, not manicured; usually near the sea with sandy, well-drained soil, thus are firm and fast; few or no trees; the first 9 holes go out, the last 9 come back to the club-house; and the bunkers are small, but very deep]. Also, it's only about 10 miles or so from home, about a mile north of Interstate 10, near Pensacola, to-ward Tallahassee. I wanted to say no to Heath at first, but I just couldn't say no to Heath *and* the Moors.

I agreed, and Jack broke it down for me like this, "You can announce yourself a pro at any time in your life, but then you start making money and you make over a certain amount, that's when you're considered an actual pro."

So I announced myself a pro. A nonactual pro at the time, but a pro. Each time I signed up to play in a tournament from then on, I'd sign up as a pro.

If I played for just that one year, made only say $4,000 or $5,000 and wanted to regain my amateur status, I'd just have to call the USGA of the PGA and say, "Hey, look, I want to get back my amateur status." Simple enough. They'd consider the amount of money I'd made and they'd probably say something like, "Alright, you've made only five thousand bucks, so we'll give you five months. Then, in five months, we'll send you a certificate saying you get your amateur status back." I wouldn't be able to enter any amateur events until I got that certificate back, but that was alright with me, because I now knew I could always get it back if things didn't work out.

So I showed up at Jack's tournament a self-proclaimed pro, and I paid like $375 to get in. I was a little nervous, and still didn't know what to expect from my first pro event. I had no idea how it would go. I didn't know what was going to happen. Would I get hammered out there? Would I look like a fool? Would I go running back to the bankrollers with my tail between my legs?

Well, I went out there and won the darn thing!

That's right, 1st place. I think I won something like $3,000, but the amount didn't matter. I'd won. I was thinking, *Wow, you've got to be kidding me!* I couldn't believe I'd actually won my first pro event, and it felt like this pro thing could really work out for me. I'd overachieved, in my mind, and I'd never be the same—same Boo, different career. I liked it, I loved it, and now I was a professional golfer (oh, and I wanted more of it).

From that day on, I was cupped and committed, as we say in duck huntin', to being a pro. There was no way I'd be returning to amateur status. No way. I was gonna chase being a pro with everything I had, and I had a helluva time playing on the minitours. I was a new man and went after it full throttle.

After playing and winning on the Emerald Coast Tour, I started looking around for other tours to play. The bankrollers had no choice but to share my talents with the minitours, though they sure as heck kept calling me. I'd get a call out of the blue, for instance, and the bankroller would say, "Hey, Boo, we got a little match going on. A three-day match. You off?"

The backer would explain the match, and if it was good enough, I'd respond by saying something like, "I'm playing in a minitour event, but if you need me, holler."

Obviously, I could make more money gambling with the moneymen than playing as a "pro" on the minitours, so I'd skip a tournament here and there if I could make $10,000 or $20,000. Once again, I ain't stupid.

Not only did the gambling produce a little extra money when I was out of work and during my time starting as a pro, but it also provided an opportunity for me to hone my skills and play under pressure. It was a way to play golf instead of work for a living cleaning sewer lines and whatnot, and my golf game got better thanks to those money matches. Honestly, it was just plain fun to be a part of something that almost no one outside our tight circle knew about. Apparently, it was a very big deal for a lot of the guys from the older days (from the late 1970s to about the middle '80s). High-stakes gambling was serious business back then, and in the middle '90s (when I got in), it was still strong, but starting to fade a bit. I caught the tail end, really, of the big-time gambling, but it was just as well. Deep down, I knew I couldn't do it forever, and I'm not sure I even wanted to. I was never golfing to gamble;

I was gamblin' to golf. Even when I really needed to pick up some cash, my main focus during those money matches was the golf. So much so that I sometimes forgot I was golfing for money. As time went by, after proclaiming myself a pro and winning that Emerald Coast event, the minitours became more and more important to me. The moneymen and the gambling sort of fell off by the wayside as I began to realize, for the first time, that playing on the PGA Tour was a real possibility for me.

I was becoming like a freight train, choo-chooing toward the PGA Tour, and nothing was gonna stop me. Well, except for maybe the winter months of November, December, and the first part of January. That's when I'd go home and hunt, and hunt, and hunt some more. Now, if I could've found a way to hustle or gamble while hunting, well, I'd probably still be doing that. Anyway, on about January 15 or so, after getting my hunting fix, I'd pack all my stuff up and head south again for more minitours. I'd head for Miami, Fort Lauderdale, Orlando, and Gainesville to play little one-day minitours. Then on around March 1, the Buy.com tournament would. crank up. Buy.com is now the Nationwide Tour, which is a step below the PGA. That was my routine as a self-proclaimed pro, before getting my card.

Some guys might've missed the swanky lifestyle that came with playing for those moneymen, but not me. For me, it was never about the swank. It was about the spank. Spankin' other golfers out there during those matches, that is. I just wanted to play golf, so it didn't matter much if it was bankrolled or not.

I loved playing the minitours, actually. I played the Developmental Player Tour and the Emerald Coast Tour, of course, which is now in Destin, Florida. I played the NGA Hooters Tour, which traveled around from place to place. I played the Moonlight Tour, which is in South Florida. I took in the rays of the Sunshine Tour and drank my fill of the Coca-Cola Tour. I mean, I played in everything I could play in across the Southeast. During those minitours, I felt like a kid firing a rifle for the first time, and I just couldn't get enough.

In reality, I wasn't like a kid doing anything for the first time 'cause the concept of minitours wasn't new to me. I'd played in some while working at Monsanto, but I wasn't really serious about 'em. I had fun as usual, though, even back then. I played on a small scratch tour while at Monsanto called the Emerald Coast Scratch Tour, which was started by Junior Ingram. Junior was once a sports writer at a Pensacola newspaper, and he left to start his own magazine. Well, he loved golf so much that he also started a scratch golf tour. It was just for scratch people (people with zero handicaps). They played fourteen or fifteen events a year, all in my area, within 30 or 40 miles of Pensacola. So I played.

At the end of 1996, they took the twelve best players on our tour and put us together, and we played a Ryder Cup–style tournament, which was very exciting and felt like the real deal to me. We played against a team from Pensacola and one from Mobile, and I often found myself wishing I could do only that, instead of working at Monsanto, as much as I enjoyed the work there. Maybe I was destined to play those money matches for the high rollers, wanting to just play golf so bad. Who knows?

I'll tell you what I do know. That little scratch tourney went a long way toward preparing me for the travel and competition of the minitours, once the high-stakes money matches went away. It also shared something with the minitours that the bankrolled money matches didn't have: It gave me the opportunity to play golf and hang with a bunch of friends who were, in many ways, family.

We'd all room together on the minitours. It certainly wasn't like staying in those nice hotels the high rollers were putting me up in, but it was honestly a lot better, because of the people around me. Having done both, I can tell you I'd take bunkin' with a few of my buddies in a motel room over staying in an empty 5-star hotel suite any day of the week. You would, too, if you had my buddies.

There'd usually be three of us in a motel room during the minitours, because it was just more economical that way. The rooms cost $40 or so back then, so we'd triple up. With tax and all, we were spending less than $20 each per day. It was more than affordable and the right kind of uncomfortable when we had that many people.

A day on the minitours was no picnic, that's for sure, but you could probably get away with calling it a potluck. Some folks bring good stuff, some bring crud no one wants to touch, and others don't bring nothing. It doesn't matter, though. Everyone eats, and everyone has a good time. So, even if a guy traveling with us didn't play well and didn't make any money, if I made a little, I'd pick up the bill. He'd do the same for me when the fortunes were reversed. The guy who could pitch in would do the pitchin' in.

My stretch of minitours ended in Atlanta with the DP Tour (the Developmental Player Tour) that Jack Slocum created. It was quite appropriate that my last minitour was one created by Jack 'cause, as I've been saying, the minitours weren't about gamblin', hustlin', livin' the high life, or even making money. They were about family—that's what I remember anyway—and there was no one on them minitours more like family to me than Jack Slocum.

Mr. Jack was really like another daddy for me in a way. I mean, he took care of us crazy golfers like it was his God-given duty or something. He and his wife, Miss Kay, cared for me like a son. Heath (Jack's real son, of course), a guy named John Cunningham, another guy named Travis Nance, and I always stayed with Jack and Kay. We were like brothers, and Jack and Kay were Mamma and Poppa. Their house was considered home during the minitours.

Their brand of hospitality didn't stop with the four of us. The odd guy or two who needed a place to crash was always welcome at the Slocum house. We'd sleep in beds, on the floor, or in the corner if needed. If the course we were playing was too far from Jack's home, he'd make arrangements with a motel, reserving forty or fifty rooms at a rate of $50 a night. We'd pair up and split the room cost, and (just like brothers might) we'd add a little incentive for the next day's play. The low scorer got the bed the next night, and the high scorer slept on the rollaway or on the floor, whichever was softer (you'd be surprised, but sometimes the floor felt softer).

A couple of other guys soon joined our "family." The more brothers, the better. Guys like Jeff Champion and Bud Steel came along, becoming my instant friends for life. A bunch of other guys came on board, too, and we all became good friends.

Of course, along with a big family comes the need to break away from time to time to be by yourself. My bros made the minitours fun, but I certainly needed my Boo time.

It ain't that I'm naturally a loner or nothing, but I like being by myself sometimes because I do a lot of thinking. During those minitours, when I could get away from everyone, I'd normally find myself reflecting on my childhood, looking back on where I'd come from, thinking about my real family and how much I missed them and the fun we had.

I have a great family. I honestly couldn't have asked for a better one (not even those guys on the minitour). My mamma and daddy raised me right, and my grandparents and uncles all played a big part of making me who I am, too. There were plenty of times when I was down and out, and it was during those times that only my real family would be there for me. Like my uncle Jim. Shoot, to this day I still owe him money, I'm sure. Even if I paid him back, I'd still owe him—for keeping me afloat when I was really struggling and trying to figure out if I could make it in golf. You just can't ever really pay back that sort of thing.

That's my family. Wouldn't trade them for all the bankrollers in the world. Those moneymen loved my talent and used it, but they didn't care about me as a person. I'm not sure if that ever crossed my mind while playing for them, but I like to remind myself from time to time these days that bankrollers are bankrollers, and family is family. Those moneymen couldn't relate with or ever bring themselves to care about the fact that I was, at one point early on, living out of my truck, for example. They wouldn't even have wanted to hear about it. They just saw me as a golfer, but I'm more than that. I'm a person. Just so happens the good Lord blessed me with some golfing talent, but I'm a person. My family loves Boo, the person, and I can honestly say, that's all I need.

To any of you bankrollers from back in the day who are reading this and don't believe me, well, I have one question for you:

Wanna bet?

6 Q SCHOOL, N'WIDE, AND K LOVE

Gambling may've been my thing for a while, but as you should know by now, school never was. Growing up, it seemed the only thing school and I had in common were the two "o's" in our names. Even studying turfgrass in college didn't make school work for me. I think school can be hard for guys like me, unless we're clearly heading somewhere with it. What I mean is, something has to have a clear purpose in my life for me to take it seriously. I won't apply myself unless there's a reason to apply myself. If there is a reason to apply myself, whatever I'm applying myself to gets my full application (if I do say so myself).

I know there are others out there like me. Perhaps you're reading this book right now. If so, doesn't it seem like school came along a tad early in life for guys (and gals) like us? We need things like school and work to come along at the right time. I don't know about you, but fortunately for me, the right kind of school eventually came along at the right kind of time.

While I was playing the minitours—every year from 1997 to 2001—I went to qualifying school. We golfers call it Q school. Now, there ain't no classrooms at Q school. There's no campus, and there sure as heck ain't no cheerleaders (dang it). Still, there ain't no detention neither, so it had its advantages, I must say.

Q school breaks down basically like this: There're three stages of play that determine who'll get their PGA Tour card, who will qualify for the Nationwide Tour, and who won't get either. It's a long, grueling process of golfing under serious pressure. Earning a passing grade at Q school is tougher than making it through any classroom I've ever had the good misfortune of sitting down in. Q schoolers are graded on a curve, and it's a short one.

Applicants who're accepted are sent to any one of several locations scattered across the country to take part in stage-one competition. The locations are basically wherever the officials can find a site that isn't filled to capacity with hopefuls. There're some seventy-five players at each location (thirteen locations when I went through). Only about twenty-five golfers (plus ties) per site advance to the second stage, but that's only if the judges think the field's strong. If the field appears weak, they'll take only fifteen, sixteen, or so. You'll never make it just because they need guys or you happen to be playing against a weak field. You have to earn it every time, no matter what.

The first stage is four days of competing in a 72-hole tournament. If you make it through the first stage, you're sent to one of six locations in four different states for the second stage. A predetermined number of golfers advance to the final stage, and let me tell you, the competition intensifies mightily at each level. It's kind of like going to high school, college, and then grad school at an extremely fast rate. No time to enjoy the summer off and get ready for the next level. Q school is everything all at once, and you'd better be ready. If not, you'll find yourself out of there and reapplying the next year, and the next year, and maybe even the next.

For five years, I sent in an application. Sometimes persistence pays off. The first four years I never made it past the first stage. This would've been disappointing and discouraging for any golfer under any circumstances, but it was particularly so for me because I was playing on golf courses I knew. I should've been able to breeze on through. The problem was, though I knew the courses, I'd never played under the pressure that Q school brought. I had only four days to prove myself out there, and that got to me more than I thought it would. (Don't think it wouldn't get to you, too, because it might.) I had to play good golf for four days instead of just going out there all relaxed and telling myself, *Okay, all I need is one good day, one mediocre day, one more mediocre day, and one more mediocre day, and I'm in.* Every day had to be good, if not great. It was a whole new ball game, so to speak.

Now, you don't have to shoot every round under par to make it or nothing like that. You just have to go out there and keep a number in your head and think, *Okay, if I can shoot two under here, I should make it.* Still, it's way harder than it sounds, and it took me a while to get it. I actually didn't fully understand what I needed to do until the first stage in 2001, when Jack Slocum caddied for me. Even in Q school, it sometimes takes the right guidance counselor or teacher to come along for things to start clickin'. Jack was that teacher (if only I'd had him for the first four years).

Jack and I went to the first qualifying stage that fifth year in and did a practice round. We went through it, and after we got off the golf course, Jack flipped through the yardage book we'd just charted and said, "Okay, this is our number, two-seventy-eight, which we're going to shoot this week. This is all we have to shoot."

"Oh yeah?" I said, thinking Jack had been in the sun too long. "Are you crazy? Have you seen the people who're here playing? These guys have been on the Nationwide Tour. There're All-Americans here who've played for Oklahoma, Auburn, Alabama, Florida. I mean, these people . . . dude, look. That's ridiculous."

I knew those other guys could do what Jack was saying, but I wasn't sure I could, since I didn't see myself on the same level as those other guys. Despite my naysayin', though, it must've sunk in a bit. After a four-round 278 (that's right, exactly what Jack called for), Jack had my attention. It was the best I'd ever done in Q school during all my time there, and it was good enough to take me into the second stage. Finally. What's that old saying? Fifth time is a charm.

Anyway, the second stage that year was at a golf course I knew fairly well. I hadn't grown up playing it, but I'd probably played it a hundred times before, so I felt good about it. What I didn't feel good about was that, though the second stage is the same 72-hole format as the first stage, there is even more pressure with the addition of golfers off the Nationwide Tour and the PGA Tour, who have played alright but not quite good enough to skip the second round and move directly to the final stage. So now all those guys were coming to the second stage and trying to fight their way back to the final stage. That was my competition.

Honestly, I felt kind of like Chris Farley in that dumb movie about being "almost heroes." He was learning how to read, and the teacher started off with a capital "A." He struggled to get it, and finally did (and was proud of himself), but then there was that second stage of learning. The lowercase "a." The pressure almost made his head explode, and he was done learning for the day. Now, my situation certainly wasn't stupid like that movie, but you get the point. I was a tad bit rattled.

Jack wasn't.

"Alright, this is what we're going to shoot here," he said, after we had finished a practice round. "We're going to shoot a seventy-one to a sixty-nine every day. I'm going to keep you straight. You just hit the shot, and I'll keep you out of trouble."

I paid attention, and Jack had me focused. I felt good and ready, and when all was said and done, I think I finished seventh or eighth. Not too bad. I was like, *Take that, you stupid lowercase "a."* Nothing to it.

Good thing I was feeling focused and ready because next we headed to Bear Lakes Country Club in West Palm Beach, Florida, for six punishing, demanding days of golf. Six rounds of golf on two different courses. I got there, did a practice round on one course, and the next day I did a practice round on the other. Now, I don't know if they were ready for the likes of me out there, but they sure as heck weren't ready for the *sight* of me.

That was the week the pro golf world got its first official dose of this small-town, redneck country boy. I wore rubber rain pants and tennis shoes, dipped snuff, and drove a pickup truck. I was there, and I like to think I belonged there, but I didn't *belong* there, if you know what I mean. I stood out like a tiger in a group of cougars. Uh, yeah, that's it. A tiger in a group of cougars.

Anyway, my approach to practice was to find the toughest course, then the toughest 9 on that course, and to play it first. If the toughest golf course's back 9 was the trickiest, then I'd go play it again to get a better feel. I kind of thought of it like eating my veggies first. Everything is tasty after that.

I'd do the same on the other golf course. I'd find the toughest 9 holes on that golf course and go play them on the same day. So I played 36 holes, more or less, or 54 holes total on both golf courses. And then I had to get ready for the 6 rounds of actual playing, getting up at the butt-crack of dawn every day, and having to practice at the driving range when I was done.

Still, as tough as the physical part was, the mental side was the most strenuous, that's for sure. If it's patience and character you want to test, I suggest going out there and teeing it up knowing you have to beat not only the golf course, but 125 other guys on that course. That'll test your patience and character plenty. I mean, they were taking only 20 spots. Yes, that's what I said. Only 20 golfers were going to get a Tour card. That was it. Twenty out of all them guys. Could I be one of them? Was it my destiny? If it wasn't my destiny, could I bulldoze my way through anyway? Man, that stuff will really mess with your mind.

I'm not sure if it was already decided for me or if I decided it out there on the course, but I played very well throughout, shooting 66, 74, 68, 67, 70, and 69, for a 6-round total of 414. My messed-with mind was starting to come around to meet up with the rest of me, which was already well on its way to making it. With everything clickin', I birdied the final hole of the tournament to seal the deal and secured my 2002 PGA Tour card. Then my mind started messing with my mind.

I made it! I thought. I couldn't believe it. I'd finally made the big leagues—golf's highest level of play. I'd finished 17th or 19th to squeak in, but hey, I was in. I'd played well enough to now play with the best in the world, so "well enough" was good enough for me. The $25,000 I won for making it was simply gravy. It was a whole lot of gravy, mind you, but it was still just gravy. Getting my Tour card was the mashed potatoes. A big ol' hearty helping, too. The PGA Tour! This country boy had made it, and he was ready to mow down!

As we walked off the 18th green after the birdie, Jack said, "That was a million-dollar putt."

I still had my mind wrapped up in the thought of mashed potatoes, and I really wasn't yet thinking about the gravy. "What are you talking about, Jack? What do you mean?"

"You'll know soon enough."

Well, I really had no expectations at all when the 2002 season began on January 10 with the Sony Open in Hawaii. I had no clue what was fixin' to happen in my life, but I charged forward into the unknown world of PGA golf with a head full of steam and a mouth full of mashed potatoes. Actually, it was dip, but you get what I'm sayin'.

I certainly didn't look like a PGA golfer headin' in there. I didn't wear slacks, and I didn't wear golf shoes like all them other guys. I wore tennis shoes and rain pants. Maybe my upper body resembled a pro golfer's, with my Cleveland hat and collared shirt. Playing Titleist golf balls and wearing a golf glove helped a bit, too, I suppose. From the waist down, though,

I didn't look the part at all. When I first got on tour, it was like I was from Mars. Shoot, I'd've been perfectly happy golfin' on Mars.

Still, it wasn't like I was making a fashion statement or nothing. A rare skin disease on one of my legs had forced me to wear those rain pants. How I contracted that skin condition, I couldn't tell you. It could've been from fertilizer or from when I was down at my granddaddy's helping him with his cows. Who knows? What I do know is the rash ran around the back side of my right knee and down the back of my calf. It looked similar to poison ivy or something like that, and it would flare up and then go away.

Every time I dressed in cotton pants, my leg would break out. I can't even put into words just how bad it itched. So I figured I'd wear rain pants with a smooth polyester lining. They helped a lot with the rash. I didn't break out, which was good, but those pants were hot as blue blazes, which wasn't too good.

Imagine wearing blue jeans when it's 100 degrees outside. I'm sure ya'll have done that. Hot and nasty, right? Now picture yourself wearing rain pants that are supposed to protect you from getting wet instead of those jeans. You're sweating profusely, and you're thinking those jeans would feel like mesh shorts compared to those rain paints. That's how it felt. When I'd get home, I'd take my shoes off and wring the sweat out of my socks.

The news folks covering the Tour liked to focus on the rain pants. I thought it might have been because, as far as rain pants go, I was stylin' out there. No cheap, shabby, school bus yellow color for Boo. No, sir. Mine were solid black, or blue, but my favorite was a pair of Mossy Oak camouflage rain pants. I imagined walking out in those camo pants, with people sort of gawking because it looked like the top of my body was floating—you know, because I had camo pants on. Okay, dumb thought, but still a fun one. Anyway, I'd picked up a couple pairs of FootJoy rain pants, too. I had some rain pants I picked up at a Cabela's retail store; Frogg Toggs is another type I wore. I thought of my rain pants as some golfers think of their shoes. Of course, it sometimes seemed like all anyone else was thinking about were my rain pants and my shoes.

The gist of the headlines was essentially, BOO WEEKLEY, THE RAIN PANTS, TENNIS SHOE WEARER. HE'S GOING TO CHANGE THE TOUR. You know, stuff like that. The media just ate it up, really. So did the corporate types. When I got my Tour card, I was sort of bombarded.

"We want to sign you."

"Titleist wants to sign you."

"Cleveland wants to sign you."

All of these companies and their representatives were coming at me like I'd just climbed under a portable building or something. I felt about as overwhelmed as I'd felt hiding under that building back home as a kid, with those flashlights shining in at me. As I said, I had no clue what to expect from the whole PGA thing, what was getting ready to happen to my life. It was something else. It's kind of like having kids. It seems scary and exciting at the same time, and everyone with kids tells you how it'll feel, but you don't know what it's like until it happens to you.

Looking back, I think in many ways the media were making fun of me. I don't know if they meant to, but they definitely were. I wasn't a golfer to a lot of them. I was more like a cartoon character. I had the name and wardrobe (some said "costume") of a cartoon character. Some in the media implied that I wasn't even really a golfer, like I was a marketing stunt or something planned by the powers-that-be within the PGA. I don't know; maybe they didn't take it that far, but I got questions about it all the time.

"Who are you?"

"What are you?"

"What are you doing here?"

And there was a lot of criticism, too, like I was making a mockery of their dignified game. At the same time, I tried to look at it from their point of view. I *was* different, I gotta give 'em that. They were trying to make a living, so I can't say their questions didn't make sense. I mean, they're always trying to get a different angle, a unique story, and I was different and unique all wrapped up in one. I mean, there I was, like a tiger in a group of . . . Well, you know.

Though I understood (or tried to understand) where they were coming from, it got (and still gets) really, really old, mostly because of where I came from. Like my nickname, Boo. It's what I go by and have gone by my whole life. So I've got a nickname for a name, and it turns out I got it from Yogi Bear and Boo Boo, from the cartoon. That's how I got it growing up. If only I had a dollar for every time I've had to tell that story. Shoot, I'd already be retired and fishin' every day, and I wouldn't have to hear the question anymore.

"How'd you get your name?"

I should tell people I'm called Boo because I'm scary. Maybe then they'd back off. Still, I can't tell them that. The truth is I'm named after a cartoon character. Ha ha! Hee Hee! So cute! Seriously, I often wanted to respond by saying, "Well, here you are a writer for *Golfers Unlimited* magazine. The dude from *Tee to Green Living* just asked me the same damn question last week at the last golf course. You can't read what he wrote? I'm gonna say the same thing to you, and you'd better listen up, because this is the last time!" Maybe then I wouldn't have to tell 'em I'm scary.

You know, I don't really get the fascination with my name. I mean, there's a bunch of guys named Boo. It's not like it's that uncommon or that funny, really. Heck, there's even another dude in Milton named Boo. Talk about a small world within a small world. In fact, when I go home, I sometimes see him in the auto parts store where he works. We chitchat and he'll say, "What's up Boo?"

"Not much, Boo," I'll deadpan back.

"You're Boo One," he'll say.

"And you're Boo Two," I'll say. "I know."

Given some of my more colorful (brown, to be exact) stories later on in this book, I should probably be Boo 2, but that's not the point. The point is we're both named Boo, and we have fun with it, but nobody's running up to him asking *him* how he got his name. It's the same name, but mine is the one that gets all the attention. I mean, look:

Boo.

Boo.

Can you tell the difference? Me neither. A rose is a rose, and a Boo is a Boo. I'm just a person like any other Boo. I'm just trying to be myself when others are trying to make me something I'm not. I reckon as long as I'm being myself, I can't go wrong, no matter what others are doing. I suppose being made into something I'm not just kind of goes with the turfgrass of being a pro golfer. I'm learning to deal with that.

Heck, there's even some of that going on with this book. But that's okay. No one, nowhere, nohow, no matter what, can take away the fact that I'm a pro golfer, even if I don't look the part.

The good news for me is that it doesn't matter what you look like in Q school. You just have to play well, and because of my rank coming out, I was allowed to play, as I said, in the Sony Open in Hawaii, which was the first tournament of the 2002 season. Let me tell you something, I learned quickly that, though it may not matter if you look like a pro golfer, you'd better play like one if you want to stay in the game. I pretty much knew I wouldn't make the cut in that first tournament after a 1st-round score of 76. Even a 67 the second day wasn't good enough for me to make the cut.

After seven events on tour as a pro, you're reshuffled according to your money winnings. I didn't make the cut in my first seven events, so I became an alternate on a lot of tournaments, which is kind of like flying standby. I'd have to stay at home waiting for that phone call from the Tour saying, "Hey, you're in. You're a part of the PGA Tour again." You never know when that call will come. I might get the call on a Wednesday. I'd be in Florida, and the tournament might be in California and start on Thursday. Well, I wouldn't be able to fly all the way to California on Wednesday night and still be mentally ready to play golf on Thursday after an eight-hour flight. By the time I got through Atlanta with a layover and changed planes again in who-knows-where, I'd be a complete mess. With no time to practice, too, that sort of stuff can seriously mess with your game (and it messed with mine). It was mentally exhausting knowing I couldn't play, but that I had to be ready to play even when there was no realistic way for me to be ready to play.

When I finally did get in, I played well overall, or so I thought. I'd do almost everything right, but I'd just putt bad, or something like that. I see the glass as half full a lot, but really, if you're trying to make it as a pro golfer, you need to see it as half empty. You really need to push yourself, and it's not enough to do "almost everything right." I played in twenty-four events in 2002 and did almost everything right, but I made only five cuts. I missed nine cuts by one shot and a couple of others by two or three shots. Horseshoes and hand grenades, as they say. Then a couple I just blew way out of the water without the help of a hand grenade, shooting 80, 81, or some other terrible number. It's tough. People don't understand really how tough it is if you don't have a very good status on the Tour. It's especially daunting as a rookie coming out if you don't play well in the first couple of events. That was me.

There were bright spots, however. I shot the lowest round of my career at that time, with a 63 in the FedEx St. Jude Classic in Memphis on June 30, 2002, finishing tied for 19th. It was also the first money I'd won on Tour: $37,724. Lots of gravy there, and it felt pretty good. I'd missed the cut in the first ten events I'd played in, though, so the gravy was hard to come by. So was the confidence. Prior to Memphis, I didn't feel like I could play with those guys. My mind was being messed with again, and I was thinking at times that I wasn't worthy of a Tour card. If not for what had happened in my personal life the three years prior, I'd probably have just packed it in.

In 1999, I practiced a lot at Stonebrook Golf Club in Pace, Florida, just a stone's throw from my house. I used their driving range quite a bit. A cute young girl worked the ball counter there, which might've been the real reason I used their driving range quite a bit. I'd flirt with her, make her laugh, and try to charm her into giving me free range balls. She wouldn't do it. She was good like that.

Just for fun, I asked her one day to let me drive her brand-new 2000 Ford F-150 pickup. It was blacked out with tinted windows and had black wheels. That sucker was fine as frog's hair. The answer was no. I was happy with her saying anything at all, so "no" was fine by me. Still, it became a bit of a challenge to get her to say anything else. I worked with one of her older brothers at Monsanto and knew another brother, but neither had introduced me to his sister before. I couldn't understand why, though I'm sure they had their reasons.

One day my income tax refund arrived, so suddenly I had a little pocket change. That afternoon I was back at Stonebrook and walked up to the counter to get a bucket of balls for the driving range. As spur-of-the-moment as anything I've ever done, I asked the cute girl if she wanted to go to the mall in Pensacola to help me spend my refund check. It might've been the smartest thing I've ever done. I mean, what woman's going to refuse that offer? She could say no to giving me free golf balls, and she could say no to letting me drive her truck, but this was an offer she couldn't refuse, right? Right.

So off to the mall we went, on our first date. I don't remember much about it, because I was mostly focused on being nervous, but it must've gone pretty well because she accepted my request for a second date. I picked her up in my maroon '94 Sahara GMC 1500 pickup to go to the movies.

We were laughing about this and that, and having a good time on the drive to the theater, when suddenly she turned to look out her window. There, staring straight into her eyes, was a green tree frog glued to the window. I thought it was funny until she realized the frog was on the *inside* of the glass and starting screaming at the top of her lungs. She made me stop to remove the frog and was a freaked-out nervous wreck until we got out of the truck at the theater. She never rode in my truck again.

That was okay, though, because she did go out with me again, and again, and even again. (Can you believe it?) One thing led to another, and Karyn and I were married in March 2000. I was twenty-six, and she was twenty. My son, Parker, was born in 2001, and what do you know? I had a family.

I've always had family around me getting me through things. Whether by blood or by bond, all of the folks helping me in life are considered family. During the minitours (and through Q school), I had the Slocums pushing and pulling me, focusing me on the task at hand and taking care of me through it all. With the birth of my son in 2001, I had my own real-life family, and it changed me. It really did. Honestly, Karyn and Parker's coming into my life is what helped me get over the edge of making it out on tour and not just packing it in, because I felt more settled. Without good relationships and loving people in my life, people caring for me and people I could care for, I seriously don't know if I would have stuck it out. Shoot, I probably wouldn't have even had a chance to stick it out.

When I was single, I'd be gone for four or five months at a time, playing golf at every stop. After I got married and we had Parker, though, I always came home within a week's time. Even playing the minitours as long as I did, I was always within driving distance. It might take two days to get home, but I'd be home for at least three or four days before leaving again to drive to wherever the next event was held. That kept me grounded and really made it work. I felt that I wasn't just floating out there on my own, so I could carry on no matter what.

Good thing, too, because I lost my Tour card after the 2002 season. I finished ranking too low and simply lost it. My golf confidence plummeted, and without family, I think golf might've left me altogether. Even with family, I started to question my career choice and wondered whether I should continue to chase the dream of playing pro golf. I'd think, *Why am I doing this? Why am I even out there if I'm not really competing with those guys?* It was time to go beyond family, to the One who gives us family.

I went to Jesus, and I sat and prayed, *Lord, what are you trying to show me here? What are you trying to give me? I know I have the talent. Why am I not out there using my gift? Lord, I don't know what you have planned for me, but whatever it is, I accept it and will do my best.*

I guess when I told Jesus I'd do my best, my best wasn't all that good, because after that prayer, I went on to play the Nationwide Tour, which is a step below the PGA Tour, and to be honest, I didn't play very well the first year. I finished 70-something. The next year was much the same, with me finishing 80-something. I was thinking, *This is my best?* Then the worst happened. The following year, 2004, I lost my full status and had to go on conditional status. It was the lowest of the low points in my life. Rock bottom. The end of the road. Decision time.

At that point, Karyn and I had several in-depth discussions about our future. The way we saw it, I could apply for the head pro position at Brewton Country Club, in Alabama, or some other country club, or I could go back out and try to play pro golf one last time. We were out of money. I mean out. O-U-T, out. Flat broke. Still, Karyn and I decided I had to get out there and try to play golf again.

Time went by, and in 2006, Karyn and I were starting to have some issues in our relationship. The stress of everything going on around us was sneaking in and making a mess of things. At the same time, I was trying to make a comeback on the Nationwide Tour. Being gone as much as I was and having to drive back and forth (unlike with the PGA Tour, where you can hop on an airplane and fly at any time) kept me away from home more and more. Since I was playing for a quarter of the money I'd played for on the PGA Tour, I figured I had to play all of the Nationwide events. I was gone from home far too much, and Karyn was working at Dad's pharmacy. It was all probably making her feel like a single mother at times, and our relationship suffered for it. Neither of us was used to being apart for so long, and we just weren't the kind of people made for the pace we were living.

It was different from anything I'd experienced before. "Country" and "hectic" just don't mix well. They're like oil and water, and there apparently ain't nothing in this world (not even BP or the government) that can fix a bad oil-and-water combo. Sometimes we just need to call on a higher power. I knew it was what I needed to do, so for me, it was time for another come-to-Jesus meeting.

In this second meeting with Jesus, I just shut up and let Him do all the talkin'. He showed me that I needed to start focusing more on my family. He let me know that He had made me to be a man, not a boy. He wanted me to quit horsing around, staying out all night, partying, and goofing off and doing this, that, and the other.

It was tough to realize all of this, but if you can swallow your pride in moments of clarity from the Lord and accept responsibility, life's a whole lot better, even if it ain't easier. I heard Him loud and clear, and instead of saying something back to Him, I decided to let my actions speak. So I got my act a little straighter and started taking this golf thing a helluva (wait, am I allowed to say that?) lot more seriously. I put my fishing poles down, I quit taking 'em with me, and let me tell you, that was a big freakin' deal. Boo Weekley is giving up fishing for golf? That's when you know I've turned a corner, and I did turn a corner. When I got up in the mornings, I worked out. Over time, I got in pretty good shape, if I do say so myself. I started feeling comfortable and felt pretty dang good about what I was doing and who I was becoming.

I had to go back to the minitours again, which was okay with me because I didn't just feel like I was starting over; I felt like I was starting anew. The first three events that I played in 2006 were on the NGA Hooters Tour.

Okay, I know what you're thinking. I had a come-to-Jesus meeting, and I came out of that meeting to play in the Hooters Tour of all things. I couldn't make this up if I tried, but hey, what can I say? The Lord works in mysterious ways.

So with the Lord's blessing, I was set to play in one Hooters event in Pensacola, one outside Atlanta, and another one in Auburn. I played in Pensacola well enough to be exempt for the next Hooters event in Georgia. I didn't play well enough there to be exempt in Auburn, though. Obviously, I was still a work in progress, but I was a work, and sometimes that's all you need to be.

So there I was back on the minitours after being on the PGA Tour in 2002 and the Nationwide Tour for three years. None of my experience mattered, and it was humbling. Maybe a little frustrating, too. You see, I didn't play well enough at this Hooters event in Georgia, so I had to go back to Auburn and Monday-qualify [i.e., pay a fee the Monday before a tournament and compete for one of about fourteen open spots]. I was like, *I have to Monday-qualify for a Hooters event? I mean, seriously.* All I could do was look up and praise the good Lord for his fine sense of humor.

By no means am I a bragging person. Ask anyone. Still, I wouldn't be being honest if I didn't tell you that maybe ten of the guys at qualifying school that final time were anywhere near my league. The point is because of where I'd come from, playing on conditional status and all, I had to qualify again just like any other Joe Blow off the street. Like I said, though, I was done talking and wanted my actions to speak. So I did what I had to do. I qualified, got in, and played.

In Pensacola, I made around $2,000. Over in Georgia I made right about $900–$1,000. In Auburn, I made about $4,000. I thought, *Okay, I'm on a pretty decent roll here. Let's keep it goin' now.* So Joe and I headed to the next event, in North Carolina. It was called the Tarheel Tour. We started driving from Auburn all the way up to Winston-Salem, which is about a five-hour drive. I was focused and ready to keep on keepin' on.

We arrived in North Carolina on Sunday for a Tuesday-Wednesday-Thursday tournament. After my practice round on Monday, I said, "Jo Jo, if we don't shoot a 66-66-66 and win this thing by ten, we need to go home. We don't belong here."

I was in the second group out on Tuesday morning. I birdied the first 4 holes and got a little swagger going. I made par on hole 5. Hole 6 was about a 530–540-yard par 5. I mashed a perfect drive off the tee. We rode the golf cart (allowed at this tourney) to the ball, and Jo Jo said he thought it was a straight 3-iron. I agreed and sent the ball on up there. It settled about 10 feet from the hole. "We're fixin' to get us an eagle here," I boastfully stated.

So there I was, standing all proudlike and feeling good and confident. Then I felt a tickle in my pocket. It was my cell phone vibrating. Let me tell you, there's nothing like a little movement in a man's pocket to break his concentration.

Anyway, I thought I'd turned my phone off (and should've), but obviously not, so I pulled it out of my pocket to ignore the call, shut it off, and get back to making eagle. The problem was I caught a glimpse of who was calling. My glimpse turned into a solid look, so I could be sure. Yep, it was the PGA Tour calling.

I let the call go through to voice mail as I tried to find a private place to check the message. I noticed the most private place of all (the bathroom), in the distance a bit, and headed on over. Looking back, I probably should've thought it was a little dangerous to be in the bathroom on a phone call. Guys like me have a way of dropping things in toilets, and I ain't just talking about poop.

Anyway, I dialed in and found I had two voice mails waiting for me. The first was from Karyn, and she was wishing me luck. The second went something like this:

"This is the PGA Tour calling. You're in the Nationwide

event in Athens, Georgia, so please call back and confirm you'll be participating."

I pressed END on my cell phone, put it back in my pocket, and rushed out of the bathroom (might've been the first and only time I've ever done that without leaving a mess behind). I quickly found Joe and said, "Hey, dude, we're in. We're in at Athens. Let's get outta here."

The hole-6 eagle I was fixin' to make had already gone, and I had one thing on my mind. I walked over to the officials at the 6th green and said, "Guys, it was great meeting ya'll. You can keep the ball. We've gotta go." I called the PGA and thought about what I'd say as the phone was ringing. Lots of thoughts raced through my head. Well, my thoughts turned to words, which came out of my mouth, went through the phone, and ended up in the ear of the PGA guy at the other end of the phone. "I'll be right there," I said.

Joe and I cut through somebody's yard (and then somebody else's) and found the guy running the Tarheel Tour. I got right to it and said, "Man, I appreciate you letting me play in your tournament. I enjoyed meeting everyone. Is there any way I can get my money back?"

He was surprised but not really taken by surprise like I had hoped. He might've been okay with Boo Weekley leaving his tournament, but he was going to hang on to that money for sure. "No," he said. "Once you've teed it up, there's no refund."

I shrugged and responded with, "Well, I thought I'd ask, 'cause nine hundred dollars is a lot of money to me right now." I was going for one little last twist of his heart to get that money back.

"I understand, but I'm afraid not."

117

With my $900 a lost cause, we quickly found my truck and headed back to Georgia with renewed gusto. This was it! This was my chance. My second chance, in fact. Once I got that call in mid-April 2006, I knew it was the Nationwide for the rest of the year, and I was pumped. Nine hundred bucks poorer, mind you, but still pumped.

That ride to Georgia seemed longer than normal. I could hardly focus on the actual road we were on, because I kept thinking about the long and difficult road I had to take to get where I was going (not to mention the rest of the way I still had to go).

I've seen it written and heard it said, "Boo Weekley came out of nowhere . . ." Well, I might've come *from* nowhere (or the middle of it anyway), but I don't think I came *out* of nowhere. Maybe to the media or the casual fan, I did. They haven't been with me the whole time, so I can see how they might think I just showed up one day and started playing on the PGA Tour. Well, it wasn't like that. No, sir, it wasn't like that at all. Let me tell you, I worked my ass off to get into that truck heading for Athens, Georgia. I was a veteran of the minitours and the Nationwide Tour. From 1997 to 2007, I traveled this country playing for pay, and without anyone really taking notice. Ten long and crazy years. Yeah, not exactly overnight, wouldn't you agree?

Anyway, there I was heading back to the Nationwide. I'd played the Nationwide five straight seasons, though I'd played only two events in 2002. I almost won as much money on the 2003 Nationwide Tour as I did on the 2002 PGA Tour. I finished 67th in 2003, and 91st in the Nationwide standings in both 2004 and '05, winning $50,000 each year. Talk about consistent. Well, consistency wasn't my goal for 2006. Besides,

91st wasn't good enough to put me back on the Nationwide Tour, and I knew it. Only the top 80 were exempt into the field, so 91st would leave me just outside the bubble. I had to do better.

Actually, saying I had to do better is an understatement. I had to improve something fierce. Sitting in that truck riding back to Georgia, I set a new goal for myself. I needed a top-20 finish to get my card back and resume my PGA career, and that's what I was going to do. Heck, at that point I wasn't even on the Nationwide yet, so heading to Georgia was the first step. I smiled a little as I thought about taking it.

It's sort of funny how a "first step" can involve a trip from Georgia to North Carolina and back to Georgia, but that's the way it is sometimes. Let me tell you, the stopover in North Carolina was well worth it, too. I lost $900, of course, but I picked up a little swagger (looking back, $900 seems like a very small price to pay for that swagger) and brought it along to Georgia with me. I shot a 71 on the par-72 course the first day and a 69 on day two. I went on to finish 42nd, which is a long way from 91st and pushed me a little closer to the bubble. "We're off and running," I told Joe. "They can't stop us now. We're going to get in the next couple of events."

I meant what I said, and I made the field the next week in the BMW Charity Pro-Am at The Cliffs in Greenville, South Carolina. I played even better there, finishing 30th. Now, the Tour reshuffles everybody after seven events, and since that event was the seventh Nationwide event for the 2006 season, we were reshuffled. That put me inside the eighty-man field. This was my opportunity to stay with the Nationwide for the rest of the season, and I wasn't going to miss it.

With the pressure off a bit, I went to the Virginia Beach

Open and kept rising. I improved my play yet again and finished 13th. For the first three events, I earned about $14,000, which helped my financial situation a bit and even helped me finally let go of that $900 I lost in North Carolina. North Carolina blue had turned to Virginia green!

Still, though I certainly needed it, it wasn't about the money. It was about doing what I'd set out to do. It was about making my thinking and goal setting on that truck ride back to Georgia mean something. It was about seizing the day and making the most of the opportunity. I solidified my position on the Nationwide and played it exclusively for the rest of 2006. That's what I wanted to do, and that's what I did.

I didn't get to play in the first five Nationwide events, but I played in twenty-four of the remaining twenty-six tournaments. I had some ground to make up on the other players, so I played every one I could. I took full advantage of the opportunity and was determined to not let it slip away again. I practiced harder than I'd ever practiced: I worked on chipping, and I worked on putting (which has always been my weakness). I even left my fishing rods at the house along with my hunting rifles. It was golf, golf, and more golf. That was it. That was what I was about. I was serious.

After missing a couple of cuts, I started making my move. I finished 5th in Raleigh, North Carolina, followed by four top-ten finishes. I settled into my game with newfound confidence and started playing like I knew I could. As the season progressed, I started getting better, and better, and better still. The next thing you know, I'd gotten myself in a position to win some tournaments.

I chugged my way to Chattanooga, Tennessee, and played in the Chattanooga Classic. Going into the fourth round (the championship round), I had a two-stroke lead. Although I shot a 3 under, three other players caught me and caused a four-way playoff. I lost in the playoff and finished tied for 3rd.

Now the old Boo might've thought, *Well, at least I was in it and had a shot.* That wasn't good enough for the new Boo. I wanted to win, and I knew I had to keep working. My Sunday scores weren't where they needed to be for me to win tournaments. So I thought about what I could do to improve.

It always seemed like Sunday's score was the highest of all the days. By the time I got to hole 13, 14, or 15, I was exhausted and just couldn't close it out. I decided it was time to get in shape. I was becoming obsessed with my golf game and doing everything I could to improve. I was constantly thinking about what I could do to get a little edge here or there. I started watching my diet and jogging every day. I lost 39 pounds during the summer months and felt so much better. I had enough energy to complete a round and make the swings.

As good as I was playing and managing my health at that time, things weren't going as well on the home front. You know that focus on the family I talked about earlier? Well, I lost it. I was so focused on golf that everything else just sort of took a backseat. Golf became everything, and life as a golfer consumed me, on and off the course. The off-the-course part got to Karyn. I guess you could say I was acting like a bachelor while being married. Not that I was doing anything really wrong, like cheatin' or nothing. I just wasn't coming home when I should've and stuff like that. I got into a routine of going out every night after a round and staying out too late, yucking it up with the caddies and other golfers. I was stuck on my golf career and on myself. It was all about me. My behavior pushed Karyn too far. She felt that she couldn't trust me. She felt as if I were abandoning her and our little boy, Parker. Looking back, I totally understand how she felt and I would've felt the same way. I was being selfish and couldn't (or wouldn't) see beyond the world of golf. I wasn't being a husband. I wasn't being a father. I wasn't home when Karyn needed somebody to lean on and I wasn't there to help when she was stressed out. It was like I was married to myself instead of to Karyn, and she was ready to let me have myself. At the time, though, I just tried to ignore it all and turned my attention to playing golf.

My breakout performance and finish came in late August and was bittersweet. At the National Mining Association Pete Dye Classic in Bridgeport, West Virginia, I went into the final round leading by two strokes and led Jason Enloe by four strokes with only 4 holes to play. I bogeyed 16 and 18, while Jason birdied 15, 16, and 18 to tie me and force a playoff.

The bitter: In the playoff, we replayed the 18th hole, which is the one I'd just bogeyed minutes earlier. I don't know if that weighed heavily on my mind or if it was just meant to be, but I bogeyed that hole for the second time in less than 30 minutes. Jason made par for the win. That was the third time during the 2006 season I'd gone into the championship round with a lead, only to see it slip away.

The sweet: It was my first 2nd-place finish in a Nationwide event and was the most money I'd won in any professional event ($64,800). The following week, I finished 3rd and won $34,000. Nearly $100,000 in two weeks! I was pretty dang excited and humbled at the same time. There were guys at the chemical plant who didn't make that much in three years.

The money was nice, and it made me think back to when I first convinced Karyn to go out with me. I had a little more money now to spend and kind of laughed to myself about how I'd asked Karyn out to help me spend my tax refund check way back then. If only money really could buy me love.

I could've made a million dollars, though, and it wouldn't have erased the trouble in my personal life. I could try to put it out of my mind, but that wouldn't change reality. Karyn had had enough, and that was that. Unfortunately, it took divorce proceedings for me to realize how serious it was and that I was missing the most beautiful thing that'd ever happened to me. At the same time, it forced me to see I was also missing out on my little boy's life. Let me tell you, when that stuff hits, it hits hard. The very thing that got in the way of my family now started suffering because of it. As the stress of my crumbing marriage built, my golf game started going downhill. My living situation was on a bit of a downswing, too.

Karyn kicked me out of the trailer we were living in, and I moved in with my mamma for a couple of months. Of course, that really made me want to be gone playing golf all the time (not because of my mamma, but because I didn't want to feel like a lame-o again), so I sort of did a nosedive even deeper into all that and away from Karyn. We went in opposite directions there for a while and sort of held each other at a distance.

I started blaming my poor play on Karyn and on what was happening with her. Misplaced anger, but misplaced with a purpose. If I couldn't put it all out of my mind (which I couldn't), then I was going to be mad about it, dang it! The realization of a pending divorce hammered me emotionally. The pain never fully went away. I hid the tension from the public and the media, but it was there. It was buried deep down inside, but I could always feel it. I always carried it.

Still, I was on enough of a roll with golf that there was just no way I could totally drop it and go find a hole to crawl in and die (even if I felt like doing just that). I knew I had to move forward and not shipwreck all the work I'd done in the first portion of 2006 on the Nationwide. I had to play through the emotional pain. That's easier said than done, but I did my best to focus on golf while dealing with lawyers, judges, pleadings, and court dates. Then came the physical pain.

I started having problems with my shoulder and wrist. Nothing major, but all the other stuff going on with Karyn just made me more sensitive to every little discomfort, whether physical or emotional. I was feeling sorry for myself.

I kept going with golf, but there wasn't really much actual motion there. It was more like going through the motions while dealing with emotions. I pretty much put my golf game in cruise control for the last month of the 2006 season, except when I went to the last regular-season event, the Miccosukee Championship in Miami, Florida. I refocused then and somehow played very well, only to lose it on the final hole and finish 2nd. It was a good closeout to the regular season under any circumstances and a fantastic closeout considering my state of mind (and heart) at the time.

Then came the tournament championship, which was to wrap up the Nationwide Tour for 2006. Some of my focus from the Miccosukee Championship carried over, and I had a good chance to win there, too. I went into the championship round in 2nd place. Then, on Sunday (my typical bad day), I hit hockey sticks (77) after shooting 69-69-68 the two days prior. I fell to 18th. Still, my number had been punched, and I wound up number 7 overall. I busted my butt that year and proved to myself that I could play with great golfers, future PGA stars. I'd won $312,843 and earned my PGA Tour card for 2007. It was now time to challenge the best in the world. Again.

So I got my Tour card back and couldn't have been happier. Of course, that's just a figure of speech. Truth is, I *could've* been happier. My excitement from doing so well and getting back on the PGA Tour was tempered by the reality that I was losing my true love, Karyn.

I didn't know what to do, and then, in early 2007, it was official. I got my divorce papers while I was back home, and the divorce was finalized. Over. I'd gotten back on the Tour, but I'd lost Karyn, and I didn't like it. Not one little bit. I missed having her around to talk with after a bad day on the course or to celebrate a good round. Everything was better with her, and nothing seemed right without her. I missed her walk and her talk, and everything in between. Shoot, I just plain missed *her*. Though I'd gotten my Tour card back and had wanted it bad, I found myself wanting to get Karyn back even more.

I think the glimmer of hope I got from thinking about getting her back helped me stay somewhat positive about things and look forward to and ride the high wave of excitement for the first PGA event of the 2007 season, the Sony Open in Hawaii. Joe and I had high expectations for that event. I mean *high* expectations. Sure, he and I were both nervous, but we truly expected to win that thing right out of the gate. We were confident. We were focused. We were ready. We didn't need a speech by Lou Holtz to pump us up. In fact, the way we were feeling, Lou might've walked away from any such encounter with a little more pep in *his* step.

Well, I didn't win it, but I did manage a top-20 finish in the first PGA tournament I'd played in since 2002. I was pleased with my performance. Not satisfied, mind you, but pleased. It was a good start. I learned I could make the cut out there and felt that I was out there because I belonged out there. I was a pro golfer, and I was ready for more.

Oh, but what a difference a day (or a week) makes.

My attitude did a 180 when we got to Pebble Beach for the next event, the following week. I just wasn't feeling it, and I told Joe this as soon as we arrived, "We're done. I can't play this golf course. It's the worst place in the world. I hate this course. I hate how I play on this course." I stayed in a foul-assed mood all morning, and Joe just took it. I carried on like a big ol' crybaby. It was 60 degrees, windy, and felt a lot colder than 60. The greens looked like someone had turned a herd of cattle on 'em. The balls plugged the fairway. I felt there was no way I could win there, plain and simple. Wah, wah, wah! Joe did his best comforting daddy impression and tried to keep me in it. "Come on, man," he said. "Let's just play golf. You can do it."

Well, he pushed and pushed until I gave in. I kept whining, for sure, but I gave it a shot, subpar as it was. I shot 72-75-69-75 and was cut from the five-round tournament.

I'd worked so hard to regain my status on the Tour, and now I wasn't playing even close to my potential. I knew I was off, and I could see myself doing the one-and-done thing all over again. I missed three of the next four cuts, and even with the one I made, I finished 54th. I felt that getting my Tour card back just wasn't enough, and I started thinking about Karyn again. I just couldn't put the divorce behind me, and my play reflected it. It wasn't enough to think about getting

Karyn back; I had to actually do it. Shoot, I'd already lost weight, so at least I had that going for me! Still, my newfound rippedness (if I do say so myself) wouldn't be enough. I needed Parker's help.

You see, the good thing (well, good in my case) about having kids with someone you're separated from is that it forces you to see that someone. More importantly, it forces that someone to see you. On one such occasion when Karyn had no choice but to see me, we got to talking. It was like old times, and I'm not totally sure how Karyn felt, but it kind of felt at times like a first date all over again for me. There was that cute girl working the counter, saying no to giving me free balls and to taking her new truck for a spin. There we were after all those years, separated, of course, but talking again, because at one point she had said yes to me. She had said yes. To me!

I realized once and for all that I needed her. Golf, fishing, and all that stuff was good, but I didn't *need* it. I needed that woman, and it was clearer than ever to me that night. Let me tell you, it wasn't just because of Parker either. I wasn't feeling like we needed to stick it out for him. No, I needed *her*. Plain and simple.

I think she realized that night she needed me, too, because she decided to let me back in the house. We fell in love all over again and rededicated ourselves to each other. We each rededicated everything to the other and got back on the right page. She's a little crazy, no doubt, but you would be, too, if you had to deal with me. Crazy or not, I'm crazy about her. I love that woman more than anything. More than golf. More than fishing. More than myself. More than anything.

With Karyn back in my life, I felt whole again. The little

things made sense and were in their right place, so the pressure was off when it came to golf. My golf game went back to its roots, and I started playing the golf I knew I could play. I told myself, *Okay, you've rededicated yourself to Karyn. Now get out there and make her proud!*

Karyn and I sat down and started making plans to build our house. It was her dream, and I started thinking about what I needed to do on the golf course to make her dream come true. Heck, it didn't matter much to me where we lived. I was just as happy as could be in that single-wide trailer. She wanted more, though, and I wanted to give it to her. When I started dreaming her dreams with her, golf became more than a game. We were feeling connected, and life was fun again.

So I jumped back into my golf game headfirst and started playing hard. I started working at it like never before, and it finally had real purpose behind it. Then I went to Mexico to compete in the Mayakoba Classic at Riviera Maya–Cancún. Armed with a new attitude and the comfort and joy of reestablishing my marriage, I was feeling I could really win that tourney. I started right in the middle of the first round playing well. I mean, really, really good golf, like I actually was trying to impress that cute girl I married all those years ago. I started hitting some shots as if golf were just what I was born to do. I birdied 6, 7, 8, 9 in a row, and I finished the day with 9 birdies and only 1 bogey, for a sizzlin' 64, which was two shots off the lead. Second place. It was close all the way, and I ended up finishing 6th, which was my highest PGA finish to date and my largest paycheck, at $126,000. Now that was sure to impress Karyn! I thought, *Yeah, that's what I'm talkin' about. I can really do this!*

Listen, playing pro golf is a dream, for sure, but it's hard work all the way there. Too many would-be golfers have the dream but little else. You have to want to work hard, and you have to have some resolve. You have to be able to stomach the sight of your dream in the emergency room from time to time, gasping for air, trying to find a way to stay alive.

You need even more than that, though. You need to have the right perspective and to put golf in its proper place. You need to have balance in your personal life and good relationships with your loved ones. You need to love people more than you love golf.

Now, don't get me wrong. When I say you need to love people, I mean you need to love your loved ones. I don't mean you need to love your competition. No, sir, you need to be able to put your competition in their proper place and that place is somewhere below you.

When I first started, a guy could send his paperwork in and might shoot 81, 81, 81 across the board. If he got paired with a guy like me (and I mean the me of right now, not the me of my pre-pro days) and he still shot 81s, but here I was with 69s, 66s, and stuff like that, his dream would be shattered quickly. If I'm not doing it to someone, someone else is doing it to that someone, or worse yet, someone is doing it to me. You're not trying to be rude or mean or anything like that. It's just the way it is out there, with so many guys chasing the dream. You have to expect guys to say things like "Hey man, you ain't ready for this. You know what I mean? You're not mentally ready, and your golf game sure ain't ready for it. Your chances are not slim, they're anorexic. Keep the dream alive and go home and work on your game."

I hate to tell anybody that, because it's a dream, you know. I'm just saying you have to be ready for it, even expect it. That's also because it's a dream. You see, if you're dreaming it, someone else is dreaming it, too. Sometimes there's room for only a certain number of people in a dream. Are you going to make it in there? Can you take the jabs? Do you have what it takes to make the cut? Do you have what it takes to do a little cutting down? For me, that last one is the hard part. Hey, the good Lord blessed me with dogged resolve and just enough talent to make it to the highest level of golf, but the rest is up to me. He gave me the will and the skill, and I'll do whatever else I gotta do beyond that to fulfill His plan for me. Think you might have what it takes to join me on the ride? See you in school. Maybe even on Tour. Always remember one thing, though: At the end of the day, I get to go home to Karyn, so I win. If you ever do make it to the Tour, get ready for a wild ride, especially if I'm still around. Funny things happen when I'm around. You'd be blown away by the sights and sounds. Oh, and the smells.

7 O CANADA, EH!

Some say I'm like John Daly, only without all that drama. Well, those folks haven't been on the road with me. When I put on my travelin' shoes there's no lack of real-life mayhem. Sometimes when I'm away from home, I can make Daly's life seem downright tranquil.

It was July 2002, and I'd never left the confines of the United States, so I marked the calendar well in advance of the 2002 Canadian Open. The idea of going to another country was intriguing. I was perfectly fine with Canada being my first out-of-country experience, even though it wasn't overseas or even all that different a culture (though, I have to point out that, really, going just about anywhere at all provides a little culture shock for a southern boy like me). I've read good things about our neighbors to the north. The scenery in magazines was breathtaking, and the fishing and hunting stories inspired many daydreams. The only hunting I was gonna be doing on this trip, however, was for eagles and birdies.

I flew from a tournament in Arizona to Canada on a private PGA charter jet. I'd always heard you needed a passport or a birth certificate to go to Canada, but somehow the Tour set it up so we could fly in and out of Canada with only a driver's license and proof of insurance. I had both, so I figured I was good to go.

It was close to midnight when we landed in Vancouver. I was a little worried about customs cutting into my beauty sleep. The next morning I was scheduled to be up and at 'em with my caddie at the butt-crack of dawn. To my surprise and relief, though, we breezed through customs.

Outside the doors, an older man met us with keys to the Buick courtesy cars we'd be driving during the tournament. Me with my own car in a foreign country? Shoot, I get lost going to Wal-Mart back home in Milton. New places and big cities really test my navigation skills, and Vancouver was both new and big. I'd even tried a TomTom GPS unit in the past, but I didn't really gel with the nice lady in the GPS. I'm more of a face-to-face, real-person type of guy.

I figured the old man handing us our keys was my 411 dude, so I pulled him to the side and asked for his help. Our accents didn't exactly geehaw. Mine has a southern twang, and his, well . . . it was a Canadian twang. I proceeded to ask him for directions to the hotel anyway.

"You go down to the next street, eh," the man excitedly explained, pointing toward the huge glass window wall. "Turn left and go perhaps ten kilometers, and then you turn right at the light, eh. Then go straight for sixteen kilometers, eh . . ."

"Whoa, whoa," I said. "How much is a kilometer? Can you break it down into miles?"

"I don't know the exact conversions," he said, "but you'll see big lights and a fancy building . . ."

They don't give directions in Canada the way we do back at the ranch. At home, if I ask directions to a hunting camp, the guy giving them might say, "Go down the road a ways and turn left at the twin oaks. You'll pass where Fat Willie's shop used to be, on your right. Take the right fork at Roy Wright's—he's always got cows in the side yard—then go past Good Hope Baptist Church and it's the first iron gate on your right." Now I can find my way with those kinds of directions.

"Okay. Thank you, sir," I said, and nodded gratefully to the old man.

"Remember to turn left at the first street, eh," he said as I walked away.

I didn't write the old man's directions down, but I thought if I could get past the kilometers/miles thing, I could get to where I was going. I guess I forgot all about being directionally disabled.

It was pretty cool to be in Canada, but I was worn out and wanted to get some rest for the next day's activities. I started driving in the direction the old man had pointed. I drove, drove, and drove some more . . . for some 30 minutes, but A Street (which is what I thought the old man meant when he was referring to streets and saying "eh") was nowhere in sight.

I figured I'd missed A Street altogether and needed to turn around, but I pressed onward for a few more minutes, hoping it was just ahead. The road turned darker by the second, and the traffic thinned to nothing.

Suddenly bright lights appeared in the distance about a

mile away. I sped up, thinking they must be the lights the old man mentioned. I thought, *I'll get into this little town and stop and ask for directions. I've gotta be close.* However, there wasn't really a place to stop. The road just kind of went through the lights, so I drove straight and passed on through 'em, too. Then there was darkness again.

I soon saw a sign that read TO SEATTLE. Seattle? Seattle, British Columbia, Canada? I wondered if they had a football team, too. Then it hit me like Bobby Boucher (pronounced Boo-Shay, like my name with a "Shay" on the end), that hard-hitting linebacker from the Deep South in that *Waterboy* movie. I wasn't heading toward Seattle, Canada. That sign was for Seattle, Washington. I'd just driven through some sort of checkpoint without slowing down and was back in the United States.

I quickly cut through the median, did a U-turn, and proceeded to the Canadian border-crossing checkpoint—but this time I stopped. It was approaching 2:30 in the morning, and I had no idea where I was, how I'd gotten there, or how to get where I was supposed to be gettin'.

"Where are you going, and what will you be doing in Canada?" the border patrol agent asked.

"I'm a professional golfer and I was just in your country, but I took the wrong road and somehow I ended up here."

The border patrol guy sort of cocked his head to side and squinted a little bit.

"Well, now, how is it that you were just in Canada and now are trying to get back in?"

"I just did a U-turn down the road and I need to get back to Vancouver," I said as I handed him a copy of my itinerary.

"Let's see your passport or birth certificate."

"I don't have either one of those, sir," I added weakly.

He straightened his head and said, "Then you can't come in."

"But sir, I'm already in." Made sense to me, even though it didn't make no sense.

"No, you aren't. You're in the United States! And you don't have proper credentials. And where did you get this car?"

Okay, I was getting offended at that time. It felt like a bit of southern profilin' was going on there at the border.

"What, do you think I stole this car, sir?" I blurted out. Okay, so using the words "stole" and "car" in the same sentence while standing in front of a border patrol agent without the proper papers to get in was a bad idea. Who knew?

"Oh, you stole the car, eh?"

"No, no, I didn't steal the car."

"Well, you said you did."

"No, I didn't. Look at the side of the car. It says 'PGA Tour Canadian Open.' Do you think I made that sticker and stuck it on the side of the door?" That went over like a turd in a punch bowl.

"Listen here, young man. You need to step out of the car. Now!"

I got out of the car while he punched numbers on his little phone thingie. He kept an eye on me the whole time, like I was some sort of terrorist with WMD in my backseat.

He hung up the phone and stepped out of the booth. "What's in the backseat of the car?"

Oh, you gotta be kidding! You know, I'm glad I wasn't actually in my car from back home 'cause who knows what would've been in the backseat? Not WMD, but it easily could've been a 7 mm rifle, a .44 Magnum handgun, or a cooler filled with a few too many largemouth bass. Would've been peculiar to this guy no matter what, I'm sure.

"My golf clubs."

"What's in the trunk?"

"WMD." Just kidding, I didn't say that. I told him my clothes were in the trunk and that I was a PGA golfer. I looked at my watch. "I have to be at the golf course in a few hours."

"Well, son, you can't just come into our country without going through the process. Open the trunk."

I popped it open, and he swiftly unzipped my suitcase and started dumping my shirts and whatnots into the trunk. Now, I'm pretty OCD when it comes to packing my bags. I fold every piece of clothing just so, and this dude was messin' it all up but good. I tried stopping him by explaining there was nothing but clothes and stuff in the bag, but he paid no attention, wrinkling everything inside, and he wasn't going to stop sifting until he was satisfied I wasn't smuggling some sort of contraband, I guess.

"Okay, I'm done here. Let's see what's in the other bag."

I thought, *Oh, man, now he's gonna screw with my clubs!*

"It's just golf clubs. Careful," I pleaded as he unzipped the bag and promptly dumped my lifeblood onto the concrete.

"Dude, you can't do that!" I didn't know whether to puke or throw a punch. Thankfully, I was able to keep my vomit and my fists to myself.

"Shut up, Yankee!"

Who, me? A Yankee? I've been called a lot of things, but Yankee ain't one of 'em. I definitely felt some profiling was going on then. Just 'cause I'm white doesn't mean I'm a Yankee. Calling a boy from Milton a Yankee . . . well, them are fightin' words.

"Keep quiet. Stop talking. You're about to be in big trouble."

"You're right, you're right," I said as I backed away. This guy's fighting words notwithstanding, I realized I'd pushed enough.

My clubs were scattered on the pavement, getting no respect. I had no one to call, and I was about to go to jail. How was I going to explain this? I was going to miss the tournament, and all because I'd driven across the Canadian border by mistake. Then it dawned on me that I could be in even more trouble for blasting past the checkpoint coming from Canada and into the United States. I pictured a swarm of blue-and-red flashing lights behind me. I could see myself facedown on the pavement in handcuffs. I imagined cameras coming out of nowhere and could even hear someone singing, "Bad boys, bad boys, whatcha gonna do?" My only defense would be that somebody in the U.S. booth was asleep at the switch or had gone out for doughnuts. My career would be over.

I snapped out of it when I saw the real flashing lights of a Royal Canadian Mounted Police patrol car. Out stepped a Mountie looking all dapper, dressed in full uniform, and appearing ready to rescue a damsel in distress tied to a railroad track. He looked the part of Sergeant Preston of the Yukon from the old TV series of the same name. The only things missing were his horse, Rex, and his faithful dog, Yukon King. Oh, and a damsel, of course. I mean, I'm purty and all, but I ain't pretty. Know what I mean?

The situation I found myself in wasn't pretty either. This was quickly developing into an international incident of sorts.

"What's the problem here?" the Mountie asked.

"Sir, I've been trying to explain to this guy that I flew into Canada on a private flight with the PGA Tour," I said. "I picked up my car, this car, and the old man who gave me directions got me lost with all this 'eh' talk." I handed the Mountie every paper I had in the car. "How I made it through the checkpoint and eventually got back here, I don't have a clue. All I know is that I have to meet my caddie in a few hours."

Thank God he knew there was a golf tournament in Vancouver. My story was making sense to him. Must've been my southern charm. He headed toward his patrol car and told me to get back in my car and follow him.

So we went by car. Two separate cars, mind you. During the police escort to my hotel, I made it a point to look at every single street sign along the way. I never did see A Street.

My hero in red got me back to the hotel just in time to change and hotfoot it to the golf course for my practice round. No sleep! Being purty and all, I like to get eight hours of beauty sleep if I'm playing golf the next day, but I hadn't gotten even an hour that night. A brief late afternoon nap after the practice round was all I got. I took a quick look in the mirror and saw a not-so-purty Boo looking back at me. Turned out to be a sign of what the next few days were going to look like.

I continued my mediocre play and missed the cut by one stroke. One lousy stroke. Stupid border patrol agent and all of his pro(golfer)filing! I just couldn't get past the previous day's events and my lack of sleep. Still, there was a silver lining. The PGA had in its lineup of perks and extracurricular activities a trout fishing trip, which is a trip I'd always wanted to take. If I couldn't keep golfing, fishing would do just fine.

On Saturday, three of us golfers who didn't make the cut drove about 30 minutes to a trout preserve. I'd been to some pretty swanky country clubs in my day, but none finer than the trout lodge I visited there in British Columbia. The finest fly-fishing equipment imaginable lined one long wall. It's what I imagine a wall in Heaven would look like. Left-handed, right-handed, 12-footers, 8-footers—they had 'em all. You might recall that I swing a golf club right-handed but chuck a fishing rod left-handed. Well, that was no problem at all. They had everything a bothpawed southern boy like me needed for outdoor adventurin'. I was outfitted and out of there.

A picturesque landscape of rolling hills with snowcapped mountains as a backdrop surrounded the series of trout ponds. Whoah. Dreams really do come true every once in a while, even for a country boy from Florida. I didn't even have to go to Orlando for it to happen on that day. I was just fine right there in the trout ponds, Canadafornia dreamin'.

They call it "fly-fishing." The only fly-rod-type fishing I'd ever done before was what we southern boys call "slash-fishing." Back home we use popping bugs—the panfish equivalent of the dry fly for trout—to catch bream. But rainbow trout was the quarry there, and I caught plenty, including several in the 4-pound range.

That day trip was exactly what I needed. The pain of missing yet another cut had met its match in a painkiller known to this country boy as fishin'.

Finally refreshed, we flew to Toronto on Sunday for the

RBC Canadian Open. Practice went well, but I played as if I had a bumper sticker on my back that read I'D RATHER BE FISHING. This time, I missed the cut by a bunch, and I was just plum ready to go home by then.

Canada was beautiful, you know, but I'd had enough and didn't want to stick around for what now just seemed like the loser's spoils. I was able to book a Friday-night flight home at around 8:00 and quickly packed and headed to the airport. I grabbed a sandwich and a soft drink and walked to my gate.

I called home to let the family know I was headed back earlier than scheduled and gave them my new ETA. Everyone said something like, "Okay, fine, Boo." Except for my daddy. He said, "Before you go, get me some of that bourbon whiskey they make up there, like Crown Royal or Canadian Mist."

It was a simple and reasonable request, I thought, so I headed for the duty-free shop and purchased a bottle of each, sealed securely in attractive boxes. He'd be mighty happy when I walked in holding a bottle of Crown Royal in one hand and Canadian Mist in the other.

I went back to the gate and relaxed, sipping on the remains of my soft drink. Mostly backwash at that point, but it didn't matter much. It was wet, and I wasn't going to waste it. No, siree.

An announcement came over the speakers that my flight had been delayed and would depart two hours later, at around 10:00. *Great!* I thought. *Now I've gotta call everybody back and give them my new ETA and hope somebody can pick me up.* I wasn't feeling like drinking any more of my backwash soft drink mess. I needed a hard drink.

It was a long walk to the bar, though, and my legs were telling me they weren't going anywhere. Seeing how I already had a cup of ice from my soft drink, I opened the Crown Royal and mixed a drink in the waiting area at the gate. Daddy wouldn't mind. Or maybe he would, but I didn't care.

I felt much better and relaxed, and before I knew it, the plane arrived and the boarding process began. I went through the slow motions of boarding. Getting up, standing there, moving a little, dragging my stuff, handing my boarding pass to the woman at the door, listening to her silly questions . . .

"What's in the bag?" she asked, pointing at my duty-free bag.

"Two bottles of whiskey," I responded.

She focused on the Crown Royal. I was thinking, *Back off, little lady, you ain't getting none!*

She didn't want any. "I see a bottle has been opened," she said. "You can't take that on the plane."

I ignored the "You can't take that on the plane" part. Or maybe I didn't even hear it. Same difference, really. "Yeah, I just mixed a drink while I was waiting."

"You can't leave the country with an open bottle."

"Look, I paid for it, it's mine, and I'm taking it home."

"Step aside, sir, so others can board."

"Ma'am, I'm ready to go home. I've had two bad weeks here, and I want to get home." Both our voices rose as we each tried to make our points. My point seemed the only one worth making, but whatever.

"I understand," she said, though I'm sure she didn't. If she understood, she would've followed that up by saying, "You're right. I'm sorry. You can have the seat next to you for your bottles. Have a nice flight!" Well, she didn't say that. She said, "You *cannot* get on the plane with your duty-free bag."

"Well, give me my money back," I snapped, "and you can have the damn stuff."

I was really hoping I'd seen the last of the Canadian authorities the week before at the border, but, come on . . . I'm Boo Weekley. The commotion of arguing with the boarding lady attracted the attention of a full-suited RCMP officer, and there I was again, face-to-face with one of those dudes. Second time in as many weeks. That can't be normal.

The RCMP officer began explaining in a little more detail why I couldn't take the open bottle on the plane. Rules and laws of some kind or another, but it was all Canadian to me.

He and I went back and forth for the longest time. Being a jack-of-all-trades, I explained that all they had to do was reseal the box the liquor was in and all would be fine. There you go—now it's not opened, okay? You happy?

"That will not work either," the now-angry officer said.

"Well, you ain't takin' my whiskey!"

"Then you're coming with me," the officer said as he grabbed my arm and pulled me away from the gate and into an elevator. We went down a few floors and into a room that resembled an interrogation cell on *Law and Order*. Another man joined the shakedown, and soon we had what seemed like a full-blown crisis. I felt like Osama Boo Laden.

Of course, I still didn't have a passport, which was obviously a problem with these guys, and that triggered a background check. Who knows what else they did outside that tiny room?

"I'm no terrorist," I said. "I just want to get home. *Home!* My plane is about to leave, and I want to be on it."

I offered a compromise. "Okay, listen, y'all keep the open

bottle, and I'll just take the other. We'll all go up there to-gether, and you can watch them re-bag the unopened bottle, and I'll be on my way, and y'all will never see my open-bottle-having ass again."

I guess they don't negotiate with terrorists.

"No! Again, you cannot take either bottle, because one of the bottles has been opened. You have two options here. One, you can wait right here until the supervisor comes in tomorrow morning, or two, you can leave the liquor with us, and you'll be free to go."

"I'll tell you what. Keep the whiskey! Just show me how to get back to my gate and I'll never come back to Canada again!"

I'm sure they were all as glad to get rid of me as I was to board that plane. Once I was in the air, though, it hit me. They were a little *too* glad to get rid of me. Hmmm, those offi-cers were back there with two bottles of paid-for whiskey. They were probably partying with my booze! It made me cringe just thinking about it. Now, who knows if they really drank my drinks? They might've; they might not've. Doesn't matter much. All I know is I didn't have that open bottle of Crown Royal anymore in that plane and had to settle for yet another soft drink. This time it was one of those dinky little in-flight Cokes. All I had to look forward to was facing my daddy with two empty hands.

O Canada? I don't think so, eh. Unless they invite me up there to do some fishing, that is.

8 SMOKED NESSIE AND CAR-NASTY

It's no secret that I like fishing. I fish for fun, but I also fish because, well, I like the taste of fish. It doesn't really matter what kind—bass, bluegill, trout, snapper, even giant sea monsters that may or may not be real.

One such monster, thought by some to be living in Loch Ness, has always intrigued me. I'm fascinated by the possibility that there's this huge beast swimming around out there that's too big to miss yet has never been clearly identified. It's like she's wearing camouflage. I'll tell you what, though, if I ever see that thing, I may just jump in the water, wrestle it to shore, and smoke it up for a fine dinner. As I said, I like the taste of fish (even if it's not technically fish).

I was thrilled that I might be getting my shot at the Loch Ness monster when I qualified for the 2007 British Open in Scotland by virtue of being among the top 50 money winners that year. It goes without saying that I was also excited about playing on a real Scottish golf course. You see, Scotland is not just the birthplace of golf and the home of good ol' Nessie; it also holds some branches on my family tree, namely the Mc-Clellans on my grandmother's side. So you've got legendary golf, legendary monsters, and legendary kinfolk. That sounded just about perfect for my first overseas trip.

The 2007 Open was held at the Carnoustie Golf Club in (you're not gonna believe this) Carnoustie, Scotland. I thought it was crazy that the Carnoustie Golf Club wound up in a place actually called Carnoustie. I mean, what are the chances?

I decided to head over to Scotland a week before the British Open to play in the Barclays Scottish Open in Loch Lomond, which is about an hour and a half south of Carnoustie. I figured I'd get my feet wet playing the week before the Open. Plus, it was a chance to pick up some lunch money.

I was really looking forward to playing real Scottish golf on a typical links golf course, firm with everything running fast. When I got there, though, the greens were built up and the fairways and bunkers were just like the ones back home. The course didn't live up to the legend in my head about classic golf courses in Scotland. The layout was great, but really, it wasn't all that different from playing in America.

Anyway, I was happy to have my Barclays experience feel a little more non-American by being paired up with Paul Lawrie, who is a native of Scotland. I was glad to hear he'd be going to Carnoustie, too. While trying to make small talk with Lawrie, who I assumed was a Carnoustie newbie like me, I asked, "How'd you get in? You qualify?"

Turns out that was one of my greater "duh" moments . . . in golf at least.

"I won it in '99," he answered, apparently surprised, or maybe even offended, by the question. I guess if you Google this guy's name, one of the first things you find is that he's no Carnoustie newbie. He actually won the Open in '99, the last time it was held in Carnoustie. Well, I hadn't Googled in a while, so there you go.

In any case, Open champions are qualified to play in the Open up until their sixty-fifth birthday, so Lawrie was automatically in.

Despite this little golf trivia mishap with Lawrie, I went on to play pretty well at the Barclays, especially the first two rounds, when I shot a 68 and a 66. Had it not been for a 74 on Saturday, I could've finished in the top 10. As it was, I finished tied for 30th place. That was okay by me, because Lawrie finished under that. Now knowing he'd won the Open, it felt pretty good to beat him.

Before the third round, I went to the driving range to hit a few. I had two to three balls left and thought I'd finish with a few punch shots. Well, I cut the club too steep, hit the ground, and buggered up my right hand and wrist—the one I broke playing basketball in high school. It was just a jam, nothing too serious.

So I left the Barclays with a hand injury and a tainted view of Scottish golf courses. Though my trip over to Carnoustie didn't do anything for my hand, when I arrived I found a true links golf course with sunken greens, sand dunes, humps, hollows, and furrows in the fairways and greens. There were lots of small, deep pot bunkers. The rough areas were covered with thick native seaside grasses. Now this was the Scottish course I'd envisioned all along, and I knew I was far from America now.

Seeing as the course is on open landscape and runs along the North Sea, wind is always a huge factor. This course is one of the most difficult in the Open rotation, and one of the trickiest courses anywhere. I was about to find out firsthand why Carnoustie is so often referred to as "Car-nasty." I looked out over the course and thought, *Let's get it on!*

With Scotland being the birthplace of golf, you can see its influence on golf courses all over the world, so I'm told. I know for a fact that some of Carnoustie's bastard children are scattered in America. For example, the Moors in Pensacola, Florida, which is basically in my backyard, is patterned after the Scotland-style links course. The only real difference is the way the bunkers were built. If it weren't for the lips on the bunkers, the Moors would be more of a true links-style course. But with lips like that, Carnoustie ain't claiming it as one of its own.

Joe and I went out for our practice round at Carnoustie. I was pumped about playing this course. On the 1st hole, I began by driving it pretty well and thought, *Here we go.* But then I hit the next two into the bunkers.

Joe said, "Listen, dude. We're going to be catching an early flight home if you keep doing that. No more bunkers. There ain't no way you're going to make pars, let alone birdies."

The only way out of those bunkers is to hit backward or to the side, so I knew he was right. I came back at him anyway.

"I understand that, dude. Now, calm down. It's just a practice round. No need to get all fired up yet." The rest of the practice round fell in line as I started laying the ball on the greens, for the most part, and making my putts. I was ready for a beer—and a little bit of Karyn.

She flew into Edinburgh that afternoon, and Uncle Jimmy did me right by driving the hour or so to pick her up. Once she was settled into our room at the Carnoustie Lodge overlooking the 18th green, we headed to the pub. It was some strange brew, for sure. There wasn't a single light beer in that place. If you walked in looking for a "drink," you'd be looking all night. It was more like "drank," and I drank me a few.

The bartender served me up something he called "cold Tennent." Uncle Jimmy drank a beer that looked an awful lot like motor oil. I still think he should've poured that mess into his car instead of his mouth. Karyn had a fruity mixed drink (I mean, "drank") of some sort. Turns out this was the best way to get ready for bed, 'cause we got close to passing out in a hurry.

I slept it off and headed back to the course the next morning for more practice. The media were there conducting interviews. One Scottish reporter asked me what I thought of the course.

"Now, this is a golf course," I said. "Any shot you can imagine, high or low, you can hit. The bunkers, though, they can go. You can fill those in with grass as far as I'm concerned. You get in one of those bad boys and you're done."

"Right, you don't want to hit it in the bunkers," she said with a knowing smile.

"That's what I'm saying," I said.

"What are your expectations this week?"

"Well, I've been dealing with some minor wrist injuries, but if we can keep my hand from hurting too much, I think I can win this thing."

After another good practice round that morning, my belly started talking. It told me to go to the players' dining room. I took along Karyn, Joe, Uncle Jimmy, and his Karen. I wasn't expecting much for my taste buds, since the food had been kind of bland up until then. Then I got to the buffet line and, oh what a glorious sight my eyes did see.

Grits.

Sausage patties.

Now, that's more like it.

I was first in line and slopped me a big helping of grits on my plate, got a couple of sausage patties and sausage links, and some other stuff that, though unidentifiable, looked plenty edible.

I sat down to my hot, steaming grits. It was just me and those grits for a minute. I salted and peppered them to a fare-thee-well. I brought the spoon to my mouth and started eating. Then I started gagging and spitting.

I yelled out to the rest of my crew, who were still in line, "*Do not* get the grits! They ain't grits! I don't know what this is, but it ain't grits."

My hungry stomach felt like it had just been sucker-punched. It was some kind of porridge or something. The Scots can sure as heck export their golf courses to the American South, but if that's their version of grits, they really should be importing our food.

So, with grits off the menu, I gave the sausage a chance. I cut into it and thought, *Are you kidding me? This stuff is red in the middle.* About that time, Uncle Jimmy sat down next to me and said, "You haven't eaten that stuff yet, have you?"

"Why? What's this stuff here?"

"That's fried blood," he said. "I think they call it blood pudding."

"Pudding? I ain't never had pudding like this. Oh man,

what I'd give right now for some fried chicken, a biscuit, and a tall glass of sweet tea."

Apparently, I went on for a bit, because the commotion got the attention of a waitress, who came over and said she'd be bringing out lunch soon, with fish on the buffet. Surely they couldn't screw up fish, right? Wrong.

Even salted and peppered, it was no better than the non-grits and non-sausage. The non-salad was bad, too. Everything was bad. I was starting to see why some of the folks over there were potbellied. With nothing to eat, all you can do is guzzle that heavy beer, I guess. I was tempted to head back to the pub just to get something tasty in my mouth and belly, but the golf course was calling me for an afternoon of practice.

Now, don't get me wrong. The people in Scotland are real nice. As I told one reporter, I had a real joyous time over there. The Scots are hard to understand sometimes, but I'm pretty sure I am, too, once we get to talking. For some of them, I just had to tell them, "Write it down," but none of that really bothered me. It was really just the food. That's where the Scots went wrong, in my estimation. I didn't get it. Not at all.

On my way to practice that day, however, I caught a whiff of hope. It smelled a little something like fish smoking. I was a bit skeptical, but I followed the scent to the backside of the putting green, where smoke was billowing from an old whiskey barrel. A man in a tent village was standing next to a drum barrel, and I could clearly see fish hanging from a rope over the smoky container. It was a shame that I had to head to practice right then, because all I could think about during practice was that fish. Whenever I closed my eyes, I could taste it.

It was all I could do to get through practice before heading back to the putting green where I'd smelled the smoked fish earlier. Turned out the man had sold it all and was gone for the day. I'd walked over there ready to let Karyn and the rest of them fend for themselves while I dined on smoked fish, but my strategy hadn't gone as planned, so I headed back to join the others.

We ended up eating some steak sandwiches, which were actually pretty good. They were no smoked fish, but at least they weren't a non-food. We drank a few more beers, too, and I went to bed with visions of smoked fish dancing in my head.

The next morning felt like Christmas. I was there to golf, of course, but it felt like I'd gone all the way to Scotland just for smoked fish. My mind made my body get up and head out to play golf, but my heart was fixed on that fish man. I started looking for him right off. Sure enough, he was in the same spot, smoking as strong as the day before. I knew right where I was going after my first round.

I played good golf that morning. I made birdie on the 1st hole and parred the 2nd. A double bogey on hole 3 made it an uphill climb from there, but 4 more birdies and 11 pars later, I was sitting at 68 and 3 under, tied for 3rd place. I felt pretty good at the end of round one, but my tummy was still rumbling.

Karyn suggested the family dining room again.

"No way am I gonna eat there," I said. "I've been waiting since yesterday to get me some of that smoked fish." I figured after such a good round of golf, I had earned at least that much.

Karyn rolled her eyes and moseyed on over to the dining room. That didn't faze me much. I honed in on the fish man.

It didn't matter to me what species this guy was smoking up, either. It was a done deal. He quickly removed the bones and handed me an open-faced sandwich with a fillet of fish in the middle. It was love at first bite, and if my heart didn't already belong to Karyn, I may've just gotten on one knee right then and there and popped the question to that fish man. As it stood, he became my new best friend.

"What kind of fish is this?" I asked as I took a second bite.

"Abroath smoked haddock."

"Okay. Well, it's good," I mumbled with my mouth full. "You gonna be here all week?"

"All week."

I took a quick break from smoked fish eating to play a little golf and was right back there chomping on another smoked fish sandwich and chatting up my new favorite Scot. I didn't even need him to write anything down.

Cold, windy, and misty rain conditions greeted me the next morning, but I was prepared, donning my camo-print thermal stretch Under Armour long johns. This set was one of my favorites with a long-sleeved high-neck top and bottom leggings printed with Mossy Oak–brand camouflage break-up pattern.

The suit fits tight. I mean, skintight. It's even tighter than that after a long day of eating smoked fish, I'll tell you. Trust me, you don't want to see me flexing in those things. No camo can hide my jellyrolls and dimples. Still, it provides just the right amount of stretch to give me full range of motion while golfing, and that's why I put those things on.

I covered the bottoms with a pair of rain pants and the top with a short-sleeved golf shirt and a rain jacket. This outfit had been so good during the first round of play in similar weather that it was worth a repeat in this, the second round.

I practiced a bit on the putting green and then went on to

start round two. I made par on the 1st hole and then followed it with a bogey on hole 2. I parred holes 3, 4, and 5. As I reached the 6th hole, the rain let up and the temperature climbed. It was getting steamy, and I started sweating like a bitin' sow. Forgetting how unflattering the camo Under Armour was on my body, I ripped my rain jacket off and threw it to Joe. A woman in the gallery instantly gasped, and I heard her say, "Look, he's tattooed up!"

"Who's tattooed up?" I said. "Who's she talking about, Joe?"

"I don't know, dude. Focus. Hit your shot."

I made my putt for birdie and started walking to the next tee box. I overheard a man in the crowd say, "Look at Boo, man! He's got tattoos all over his body! Down his arms and up his neck!"

"What's he talking about?" I asked Joe. "I ain't got a tat anywhere on my body."

"No clue, dawg."

I looked down at my arms. I still had no idea what the crowd was seeing. I mean, my arms weren't even exposed. I was wearing those camo long johns. No tats anywhere.

Then it hit me. My arms and neck weren't covered with tats, but they were covered with camo print. I looked at the crowd and then back to my arms. Then back to the crowd and smiled a bit.

I turned to Joe and said, "Hey, I bet they all think these here long johns are tattoos. I guess they've never seen a golfer wearing camo-print underwear before." I could only snicker and shake my head as we walked to tee it up.

As I stood there, I began to think about how nobody there had really seen my arms since we arrived—mostly because we'd hardly left the hotel room, but also because when we did leave the room, I'd wear a jacket. I felt like Jesse James out there, with a bit of Tiger Woods. You know, a pro golfer with tats.

"I can't believe these people think I'm all tattooed, man," I said to Joe with a grin.

"Well, I guess it does look like that from a distance," he said.

I shook my head again. "Seriously, Joe, you know me. Do you think I'm a tattoo kind of guy? Do you think it would make me look tougher?"

"No, dude. You'd look like a punk. Don't even think about it."

"Well, I ain't got no tats, and I ain't getting none, so there."

Through the rest of play, all I heard from the crowd was stuff about my tattoos, nothing about my game. Whispers of, "I can't believe Boo's such a freak." "Boo's a weirdo." "Next thing you know, he'll have a ring in his nose." "He looks like Jesse James out there." You know, stuff like that.

My amusement with the situation turned into annoyance, and I wanted to scream out to the folks in the gallery, "These are clothes, not tattoos! I'm no weirdo!" I was distracted enough as it was, though, and I didn't want to get into it with the hecklers.

Considering the bad weather and the tattoo talk, I played pretty well and finished the day at 1 over and 2 under for the tournament through the first two days. That was good enough to keep in contention for a top-10 finish, and if I played well enough . . . well, you just never know.

I put my rain jacket back on, covering my non-tattoos,

and headed off to sign my scorecard. I then put fresh dip in my mouth, as I like to do, and headed to the driving range to hit a few balls. When I got there, a TV lady stopped me and asked for an interview. I told her I'd be happy to, after my practice, but she insisted and pressed me for a sit-down interview. "I have a deadline. I need to interview you now to find out why you have so many tattoos."

"Look, lady," I said, having reached my limit on the tattoo thing. "I don't have any tattoos."

"But I saw them."

"No, you didn't. You saw my underwear."

It felt kind of weird to say that to her, but that's how it went.

"You are funny, Mr. Weekley."

"I'm not trying to be funny, ma'am. No joke, I ain't got no tats, okay? I'll catch you later."

"Okay, okay, I believe you. Please, Mr. Weekley, can we talk now? It won't take long, I promise."

"Alright, fine. For just a couple of minutes. Let's go."

I removed my jacket and sat down for the interview. "See, look," I said. "This ain't tattoos, it's Under Armour." I held my arm out so she could get a close look. "You can feel it if you want." She rubbed her fingers over the material and was astonished, acting like she was a little kid petting the alligator for the first time at the zoo.

"Wow," she exclaimed. "You really can't tell the difference. It looks like it's your arm. I mean, I was certain your whole body was tattooed. It looked that way on the links for sure."

With her satisfied and finally knowing the truth about my not being a freak, she began the interview. "So, how do you like the course so far?"

"I like it. I actually feel like I played a little better today even though I was one over. If I can keep this up, I can be in contention on Sunday."

She began to ask another question (I can't remember what it was) when I stopped her. "Hold on to that thought," I said right before I leaned over and spat on the ground.

"Oh my," she blurted out with the cameraman catching it all on film. "Did you just spit? Why did you spit on my set?"

"Because I dip, I have to spit."

I noticed the cameraman leaning around his camera, signaling her to move on to another topic and not to make a fuss over my dipping and spitting, but she wouldn't let up. She was plain disgusted. "I can't believe you would dip on my set during an interview."

"Well, you're the one who wanted me to come over here in such an almighty hurry. If you'd given me a little time, I could've finished my dip."

She decided to move on to her next question, which wasn't nearly as exciting as the conversation we were having about dipping and spitting. "What all have you experienced since you've been here?"

"Well, I'll tell you one thing, that couscous or porridge or whatever mess that is, it ain't grits. It looks like grits, like my arms look tattooed, but that stuff is awful, awful, awful. I honestly don't know how you people survive over here on this food. I'll tell you something else I have discovered over here: the best tasting smoked fish you'll ever put in your mouth. That must be what ya'll eat. It is some kinda good."

"Really? Fish?"

"Yeah, fish. If you'll go to the other side of the putting green, you'll see a guy smoking some fish," I said as I pointed to the tent village across the way. "You can smell it from here. Smell it?"

"Yes, I smell it. What is it?"

"It's fish!"

"But that doesn't smell good to me."

I slumped back in disbelief. "This is your heritage. This is what you should be eating here. You don't like fish?"

"No, I don't eat fish."

"Oh my gosh. Well, that's the only thing I'm gonna eat from now on, because everything else I've eaten has been nasty."

I leaned back over and spat again. I don't think I realized just how close she was to stopping the interview before that second spit, but that did it.

"You and I are done!" she said with some serious oomph. "This interview is over."

"Yes, ma'am, that's fine by me. When I come back, I'll show you what that fish looks like."

With the TV lady utterly flustered and through with me, I decided to go to the putting green, instead of the driving range, and hit some balls. I looked over to see the fish man packing up for the day, and my mission changed. I rushed over and asked if he had any fish left. He said he had three, which was music to my ears. I bought all three.

I decided to take the fish back to where the TV lady was conducting her interviews, and lo and behold, there she was interviewing another golfer. I just couldn't resist.

I took a fish in each hand, stood directly behind her

interviewee, and I began waving my arms as if I were guiding an airplane to its final destination.

She stopped the interview and gave me her version of "the look."

"Did you smell that when I waved it just now?" I asked.

"Yes, I smelled it, and it stinks," she said, smirking.

"It's the best thing ya'll have over here. You really ought to try it."

She didn't cotton to my humor, though, so I took my three fishes and went to the main restaurant. I laid my "catch" out on the table, and the waitress came over. "Where did you get those?" she asked.

At first, I thought she might've been talking about my non-tats, but she wasn't. She was talking fish.

"There's a man down there selling fish at the tent village. I got 'em from him."

"Sir, you can't bring that fish in here. We don't allow people to bring in their own food."

"Well, I'm staying here in the hotel, and this here is what I'm going to eat tonight. Now, could you please bring me a cold Tennent?"

The waitress kept arguing with me about whether I could bring my own food into their restaurant. She went on and on, but I didn't let up. I just kept eating. By the time she was ready to give up, I'd finished my meal.

Karyn caught the whole episode.

When we got back to the room, she lit into me with claws extended for what she called "acting a fool." "You need to calm yourself down and start showing some respect and manners around here."

"Karyn, you know I don't mean anything by it. I'm just

having fun with these folks. I guess they just don't understand me or something."

"They don't understand you? Are you kidding? Boo, nobody understands you."

I looked down and thought about the tattoos, the fish, the dipping and spitting, the arguing, and everything else. I looked back up and said, with some heavy sarcasm slapped on it, "I guess I'm just misunderstood."

Well, one thing I know for sure, I understand golf, and golf understands me, and it was time to play golf. Starting the next day (Saturday), I was in solid position and only four strokes off the lead. I really wanted to get off to a good start that day to keep it going. I was hoping to make a couple of birdies right out of the gate, so I could move up the leaderboard and maybe put a little pressure on the leaders.

I made par on the 1st hole and thought, *Okay, here we go. We're fixin' to make some noise.* Hole 2 on that course is a par 4. I hit a good tee shot, but drove my second shot into a divot. I thought I could take another club and hit a little punch shot and let it bounce onto the green. Joe said, "If you can land it fifty yards short of the green, it'll run right up there."

I got ready to do what Joe told me, but I stuck my left hand a little too deep in the ground. I hit it bad and got that tingle back in my injured hand. I tried to rub it out, shake it off.

"Hey man, what's wrong?" Joe asked.

"That tingle's back."

I told myself to ignore it. I'd been ignoring things all day. I'd ignored the fact that I didn't look right in skintight long johns and ripped my jacket off anyway. I'd ignored the folks calling me a freak for being all tattooed up, even though I wasn't. I'd ignored the TV lady who didn't want me spitting on her set. I'd ignored the waitress who told me I couldn't bring my own food into her precious little restaurant. I'd even ignored my wife a little when she said I needed to stop acting a fool. Shoot, with all that ignoring going on, I figured ignoring a little tingle in my hand was nothing.

So I stepped up and played golf.

I managed to make birdie, and followed with pars on the next two holes. Going to the 6th hole at 1 under was decent, given the circumstances, but I still wasn't hitting the ball very well. I was striking it, but I had no idea where it was going. I was doing my best to ignore the tingle in my hand, but I just couldn't ignore the fact that I felt like I couldn't hold on to the golf club. It was slipping right out. Still, I played on and actually did better than I thought I would. Three straight bogeys to finish the round gave me a 75, 4 over for the day. That put me out of the running for a top finish.

I was still feeling pain in my hand on Sunday, but it wasn't as bad as the day before. I played decently and finished the day at 73, 2 over, and 4 over for the tournament, good for a tie for 35th. That was respectable, in my view, for playing in the British Open for the first time. Once again I'd beaten my Barclays buddy, Paul Lawrie, so I couldn't complain much.

I came to Scotland and did my thing on and off the golf course, so the Loch Ness monster wasn't about to raise her head out of the water for me to see. She didn't want to be smoked up and eaten by that freak with all the tats! She'd better look out, though. Next time I'm there, I might just team up with that fish man and have me a little smoked Nessie.

9 FINISHING NUMBER TWO

There are all kinds of people in this world. There are Canadians, Brits, and Scots (are they the same thing?), and there are country boys like me from the American South. There are golfers all over the world, and there are folks everywhere who can't stand the game. Thinking about my coming up as a golfer makes me realize that even though we're all different in a lot of ways, there are some things we all have in common. Like pooping. We all poop. Don't act like you don't. Some guys swear their mammas don't poop, or fart, for that matter, but trust me, they do. Despite the lack of evidence, they definitely poop. We all do.

You know what? Pooping is a lot like golf. You want to get the ball in the hole, and you want to get the poop in the pot. Sometimes, I just can't do either.

Seems I finish number 2 more than my fair share of the time. I mean, sure, I've finished number 1 many times while playing the minitours and a couple of times on the PGA Tour, but 2 really seemed to be my number there for a while. And I ain't just talking about golf.

I remember back when I was headed to Qatar for the 2009 Race to Dubai. I was facing a 29-hour flight. Now, I don't care what kind of frequent flier you are, that's a long flight. There ain't no way I can sit through a flight that long without some goings-on in my belly region. We were flying on a Qatar airline, which was one of the nicest planes I've ever flown on. Still, there ain't no kind of nice that can keep your belly from feeling that "uh-oh" pinch everyone feels from time to time. I knew I was going to have to deal with it at some point on that flight, but there was a guy on the plane I had to deal with first.

This man was seated next to me during the flight, and he'd told me earlier that he was a Qatar citizen. We hadn't really talked the whole trip, though, until near the end. He had a dark complexion, was clean-shaven, and sharp-dressed. With about three hours left in our flight, the man nudged me and said, "You look familiar. Can I ask who you are?"

I removed the earphones I was using to listen to the movie I'd been watching, *Appaloosa*. The man, who was dressed in an expensive-looking business suit, had been standing up, moving around, and steady drinking for 20-something hours, and I could smell it on his breath.

"Sure, I'm Boo Weekley," I said, as I was nudged again, only this time not by the man. Seemed like something was nudging me from the inside, too, down in my stomach.

"I thought that was you!" he said in his drunken excitement.

"Okay, cool," I said. "I'm going to get back to my movie now. It's almost over."

A few more minutes of *Appaloosa* passed, and he bumped me as he pulled a piece of paper from his wallet and said, "I want you to sign something for me."

"Okay," I said as I quickly signed the folded paper, handed it back to him, put my earphones back on, and turned once again to watch the movie. Apparently, he wanted more than an autograph, because the guy immediately started tapping me on the shoulder. I was starting to get a little annoyed at that point. The movie was just getting good, I was starting to feel a little like I might need to take a crap, and I didn't need to deal with a drunk hounding me for more autographs or some stories or whatever it was he wanted from me.

"Give me my wallet," the man mumbled.

Now, I've gotten a lot of requests from fans for a lot of things in my time, but that man's request was the strangest, and it certainly hit me the hardest.

"Do what?" I asked, not believing what I'd just heard.

"Give me my wallet," he repeated a little louder.

"Man, what are you talking about? I don't have your wallet. What makes you think I have your wallet?"

"You signed the paper from my wallet," he said, as if that cleared it all up.

"Yeah, and I handed it back to you, but I never had your wallet."

I turned again to watch my movie, but I felt like I was his movie. Have you ever had that feeling? You know, like someone is just staring at you, and it bothers you and eats at you until you can't take it anymore and you have to jump up in a frenzy and beat the guy up? Well, I didn't beat this guy up, but I certainly couldn't take his sitting next to me staring at me while I watched my movie for very long. I yanked my headphones out of my ears, and it was déjà vu all over again, as Yogi might say.

"Just give me my wallet. It's my life!" he shouted at me.

At that point, I was like, *What the heck is going on here!* "Listen, man," I said. "I ain't got your wallet!"

This exchange went on for about 10 solid minutes. He'd ask me for his wallet. I'd say I didn't have it. He'd ask me for it again, claiming I was trying to steal his life from him or some such nonsense. I'd tell him again, not so kindly, that I didn't have his wallet, and all this time, the pinch in my belly was growing. I was getting upset and very angry and I offered one last volley. "I ain't got your damn wallet, and if you ask me one more time, I'm gonna bust your nose."

"I don't care what you do, just give me my wallet."

Though I wanted to get up and send my fists a-flyin', I think my building stomach issues kept me in my seat. The only things that went flying were more of the same words.

"For the last time," I said, "I ain't got your damn wallet. Maybe you dropped it. Why don't you go ask the flight attendants. Maybe you left it up there, you drunk!"

"Fuck you!" he said.

Oh no he didn't.

"Well, fuck you!" I yelled as I began unbuckling my seat belt, fully intending to let more than words fly at that point. "I'm fixing to bust your nose now! Get up!"

"No, I'm not getting up. Where is my wallet?"

"Look, you are drunk." I thought for a moment and gathered myself. I decided to sit back down, not really wanting to punch a drunk on the plane. That probably wouldn't turn out good for me, no matter how it turned out. I put the earphones back in, rolled my shoulder away from him, and started watching the movie. Again.

Then he got up. He stood and started walking around looking for his wallet. He peered under the seats for a bit and then walked up to the flight attendants' station. I knew what was coming next, and my attention was off *Appaloosa* once again. *Can't I just finish this dang movie!* I thought.

Sure enough, a flight attendant came down the aisle toward me and said, "Sir, do you have this man's wallet?"

I just shook my head and gave my best I-have-no-freakin'-idea-what's-going-on-here look. Then I proceeded to spell it out for her nice and slow. "Ma'am . . . I . . . do . . . not . . . have . . . his . . . wallet."

About that time, the man spotted his missing life-filled wallet safely tucked between our seats, on the floor in a very dark area of the plane. I just rolled my eyes and threw up my hands. Then he started apologizing in the same annoying way he seemed to do everything. "I am so, so sorry. So sorry."

He kept on and on and on and on, which didn't surprise me given how he kept on and on about my taking his wallet. Finally, he wrote his phone number on a small piece of paper, handed it to me, and said, "You call. I will make it up to you. You will see. I will take you out."

"Yeah, I bet you will," I said. "You'll take me out alright. Nah, we're good. You just sit in your seat and leave me alone. You've made it clear you're an ass, so we're done. Glad you got your life back and all, but I'm going to watch my movie now."

I felt a few more stomach pinches here and there, but it all sort of went away, probably due to all the excitement from the wallet fiasco.

Once the movie concluded, I dozed off for an hour or so and was wakened by the familiar "ding" of the airplane intercom system. Finally, I was hearing some encouraging words, something like this:

"As we start our descent, please make sure your seat backs and tray tables are in their full upright and locked position. Make sure your seat belt is securely fastened and all carry-on luggage is stowed underneath the seat in front of you or in the overhead bins. Please turn off all electronic devices until we are safely parked at the gate. We will be landing in thirty minutes. Thank you."

I looked over to Caddy Joe, who'd been sleeping across the aisle during the altercation and was now awake and giggling. I was a little surprised and curious about that.

"What are you laughing about, dude?" I said.

"Hey, man," Joe asked, "did I dream you were arguing with that guy sitting next to you?"

I couldn't believe Joe was acting like he'd been asleep during all of that. "Yeah, you were dreaming alright," I said with some disgust in my voice.

"No, I wasn't," he laugh-talked. "You were arguing with him, weren't you?"

"Yeah, I guess you could say that."

Joe stopped giggling for a minute and got all fake serious on me. "Look, dude, you'd better hope we get there fast and get situated, 'cause he's probably got a bunch of buddies who'll come get you," he said, trying to egg me on.

"Man, I ain't worried about that joker."

"Just don't you do anything else to get us in trouble. That's all I'm saying."

The "ding" went off again, reminding us we were about

to land. It also must've reminded my stomach that it was pinching and rolling earlier because it started doing all of that mess again. Only it felt worse at that point. Way worse. Like it had been building and building in secret, and all of a sudden, the floodgates of my hind end were fixin' to crack. I thought, *Uh-oh, this ain't good, but I can probably just squeeze and hold it until we land.* The longer I sat, though, the more my stomach rolled and began to taunt me, saying, "Yeah, good luck holding all this in, pal!" The plane banked and turned a bit back and forth, and that sort of put it all over the top, so to speak. Squeezing and holding it until we landed just wasn't a viable option anymore. I had to go to the john 'cause a flood was a-comin'!

I unbuckled my seat belt and started down the aisle to the restroom, pretty much in emergency mode. As I approached, a flight attendant seated in her chair all buckled down said, "Where are you going, sir?"

"I'm going to the bathroom."

"You can't go now," she said, as if I were in any condition to listen to her. "Please take your seat, and buckle your seat belt."

"I've gotta go. I'm sick." Trying to be helpful, she responded by telling me there was an airsickness bag in the seat pocket in front of my seat.

Under other circumstances (if it'd been happening to Joe, for example), I might've laughed at her comment. I was deadly serious, though, and in no laughing mood.

"I don't think you understand," I pleaded. "I don't need a barf bag. I gotta do number two! And I ain't doing it in no bag." I started walking fast and came to another attendant, who was as stubborn as the first one. I guess part of their

training is to be stubborn about all of the rules, even if someone is about to make a mess of the plane.

"We are about to land. Please take your seat," the second
flight attendant commanded.

I was having none of it, though. "I'm going to the bathroom, and that's that. Tell the captain to land the plane. I'll
be okay. Heck, I'll buckle up on the john."

I went full steam and simply bulled my way into the bathroom, locking the door for fear that a group of stubborn, out-
of-control flight attendants might come in, overpower me,
pick me up with my pants down, and carry me back to my seat
dripping brown droplets all along the way. One of the attendants immediately started banging on the door. "Come out,
you have to take your seat."

I was right next to the cockpit and could hear the pilots
talking, too. They were saying, "Three thousand feet, two
thousand feet." The attendant kept banging on the door and
yelling, "You've got to get in your seat, we are going to land!"

"Great, tell the pilot to land it gently," I said loudly, kind
of hoping the pilot would be able to hear me. "I'm going to be
a while. I've got some serious issues in here!"

There's really nothing like sitting on a toilet when you
need to lighten your load, and it felt good to be in there on
that plane. Only thing was, those dang flight attendants kept
breaking my concentration. Relief for ol' Boo came slowly
thanks to the circumstances, that's for sure, but it came nonetheless.

"My eagle has landed!" I screamed through the door to the
attendants. "Tell the captain to land his!"

I don't think the pilot got my message, because I felt the
plane suddenly pull up and bank to the left. I thought, *You*

can't be serious. This guy ain't gonna land until I get out of the crapper! The plane felt like it was circling, and I started shaking my head. Seems if there's an international incident to be created, I'll create it, and I was thinking this one was of major proportions. Man, oh man.

I just sat in there on that toilet scared to make a move. It seemed like forever before the plane felt like it was making a descent again, but I didn't budge. I kept my seat and held on to the sides of the toilet. There wasn't a seat belt in there, but I wasn't going anywhere.

Then a loud "ding" went off again, followed by a voice over the intercom saying, "Ladies and gentlemen, we have just been cleared to land. Please make sure one last time your seat belt is securely fastened."

Ha! I thought. *Well, put a dang seat belt on your toilet next time!* Seat belt or no seat belt, that landing was perfect. Perhaps it was because I was freshly relieved (if you know what I mean), but I've honestly never experienced such a soft and bump-free landing in all my life.

There was a final "ding," and the voice on the intercom came back on. "Ladies and gentlemen, welcome to Qatar. For your safety and comfort, we ask that you please remain seated with your seat belt fastened until the captain has turned off the FASTEN SEAT BELT sign. This will indicate that we have come to a complete stop."

Yeah, okay, I thought, as I began to plan how I was going to make my exit. I think I decided to just wing it, because once the plane had taxied a few hundred yards, I came busting out of there. The in-flight announcement was still playing, and the plane was still rolling. I stood there for a moment, not really knowing what to do as I stared into the eyes of an obviously annoyed (she actually looked disappointed, like my mamma might've been) flight attendant, who said nothing. I then turned toward the cockpit and, though the captain couldn't see me from behind his closed door, I tipped my cap to him and said, "Thank you, buddy, for making that one gentle." I'm not sure if the flight attendants laughed, but they should've.

I wish I could say that was my only experience dealing with the urge hitting me at a bad time, but I can't. Back on the minitours, it seemed I always had something like that happening to me. Always.

Like the time I was in South Florida playing in the Moonlight Tour. We'd finished one of the events of the Tour and were headed to the next one when the urge hit me. After driving for many miles, we came to a small Exxon station, but it didn't have a public bathroom. I absolutely couldn't wait any longer, so I spotted a big Dumpster, went around to the backside, and proceeded to take care of business. I was propped up by placing both of my hands behind me with my palms on the Dumpster. I mean, taking a dump next to a Dumpster seemed appropriate to me. Why else would they call it a "Dumpster"? Anyway, I was comfortable back there and hidden. At least I thought I was.

Well, there was this cop who apparently peeked-a-Boo back there, because all of a sudden, there he was in my "bathroom." He looked slightly entertained, but not really all that amused. "How's it going back here?" he asked sarcastically.

I didn't know what to say, but I said it anyway. "It was goin' pretty good a few seconds ago, but not too good now," I quipped, just looking down at the ground.

"Well, when you finish up, I've got some extra paper for

Baby Boo.

The Weekleys:
(left to right)
Patsy, Tom, Ali,
and Boo in 1980.

A young Boo with a
whitetail buck.

(Courtesy of Patsy Weekley)

Boo with a nice eight-point buck. *(Courtesy of Patsy Weekley)*

Boo shows off a spring turkey harvest.

(Courtesy of Patsy Weekley)

(Left to right) Another winning angler and Boo pose with a day's catch.

Boo *(top left)* after earning his tour card on the Nationwide Tour. *(Courtesy of Patsy Weekley)*

Sign in Milton, Florida, after shooting his career best 63 at the St. Jude Classic in Memphis. *(Courtesy of Patsy Weekley)*

Boo and wife, Karyn, in 1999.

(Courtesy of Patsy Weekley)

Sign at Milton High School after Boo's first PGA win at the Verizon in 2007.

(Courtesy of Patsy Weekley)

Boo at the Verizon Heritage after his first win.

(Courtesy of Patsy Weekley)

Boo sits with his father after his second Verizon win.

(Courtesy of Patsy Weekley)

(Left to right) Heath Slocum, Tyler Kirby (Boo's cousin), and Boo Weekley in 2008. Milton High School started an annual golf tournament named Milton High T.P.C. (Triple Pro Classic) in honor of Bubba Watson, Heath Slocum, and Boo.

Boo with his son Parker.

(Courtesy of Karyn Weekley)

It's easy to see how Boo's underwear was mistaken for tattoos.

Boo gives autographs during a practice round at the TPC (Tournament Players Club) Sawgrass.

Boo poses with two young fans at his charity event in Brewton, Alabama.

Boo sports his favorite golf attire.

Boo with his grandparents Abbie Jean and Ed Weekley and uncle David Weekley.

(Right to left) Boo's agent Jimmy Johnston, Tom Kennedy, and Boo discuss a putter at Boo's annual charity event.

Boo modeling his Mossy Oak camouflage.

you." His comment was clever and got a chuckle out of me, but come on now, it's kind of hard to "finish up" when you've got a cop leaning against the other side of your "outhouse." Still, I did my best to finish up quickly and made what was now a very long walk around the Dumpster to face my fate. The cop turned out to be cool.

"I'm just gonna issue you a written warning this time," he said, "but next time it'll be an expensive ticket at best and an arrest at worst for indecent exposure. Now go back around there and clean it up."

"Yes, sir, and you don't have to worry 'cause it won't happen again," I promised as I hustled back there to clean up yet another messy issue. If only that cop had known how familiar I was with cleaning up crap. Still, a promise is a promise, right? No way I would do something like that again, right? Come on, you know me better than that.

Not long after the Dumpster incident, I was returning home from a developmental players minitour event run by Jack Slocum. I was traveling through Atlanta in my maroon pickup, with its license plate that read, THE BOO, along with all my fishing and golf paraphernalia in the back of the truck. It'd been raining the last day of the event and, of course, I was wearing my usual rain pants over a pair of Umbro shorts and my underwear (briefs, if you must know). I took the rain pants off for the trip home, was driving along all comfortable like, and yep, you guessed it, the dreaded urge hit me.

I immediately started looking for a place to stop, but I was on the interstate, and you know how that can go. Seems whenever you're on a road trip and spending a lot of time on the interstate, there are plenty of spots to stop when you don't need to go, but nothing in sight for miles when you do. In my case on that day, it was one traffic jam after another. So there was nowhere to stop, and I was getting there fast.

Well, I guess on the interstate of my intestines, whatever is travelin' along doesn't really feel the need to find a place to stop. When it's ready to drop, it drops. And when the "it" is diarrhea, it's like a semi, and there just ain't no way to hold it back. Seriously, there ain't *no* stopping it. You know what that means. That's right, I couldn't stop it. I didn't stop it. It must have thought it was on the *Price Is Right* or something 'cause it came on down, in my drawers and down my legs. I thought, *Oh man, this just ain't right. I can't drive like this, sitting in muddy waters. I've got to stop soon.* I spotted an overpass and pulled up next to the guardrail, under the bridge on I-285.

I sort of oozed out of the truck and crept around to the passenger side kind of bent over, trying to keep the chocolate river from running farther down my leg. Then I opened the passenger and extended cab doors to create a sort of make-shift "stall" to hide in as I cleaned myself off.

I got situated down there and pulled my Umbros off. I leaned into the truck, grabbed a hunting knife from the console, and began the nauseating task of cutting off my underwear. It was like cutting through a tar-filled diaper. I used the clean part of the underwear to wipe my behind as best I could, then I chucked them over my shoulder and onto the slop pavement under the bridge. I found a roll of toilet paper under the truck seat (I probably don't need to explain why I had a roll of toilet paper under the seat), so I was ready to finish it off and get everything as good as new.

Then I heard something, and it wasn't my stomach tossin' and turnin' again. It was a voice, and it asked, "Is there a problem over here?" I looked up and saw the owner of the voice. He was a law dawg, a Georgia Highway State Patrol trooper, and he was staring down at me through my passenger door window. "You might want to pick up whatever that is you threw on the concrete, or I'm going to ticket you for littering," he continued.

There was no way I was going to revisit my soiled underwear, and I figured the best thing to do was to let the trooper know it. "Sir," I started, "let me finish what I've got going on here, and me and you can have any kind of chitchat you want, but I ain't touching them undies 'cause they've got shit all in 'em."

"I'm going to write you a ticket then," he said matter-of-factly.

"Fine, but I've really got to get back to wiping right now." So I finished cleaning myself and put my Umbros back on with the law dawg watching my every move. I froze for effect before stating emphatically, "Seriously . . ." What I meant was "Give me a little privacy."

I must've forgotten for a moment that the trooper was keeping his eye on me, 'cause I was dropping the tissue to the ground as I wiped, and every time a car passed, the pieces would blow all over the place. So all these little flimsy tissues with my poop (which I'll call Boop) on 'em were flying around.

"And pick up that paper, too," the trooper demanded.

That's when I knew this guy was going to be giving me an extra hard time with this one. Still, I had to fight him on it, 'cause it just didn't make no good sense to me. "Dude, it's biodegradable," I argued. "It's just tissue."

"I don't care, son. You pick it *all* up."

I knew I wasn't getting out of it, and I also knew I was

already pushing my luck with my dirty undies on the road, so I figured I should do what he said. I went around picking up the brown toilet paper and threw it into the back of the truck.

The trooper watched the whole time, and when I was done, he sort of twisted the knife in and said, "Now, I'm fixin' to follow you, and if any of that paper blows out, you're getting a ticket."

At that point, I was in a pretty foul mood (no pun intended). In the process of "cleaning" myself up with the trooper watching, I'd managed to get Boop all over my left hand. It started on my hind end and ended up on my hand, and I had no idea how I ended up in that mess. I thought, *Great, and now I have to get in my truck and have this patrolman follow me to see if I'm littering? I've heard it all now!* If I was going to have to do that, I at least wanted a clean hand to drive with, but I didn't have water or any other means of washing my hand. *Serve, protect, and help wash, maybe?* I thought.

"Sir, do you have any water I can use to wash the poop off my hand?" I asked simply.

"Nope," the trooper responded more simply.

I mumbled some angry nonsense and shook my head as I looked in the back of the truck, snatched my golf towel, and fortunately found a bottle of water in a bag in the truck. I washed the Boop from my hand the best I could, then climbed over the guardrail and rubbed my hand in the dirt. Might seem silly to finish cleaning something by rubbing it in the dirt, but that's how we do things where I'm from. Apparently that's how you do things where that trooper was from, 'cause he watched me without saying a word.

That incident will go down in history as one of my better

stories on finishing number two, but it'll also go down as probably the most inefficient use of time (in my opinion, anyway) by a law enforcement officer. Ever. He didn't even issue a ticket or nothing, but he dang sure was going to make sure I didn't litter. Pure nonsense.

Anyway, that may've been one of the better stories on my finishing number two, but it's not the best. Not even close. I've saved the best for last, but I have to go back just a bit for this one. It happened during my rookie year as a pro on the Tour, 2002 . . .

A buddy and fellow rookie, Jason Hill, and I hooked up and roomed together much of the Tour to cut down on expenses. He and I'd played on the Nationwide together and got to be good friends, so it was an easy call. We were both struggling financially and needed to cut every corner we could. Neither of us could make the cuts that count as a pro golfer, and we just weren't playing good golf like we did on the Nationwide. We had a good time with one another, though, and it just made sense to room and travel together full-time. We'd get two courtesy cars, but for the flight home, we'd book our flights for the same time and ride to the airport in one.

We played a tournament in Connecticut and both missed the cut, of course. I shot like 77, and I would've had to shoot a 61 the second day to make it. My start time was sooner than Jason's that day, so I finished before him. He was a couple of groups behind me, so I had to wait for him since we'd be riding in one car. I put my golf clubs in the trunk and walked over to the caddy shack.

I mostly hung out with the caddies when I could. I didn't hang out much with the pros. As I've said, I just don't fit in with them all the time. The caddies were my guys. Only difference between them and me in my eyes was that I was playing golf. I didn't feel like I had to hang with the pros just 'cause I was one. I hung with who I wanted to hang with. Always have, always will.

A bunch of the caddies were having lunch, so I stopped by and ate some greasy fried chicken with them. It wasn't that bad, so I kept stuffing my face. Jason finally finished up and walked over to join our finger-lickin' chicken lunch. We already had all of our clothes packed up in the car, so all we had to do was get Jason's clubs and we were outta there.

Jason said, "Well, I'm just going to grab me something to eat here. We've got an hour before we have to leave for the airport." Hey, if you say something like that to me, I ain't never gonna tell you no. I understand when a man has to eat. So, I had a beer with Jason and the caddies while he finished eating. Then Jason got his clubs and placed them in the trunk. About that time, I rehungerized and reached over to find one last drumstick. I gobbled it down as fast as I could, and it hit the bass drum of my belly with a boom!

"Man, are you ready to go?" Jason asked.

"Yeah, let's go."

"We can go to the bar at the airport and have a couple of beers while we wait for our airplane," he said.

"That's fine with me," I said.

We got in the car, and I realized the keys were in my back pocket, so I got out to get them, and that's when it hit me. You know, the urge I've been talking about this whole chapter. This time, it felt as if that bottle of beer I'd had with Jason and the caddies was running straight through me. I leaned in the car and said to Jason, "Uh, hey, listen, man. Let me run over there to the bathroom real fast." Jason said he had to go, too, so we walked over to the nearest Porta-John.

I was wearing rain pants, tennis shoes, and a short-sleeved collared shirt. The rain pants had only one pocket, and it was in the back. I had all of the important stuff in that one pocket: snuff, cell phone, and wallet. There was no room for the car keys, so I had them hooked on my shorts underneath the rain pants. Seemed like a good idea at the time.

I went inside the vertical coffin, as some call those Porta-Johns, and locked the door. Those rain pants I was wearing ain't got no zipper, so I pulled 'em down. When I did, my keys went flying, hit the side wall, bounced up, centered the toilet hole, made a nice entry splash, and sank to the bottom of the pit. Larry Bird couldn't have shot it better. *You've got to be kidding me. Our keys just sank to the bottom of a Porta-John*, I thought.

The sad part was that, at one time while they were flying, I actually had my fingers on the black Buick key chain holding the keys, but that fried chicken grease was still on my fingers, and they just slipped right off. It was like it was all in slow motion. I could just see 'em going doooown.

I came out of the Porta-John and looked around for Jason. I spotted him up the hill waiting for me.

"Hey, come 'ere buddy," I hollered, and I gestured him over.

"What?" he asked as he started walking my way. "I hope you don't need my help in there."

"Man, you ain't gonna believe what I just did," I said, ignoring his comments about needing his help.

"This'd better be good," he said. *If only he knew*, I

thought. It was good, all right. I mean, it wasn't good good. It was bad good, and I don't mean like Michael Jackson bad. I mean it was bad like in the short term and bad that we were going to have to deal with it, but it was good in that we'd be laughing and talking about it for years to come.

"I just dropped the car keys in the shitter."

Jason looked annoyed, but not because our car keys were somewhere in the middle of all that poop. He looked annoyed because I don't think he believed me. "I don't feel like one of your jokes now, Boo. Where are the keys?"

"Man, I'm serious. I just dropped them in the pooper right here," I said, shaking my head. "We've got to find a coat hanger."

Okay, so *now* Jason looked annoyed because I'd dropped the keys in the portable toilet, but he agreed instantly with my coat hanger suggestion, so we went up to the clubhouse to try to find a coat hanger. We went all over hunting one out. We couldn't find a dang coat hanger for love or money. Our search broadened to whatever might work. We went into the locker room looking for anything to go fishing for keys. Couldn't find so much as a piece of wire.

"Well, there ain't but one thing to do, buddy," I concluded. I looked Jason right in the eyes and told him my plan. "I reckon you're going to have to dig them out."

He said what I would've said had he said to me what I'd said to him. "I ain't digging them out. I didn't drop them in there."

"Okay, so neither one of us wants to dig 'em out," I admitted. "So how are we getting to the airport?"

"We'll go over to the car lot. Maybe they have a spare set of keys and we'll just tell them that the other ones are in the

178

john. They can get them out later. We'll just tell them, 'Hey, look, your keys are in the pooper. Just give us another set. We've got to get to the airport.' But Boo, man, you're telling them you did it."

I was okay with that, so we grabbed our clothes and clubs and walked over to the car lot. Nobody there. We should've known we couldn't have been that lucky. Our options had run out, and I knew it wasn't reasonable to expect Jason to get in there after the keys, since he hadn't dropped them in there. There was only one thing for me to do.

"Look, buddy, just hold the door open," I said to Jason, ready to be a hero. "I'll reach down in there and get them keys, okay? We have to get to the airport. We ain't got but fifteen minutes, so I'm just gonna do it."

"Okay," Jason agreed quicker than anything Jason had ever done before.

So I took some snuff out; at least that was still in my pants. To be honest, if I had to choose between the keys and the snuff, I would probably have chosen the snuff. Anyway, I took it out and rubbed it on my upper lip, under my nose. I was worried that the smell plus sloshing my hand around in that gook might be enough to trigger my gag reflex, adding barf to the mix.

"Alright Jason, hold the door open," I said, preparing myself as if I were getting ready to jump out of a plane without a parachute (actually, it sort of felt that bad). "I'm going in! As soon as I find 'em, I'm hauling butt out of here, so stay out of my way, buddy."

Then I did it. I just did it. I had to do it, and I did it. I reached down in that smelly blue goo and started fishing around with my hand and feeling for anything solid. I felt a lot of solid things that I knew weren't keys. Also felt a lot of soft things and a whole lot of mush. I swirled around with my arm submerged past my elbow and finally . . .

"I got 'em!" I screamed, as I jumped up and took off running like a wild man, out the Porta-John door and toward the cart barn. I ran right by the caddies with blue slime dripping everywhere. Jason's caddy, Peter Van Der Riet, yelled out, "Ooh, what in the hell is wrong with your arm?"

"Man, don't ask!" I said as I whizzed on by.

I then heard one of them say (and I ain't kidding), "Man, what you been doing, jacking off Poppa Smurf?"

Looking back, that was pretty funny, but it was no laughing matter at the time. My arm was literally blue from the chemicals used in those Porta-Johns, and my life's mission right at that moment was to get my arm cleaned, sanitized, or even amputated if need be. An attendant at the cart barn found some spray bleach for me, and I washed and sprayed and washed and sprayed. I think I cried the whole time, too. A whimpering sort of Boo-hoo. I'm a little OCD about cleanliness, so you can bet I overdid it on washing my arm. Drastic times call for drastic measures, and drastic dirtying calls for drastic cleansing.

Now, I said at the beginning of this chapter that you want to put the ball in the hole and the poop in the pot, and that sometimes I can't do either. Well, that was definitely true of my rookie year, 2002. In addition to it being the year of Boo, the Blue-Armed Bandit, it seemed my whole 2002 season went the way of those keys: in the crapper.

There was just something wrong with me that whole year. It might've been those blue chemicals seeping into my arm and getting into my blood or something. Or it could've been the psychological impact of having my arm submerged in OPP (other people's poop). It's hard to shake that off, in more ways than one. Whatever it was, I never could get any momentum in my golf game that year. I just couldn't get the ball in the hole. I'd hit sprinkler heads when you just didn't need to hit a sprinkler head. I'd make a bad swing and it'd hit a tree, and instead of kicking it either straight down or back out, it'd go out into the woods and get lost. I'd be 20 yards from the green and hit it so hard it'd go straight out of bounds. It was just one of those years. Every single part of my game reeked.

Though one of my greatest Porta-John memories of all time came out of 2002, it wasn't a year for me to remember in terms of golf. At the end of that mess I felt like I needed to wash a whole lot more than my arm. I told myself, *Okay, I'm washing all this crazy shit out of my head. I've got to get rid of it all. I've just got to. I've got to look forward and improve my game. Things have to get better. I'm done finishing at number two.*

10 TWISTS, TURNS, AND TIES

Have you ever been on one of them huge rollercoasters? You know, the kind you have to be a certain height to ride? You stand in line, excited about the thrill you're about to get, thinking that monster of twisted metal (in some cases, wood) is going to be nothing but fun. Then you get on. It starts off slow, you turn a corner, and you see a big hill in front of you. The exhilaration builds as you inch your way up the hill, taking in all the sights of the park as you get higher and higher. Then you reach the top and feel like nothing can touch you up there. You're literally on top of the world.

Then you fall.

Just like that, you're at the bottom again, and you might even feel like throwing up. Oh, and that's not the end of it. You then proceed at break-neck speeds through twists and turns and loops and such. There're a few points where you wish the ride would end. There're a few points where everything's blurring and you can't make heads or tails of nothin'.

There're even a few points where you get pretty darn close to blacking out.

Well, that's sort of how golf's been for me. Ups and downs, and twists and turns. High points and low points. You know, one of them huge amusement parks should build a ride called Boo Weekley's Pro Golf Ride of Mayhem. Yeah, that'd get the thrill seekers.

One of the high and low points of my roller-coaster golf ride came when Joe and I turned our attention to the Honda Classic in Palm Beach Gardens, Florida, from February 26 through March 4, 2007. Once again, I was riding a high, having played very well in Mexico, but it was time to play consistently at a high level and get off the roller-coaster ride that was making me dizzy.

After playing a practice round, I said to Joe, "Man, you know this golf course here sets up pretty good for us."

"Yep, as long as we keep it in play and keep it out of the water, it shouldn't be that hard," Joe said.

"Yeah, I guess there's a lot of water out here, huh?" I asked, though it was more like a remark. I was starting to rethink my first statement about the course setting up good for us.

"Yeah, there's a lot of water," Joe said, looking like he was in deep thought or something.

"That's alright," I said, reassuring Joe of my confidence. I was ready, and no amount of deep waters (or deep thoughts, for that matter) was going to get me down.

I must've been making some sort of subconscious prediction when I said, "That's alright," because day one was pretty much just alright. It ended better than it started, that's for sure. I started off by bogeying hole 10 and finished the front 9 (holes 10–18) at 3 over. Thanks to three birdies to one bogey on the back 9 (holes 1–9), I finished day one at 1 over and six strokes off the lead. Not insurmountable by any stretch, but a pretty far piece after only one day of play.

Round two started out much like the day before, with more bogeys than birdies (2–0) on the front 9, which put me back to 3 over. I thought, *Here we go again*, and started to have visions of a bunch of construction workers putting together that Boo Weekley roller coaster. Thank God for the back 9, though, where I made four birdies to no bogeys to put me at -1 after two rounds. That back 9 felt good, like I was shooting me a perfect bow and arrow. My second-round 68 was only 2 over the low 66 shot by Mark Wilson. Still, I had a long way to go to be in contention for a top-10 finish.

Then came day three, and what a difference a day makes, as they say. I ain't talking about any ol' day. I'm talking about Glen Day. You see, I was paired with Glen for the third round, and that was more than alright. I was staying with Glen at a house he'd rented about 7 miles from the course, so I already knew we had a lot in common. I'm not sure what he'd say, but I guess I'd say you could say we're both rednecks. He's from Mississippi, and I'm from Florida. Now, of course, being from Mississippi and Florida doesn't necessary make someone a redneck, but being from the parts Glen and I are from in those states goes a long way toward reddening the neck. Anyway, the point is that Glen and I are a lot alike and we got along well. While staying at the house, we cut up with each other, grilled out, and swam almost every night. It got my mind off golf and roller coasters for a few hours and helped me to relax a bit.

So it was nice being paired up with Glen on that third

day. It's definitely true what they say about the difference a day can make.

I began the third round by parring holes 1 and 2. Then I made eagle on hole 3. I bogeyed that same hole on day one, so day three was obviously much improved. That's why we play the game each and every day. That's why they go ahead and play the Super Bowl even if one team is figured to run away with it. That's why they run the race even if Usain Bolt is one of the runners. That's why they have the fight even if it's David matched up against Goliath. In golf, each day is different. The player and the course can be worlds apart from one day to the next. The holes can be like canyons one day, and as if someone filled them all up the next. I can be Boo one day and just plain scary the next. You never know, and it's different every day. Sometimes it's different every second. Heck, I could triple a hole and then turn right around, play it again, and make birdie. Out here, you're always just one bad swing away from a horrible one-hole score.

Anyway, after the eagle, I was -3 for the tournament and feeling a lot better about my chances. I went on to close out the front 9 holding the 3 under. The back 9 only served to improve my position. With no bogeys along with two birdies, I finished play on day three with a 66, which tied Mark Wilson for the best score of the day. My -5 after three rounds gave me the confidence I'd need for the rest of the tournament. I felt as if I'd gotten to the top of the hill and just stayed there, looking out without fear of falling anytime soon. I felt like a bird.

Now, don't get me wrong. I didn't feel like Larry Bird. That guy was ultra-competitive in terms of other players and, from what I understand, checked the box scores a lot in his days of competing with Magic Johnson. Well, I'm a little more laid-back than that. I'm not one who watches the leaderboard. I'm usually so into my own game and competing with the course itself that I'm not worried about what the other players are doing. Besides, it was a darn good thing I didn't check the leaderboard after the third round. I'm sure Joe kept a hawk's eye on the board and knew where we stood, but it was good that I just focused on playing golf.

As we walked toward the first tee box at hole 1 for the final day of the tournament, I decided it was time to glance up at the leaderboard. I looked up at the top and didn't see Larry Bird and Magic Johnson up there fighting it out for first and second place. I saw my name, Boo Weekley. Right up there near the top. I was in second place!

My mind started racing so fast that I'm pretty sure it could've beaten Usain Bolt in the 100 meters. I was like, *Wow, here I am! I've got the opportunity to win my first PGA Tour event! Never won one on the Nationwide Tour; won 30 on the minitours, or at least 30 on the minitours. How am I going to handle this? Come on, Boo.*

Joe walked up, and I leaned toward him and whispered, "Man, do you see this? We're in second place, man." Joe gave me a look and a smile that said something like, *Yeah, I didn't want to tell you.* I was a nervous wreck. I was ready to rip my sleeves off, and I didn't even care if I had camo under there that would make folks think I was all tattooed up. I started panicking a bit, which is probably why Joe didn't want to tell me I was in second place. I could've bitten the head off a 10-penny nail, I was so nervous. So I did what I do when I'm nervous and dipped a can of snuff. That's right, a can. A whole can. Normally I'll dip one can of snuff during a whole round of golf, maybe, but that day, I done dipped a whole can of snuff right then and there before I teed off. You know, I was about to have an anxiety attack, and I guess I was drowning my anxiety in snuff.

"Wow, dawg." I hemmed and hawed. I was making no sense at all. "Dude. Well, you know. What are we . . . ?" I might've even thrown a "*wheeeeeeee!*" in there.

"Hey, man, just calm down," Joe said, probably talking as much to himself as to me. "Man, it's just golf. Let's just go out, have fun, and let's play the best we can play. It's going to happen. Eventually it's going to happen to you."

"Yeah I know. We've talked about it, but, Joe—"

"They can't keep you from winning. They can't like say, 'Hey, you can't have this trophy even though you shot the best.' That can't happen. You just go out and play golf."

Well, I listened to Joe, stopped listening to all those thoughts in my head, ignored the urge to throw up, and just got out there. I played golf alright. I played and played and played. I played my game, me and the course. I made the turn, and all the noise around me sort of went away as my ears picked up a familiar voice and I focused in on it. I smiled from ear to ear when I realized who it was. I looked at Joe and said, "Man, that sounds like Parker."

"Yeah, man, your family's here," Joe revealed.

"How long have they been here?" I asked with the excitement of a kid opening a gift on Christmas morning to discover that awesome toy he didn't think he was getting.

"Man, I think they got here like the second hole."

"You're kidding me! How have I not seen them?"

I had no idea my family was even thinking about coming.

I wanted them there (I always want them there), but it just hadn't crossed my mind that they might come. Why would it have? They'd seen me play golf many times before, and how could anyone have known I was going to have a shot at winning? Also, I was so focused on my game that I never looked into the crowd or heard a recognizable voice, really. It was mostly just a jumbled buzz of voices until Parker's voice jumped out at me and took complete control of my heart and mind. Well, it got a whole lot sweeter when I realized my family was there. It all made sense. It all came together. It all felt right.

"Really, they're here?" I asked, still like that kid on Christmas morning.

"Yeah, there's Parker, right over there," Joe said, pointing.

"Ha ha! Oh, wow, there he is!" I ran over and gave Parker a big Boo bear hug. Gave my mom a hug and a bunch of other folks some hugs. I was giving out hugs like they were going out of style (not that I'd know what's in style). I lost track of how many hugs I handed out. (Or do you arm out hugs? I don't know, but I did a lot of huggin', and it all started with Parker.)

So with all the warm fuzzies we picked up from family time, we made our way through the course playing golf. I wasn't playing as well as I'd played the two previous rounds, but I was playing good golf, no doubt. I was playing good enough to be tied for first going into the 17th hole.

My second shot was 165 yards to the hole. I pulled out an 8-iron and told Joe, "You know the pin's only seven steps on the green. There's a lake in front of this green. It's got a bunker about fifteen steps behind the pin, and like I said, the pin's only seven steps on the green." It was tucked right over the water, and there was a little bailout area over to the left side of the green that was reachable. I paused for a moment. "Alright, Joe," I continued, "how do you like it?"

"We've got a little bit of wind helping us off the right," Joe said, looking off to the side. "All you have to do is just get it in the air, start it."

We were trying to pick a spot, and I said, "Where do you want me to start?"

"Well, can you draw up a little bit?" Joe asked. "Let's start it right over the edge of the bulkhead." The bulkhead's part of the wooden decking that goes around the green. Joe continued, "Just start it right on that corner there and just let the wind—"

I cut him off. "Well, what if I just push it, man?"

Joe looked a little disappointed, like I was losing it. It was as if he could see all those warm fuzzies flying away from me, looking down, laughing as if to say, "Ha ha, you thought we were just going to stick around forever and keep you feeling all warm and fuzzy for the rest of the day!" Well, Joe scolded me a bit and said, "Don't think like that. Here, let's just step back and regroup, okay?"

So I stepped back. We regrouped. I tried to grab some of those escaping warm fuzzies by their fuzzy little legs and pull them back. Joe and I had to go back all through our whole routine again just because of that one little bit of negativity. You know, my "What if I push it?" comment. That'll make a guy like Joe pull you back and make you go back through the whole tee, take some grass and throw it up. Everything.

"Alright, listen," Joe said, now that he'd started over and begun laying out his strategy again. "Start it over the bulkhead, at the pin, but just hit it, okay?"

"Okay," I said with as little negativity as possible. We had a little window that we were looking at, kind of like when you're shooting a bow. You have to slide it through a little window, and we started at the pin, but we wanted it to end up over on the left edge of the bunker that was kind of behind the green. That was the bull's-eye I was aiming at.

"Just get it between the pin and that bunker. Just start it at the pin and let the wind just push it a little left," Joe advised.

"Okay," I said again, with even less negativity than the first time. I started it just to the right edge of the flag. The wind got it up there and it pushed it. I mean, it pushed it. It pushed it every way a shot should be pushed, landing it about 15 feet just left of the hole. It was one of the prettiest shots I've hit in my life. You know, it was just one of those shots you dream of. Well, this time, I didn't just dream. I hit it. Bull's-eye.

"Now, that's what I'm talking about!" Joe yelled out. He was now the one overtaken by the excitement of a little kid opening a present on Christmas morning he wasn't expecting to get. "Now, that's a golf shot!" The best part about the shot was that I made it during a pressure moment. That really magnified the feeling. I was on the verge of my first PGA Tour win, so it was a real pressure moment. It's like the kid who hits the game winning 3 in the NCAA tournament. Hitting a 3-pointer is always a good thing, but when the game's on the line, a 3-pointer packs a little more punch. That's how this shot of mine was. It packed some serious punch.

We got up there, and Mark Wilson, the guy I was playing with, hit it just to the left edge. He rolled it up there real nice and almost made it. He tapped it in to put him at 5 under.

There were two guys who'd already finished at 5 under: Camilo Villegas and José Cóceres. They were in the clubhouse, and Mark and I were both still out there at 5 under. So that made four of us bottled up together, and I had a 15-footer remaining for birdie after the Mark Wilson putt.

"Did you see that putt?" Joe asked.

"Yeah, I saw it," I said, not really sure if it mattered that I'd seen it, but I think it mattered to Joe.

"Just slide a little to the right, just a little," Joe continued.

"Alright, where would you like it?" I asked, wanting Joe's advice more than ever before. Nerves were creeping up on me again.

"I like it just maybe outside of the left lip a bit."

"Yeah, you like that?" I asked, just to keep the talking going.

"Yeah. Okay, let me line you up."

"You going to line me up?" I asked, now simply taking everything Joe said and repeating it in the form of a question. I guess that's a nervous habit of mine.

"Yeah, I'm going to line you up," Joe said as our nervous chatter continued.

"Okay," I said, resisting the urge to ask again if he was going to line me up. My heart was pounding. Everything seemed heavy. Even my golf ball felt like a heavy weight. Then I took a look at it.

On one side of my golf ball, I write my little boy's initials. So there it was, TP, for Thomas Parker. Every time I pick up that ball, no matter how bad I feel or how mad or nervous I am, I can look at that ball, see my boy's initials, and think, *Hey, they're having a good time right now. They're having fun. TP loves his daddy, win, lose, or draw.* I use that as a mental exercise from time to time so that I can get perspective and calm down when I'm all hyped up like I was that day, in that moment. About 90 degrees to one side of Parker's initials, I draw a straight line that I use to line up my shot. I started writing Parker's initials sometime in 2003. Now it's habit. Plus, now I have another son, Aiden O'Neil. So, it's TP on one side and AO on the other. The only time I write TP and AO on a ball is during actual tournament rounds. I had the line pointing right out the left, outside of the hole. I have a line on my putter that I line up with the line on my ball. I try to get them together as best I can.

Joe will usually stand about five or six feet behind me and squat down to line me up. That day, Joe stood there as usual and said, "Okay, buddy, you've got it lined up, but you're a little too far right."

"Okay," I said, this time with no negativity at all. So I picked up my putter and I read it myself and then sat my putter back down. "Alright, that's it."

Everything went silent around me, and Joe nodded in what seemed like slow motion. When he stepped away, I looked back at the hole one more time and then just stroked it. No more thinking, no more talking, no more lining up, no more being nervous. I just stroked it—and it was perfect.

It rolled—I mean picture perfect. It was as if the air just sort of grabbed the ball, helping it along. Something was pulling it to the right spot. I watched it with pure contentment, like it was on a track, and there was nothing anyone could do to knock it off course. That ball was meant for one spot, and it was going to get there. Then, all of a sudden, it just made a right turn, right into the hole. Yep, that was the ball's spot.

Now I had the lead. Six under going to the 18th hole. First place. That was *my* spot.

The silence was gone, and the noise around me was back. It was louder and now focused on me. The crowd started chanting my name. "Boo, Boo, Boooooooo." They were hollering. They were whooping it up. They were rowdy. I could hear my mother's cheers among the others. That's my rowdy mamma! I was taking it all in, and I could hear some folks saying, "Hurry, let's go to the eighteenth hole and watch Boo win." I mean, it was just amazing. I felt like a rock star. One guy looked at me and said, "You tha man, you tha man." That had me so fired up I could've run through a brick wall.

I just smiled and gave the throngs of folks the number-one signal with my index finger pointing skyward, shaking it back and forth. I kept my mouth closed and let my finger do the talking, and boy, did it ever talk. It wagged back and forth as if to say, "Alright, I'm number one; I'm going to close this thing out." I smiled, tipped my hat, and waved to the crowd.

The 18th and final hole is a par 5. It sits 604 yards to the pin. The green's reachable in two shots. We got to the tee box and Joe said, "Alright, Dick, here's what we've got to do." Joe calls me all sorts of names, and I think nothing of it. Not sure why he called me Dick at that moment, but that's what he called me. Anyway, he continued, "We've got a bunker on the left. We've got a little bit of a rough on the right. Let's start it right down the middle here. If it draws a little bit, you're fine. You ain't quite going to get to that bunker. If you cut it just a little bit, it's going to be perfect. It's going to be in the fairway."

The fairway makes a little doglegged left turn, and then

another when it gets down there in the bottom. Another big lake surrounds the green as the green makes a little turn back to the right. So it makes almost a snakelike twist.

I was so nervous about closing it out that I hit the son of a gun 20 yards off line. I just stepped up there and *wham*. It went way right, and I knew it was off. I felt like a little kid who'd just done something stupid like try to punch through a wall or shoot a knife out of a slingshot. You know, when you're young, you do some dumb things without thinking and then wonder what the heck you were doing right after you break your arm or slice your finger. Right when I hit that ball, I was like, *Why did you do that? Oh my gosh, don't go in the water.*

I hit it way right, that's for sure, but somehow it didn't get near that water. I'm telling you, something was guiding it. It was a thicker rough. We got to the ball, and it was sitting perfect. I mean, it was sitting up, just waiting for me, as if to say, *No need to worry, Boo. Your arm's not broken. Your finger's not sliced.*

"Man, this is like sitting in the fairway," I said to Joe.

"Well, good. Let's get this down there where we can have a good drive."

"How far do we have down to the water there?" I asked Joe.

"You've got a hundred thirty yards," he told me.

"You don't like a five?" I asked, referring to the 5-iron.

"No, I don't like a five here."

"Well, what do you think?" I said, fully trusting his judgment.

"Well, I tell you, man, I like a four-iron."

Okay, maybe I didn't *fully* trust him. "Four-iron?" I

asked. "God dang, Joe, that pin's tucked from the right-hand side over that bunker. There ain't no way. We ain't gonna make it."

Joe got serious, and he was ready to help me win. "Look, Boo, you have a one-shot lead. Make him make birdie. You don't worry about trying to make birdie. You just focus on you getting this ball down there where we can get the next shot onto the green. That's all we need to worry about right now."

"Dude, I just don't know."

"Don't worry about what distance we got. Let's just go. Here's a four-iron. I want you to hit this four-iron, and I want you to hit it right at that TV tower right there at the edge of the grandstand." I could tell Joe was fully confident in what he was telling me, and I had to be honest with myself at that moment. Joe's the man, and when Joe's fully confident, I'm fully confident. I decided to go with Joe.

It was an easy decision, really. The 4-iron actually made sense. I had just wanted to be sure, and I think my mind was messing with me. We knew if I hit the 4-iron and I smoked it, I couldn't get it in the water. Still, I knew if I hit it bad, I'd leave myself too far back, where I'd have to hit probably with the same club or something a little less onto the green.

The wind was blowing off our right side, kind of down and off our right a bit. So, taking Joe's advice, I hit the 4-iron—and I hit it perfect, just the way we drew it up. I just laid it right out there in the fairway. Joe'd been right, and he knew it.

"Alright, let's go," he said excitedly and with a great deal of pride. It was a job well done, and that's why he's my guy. "We're going to go down there and finish this thing," he said with a healthy dose of attitude.

Joe had already figured what we were going to have. Coming off that shot, he said, "you're going to have anywhere between one-seventy to a hundred fifty yards to the hole."

"Okay," I said, fully trusting he was right. This time really fully trusting him.

We watched Mark Wilson hit. He hit it down the fairway on the left-hand side and left it where he had a good little approach shot onto the green. Not bad at all, and I knew I had to step up on the next shot.

I was first to hit, of course, and when we got up there, Joe figured it was 155 yards to the hole. He was pretty much right on the money, but I thought we had a problem. You see, I normally hit an 8-iron at 160 yards and a 9-iron at 150 yards. So what was a Boo to do? Joe knew.

"Alright, this ought to be a perfect little eight-iron shot," he said.

Hey, that was good enough for me. "Okay," I quickly agreed. This was no time to dicker, so I was totally on board with whatever Joe said. I took two practice swings, and then I stepped up to hit my shot.

"You see that palm tree over there, just to the left of the pin?" Joe asked.

"Yeah."

"I want you to start this ball right there."

I don't know why I doubted Joe at that moment, but I did. Or maybe I doubted myself. "Gosh dog, cuz," I commented, "that's ten, fifteen feet right of the hole."

"That's what I'm talking about," Joe insisted. "You gonna start it right there."

I was starting to see eye to eye with him. "Before it's said and done it's going to end up about another ten or fifteen feet," I said, "but we're gonna have a twenty-five- to thirty-footer max. We're putting good. We ain't had but one three-putt this whole week. We're okay. This is what we've got to do to win this tournament."

Joe smiled. "You got it, dawg."

I stood up there, got ready, and cleared my head. It came down to this, and I knew it. Before I could think about it too much, I stroked it. I really sent that ball flying. Perfect. Right at the palm tree, like Joe said, but just kinda hooked a little bit. It was exactly what I wanted to do. Couldn't have been better. Bam, center of the green.

That's when the crowd took it to a new level. I could see my mamma, and she was going nuts. Ha ha! It was awesome. Everybody was back there jumping up and down, screaming and yelling. Clapping like I've never seen 'em clap before. Not for me, anyway. Yet all this noise and clapping was for me. They were all hurling praise my way. "Boo, it's your time, it's your time. Boo you're going to do it this time. You're the man, Boo."

The grandstand starts out about 100 yards from the green and goes almost all the way around the backside of the green. It sounded like the entire crowd was hollering my name, chanting "Booooooo." I mean, I got the biggest goose bumps I've ever had. My hair was standing up. I walked down there just shaking my club and with my hand just waving at them and smiling. It was my time, and the crowd sure did a heck of a job letting me know it.

I got up on the green and still had a big ol' smile on my face. Mark had hit it just over the back, and he chipped it up and almost in the hole. As I remember, he had about a 5-footer or so.

I had a 30-footer for birdie, and it was time to take care of business. So I got up there, and we looked it over. There was a little ridge in the green. It kind of went downhill, but it went right toward the water. The grain was pulling that way on the green. I remember it going downhill a little bit, then going up just a little, in a little ridge, and then going back up a ridge.

Joe and I were talking as usual, and he said, "Alright, it's about a foot out on the left." I always pick something as a ball marker when I have longer putts on the green, so that's what I did here. This was definitely a long putt. I picked a piece of grass that I could start my ball toward. Now, keep in mind that even though that's where I wanted to start, I wanted to end up in a different place. That piece of grass was the apex of the turn, and that's what I mean when I say it was a marker. I looked at Joe and said, "I like this mark."

"I do, too," he agreed. "I like that. Alright, let's stroke it then."

My nerves were beginning to fire up because I knew this was it, but I felt under control. I felt I was in charge and that my nerves could be used to my advantage for once. Like I had a little army of nerves that had accepted me as their commander. My adrenaline was pumping, and I felt good and energized.

I hit the putt, and it just felt right. I immediately thought, *Boy, that could go in. That thing could go in.* Then, all of a sudden, the air that had seemed to be on my side up until that point decided to play with me a bit. A gust of wind came out of nowhere as if to say, "Not so fast, my man." Seriously, that ball was going right toward the hole, and then it started back up that hill. And that wind just came across, and it was just like that ball hit Velcro. It was just barely creeping and didn't look like it was going to creep out to the down slope. Well, some other force must've been out there working against that wind, because all of a sudden, the ball caught the down slope and barely crept out of there.

From the top of that slope to the hole, I probably had about 6, maybe 7 feet. Well, like I said, the ball rolled out, just barely, but it stopped short of the hole. It was 3 feet and 2 inches to the hole for my next putt. Should be a piece of cake.

My mamma was crying. I could hear a lot of things going on around me, but I could really hear her crying over there above everything else. Sniffling and crying there above all the other noise. I mean everything was so loud, but I could hear certain things like my mamma's crying. It was almost as if I had a bionic earpiece in my ear. There were certain things I would pick up on, without even trying. Just all of a sudden, *bam,* I'd hear something. For example, there was a floating dock with a scoreboard out in the water. I'm not sure how, but I could hear the guys working on the dock talking and saying, "I bet he makes it. I bet he . . ." Then I'd hear another person over in the grandstands: "I don't think he can make it." Then I'd hear my mamma crying in the middle of all that.

Then I heard a news guy covering the golf tournament: "He's got a test here. He has a downhill, you know, and it's pretty speedy going down that hill. You know the wind kinda . . ." I was listening, not really sure if it meant much to me. But I'm telling you, I could hear all that stuff at one time, and it was a little overwhelming. Fans, doubters, analysts, crying. It was all getting to me and pulling my mind in different directions.

I backed away, and then Mark backed away.

Joe could tell something was up. He came up to me, threw his arm on me, and said what I needed to hear. "Hey, man. Shit, you done made every one of these. You've missed only one of them this week. You ain't going to miss this one. All this is, is an inside left, left putt, dude. All you got to do is roll, baby."

Joe was just trying to keep me from thinking too much, because he knew better than anyone what overthinking something can do to me. He wanted me to just get up there and get it done, and he was right. He could tell I was starting to get very nervous, so he was dead on about what I was feeling. He knew I needed a bit of a pep talk to get my mind back in the game.

Mark had to putt first, so I watched. He was sitting at 5 under, as you know. Then bam! He putts it, he makes it, and everybody cheers. Mark made par to stay at 5 under. They're hollering for him. They're cheering for him. They're clapping for him.

When Mark took his ball out of the hole, I said, "Good playing today. Good round."

He looked at me and said, "Okay," and that was it. He didn't say another word to me. "Okay" was all I was going to get. I could tell something was different about that moment. I'd never been there before, of course, and it definitely felt different. Usually we golfers say to each other things like "Knock this in." If it's down to the final putt, we'll say to the one putting, "Alright, knock this in, tap this in." Yet Mark just walked away. If "okay" was all I was getting, well *okay* then.

I went around to the other side of the hole, and I looked it up and down, sort of acting like I was really studying the situation, but really I was trying to catch my breath. Anxiety was starting to take over. My hands started pouring water. I sweat an awful lot in my palms anyway, but my hands were getting to where I couldn't hold the putter, and it's rubber. I mean, that's some serious sweating. You can hold rubber when it's wet, but this was poles apart from any kind of sweating I'd done in the past.

I motioned for Joe to bring a towel over, and I wiped the grip off. Then I wiped my hands. Then I wiped them on my pants. Then I did it all again.

"Do you like an inside lefty?" Joe asked, ignoring the sweat and trying to break through the anxiety.

"Yeah, I like an inside left."

"Alright, well knock it in," he said, urging me to get on with it. I looked at him and knew I had to do it. I knew this was my moment. I picked up my mark and placed the ball down. I stepped back and looked it over again. I got up there and took my practice strokes. I put the putter down behind it, and I seriously felt like I was choking. My throat felt like it was closing, and my breath quickened. I just couldn't seem to get control of it. The anxiety just wouldn't be defeated. I mean, my knuckles and fingers were death-grip white. I looked down and could see the pressure I was applying to the grip, but I couldn't back away. I should've been able to step back and get my composure, but I just couldn't make myself back away from that ball. I told myself, *Just take a deep breath, and regroup. Try it again.* But I couldn't. Or I wouldn't. The bottom line is, I didn't.

So, finally, I took my putter back and hit the ball, and I'm telling you I hammered it like I was trying to hit a drive. The crowd's roar instantly turned to a collective gasp as the ball skipped over the hole. I'd missed the putt. I'd hit a chicken truck! It went right across the top of the lip. It was now far-ther from the hole than it was before the putt. It was sitting there about four feet back from the hole.

As soon as it went by the hole, I threw my putter up against my head. I just tapped my hat and looked straight up in the sky. I said, "Why me, Lord? Why me? I just want one, just one! Please just let me have one. Why me?"

After that putt, it was a four-way tie! Camilo Villegas, Mark Wilson, José Cóceres, and me, all at 5 under. And now here I was, needing to hit a putt to be part of a 4-way tie when just moments before I could've won it. I threw my putter down, disgusted with myself, and I walked around to the other side. I marked the ball and threw it to Joe. He cleaned it off. I cleaned my grip. I cleaned my hands. Then I stepped up for the second putt. I knocked it in to bogey hole 18 and create the quad tie.

Then my bionic ear started up again.

There was this guy standing right on the corner of the grandstand just behind the green, and I could hear him clear as my bald head. "He choked," the man said. I don't think he was saying it loud enough for anybody else to hear, but *I* could hear it. "He choked. He's a choker. I can't believe he choked. He cost me money."

I had visions of Reggie Miller giving the choke sign to Spike Lee on the sidelines. Little did this guy know that I'd been literally choking right before that putt. Still, it was as if I were onstage and everybody was staring a hole right through me. The guy was right. I did choke. Then I heard my mamma again, and I was thinking to myself, *My poor mama. She's really crying now.* I could hear her loud and clear. I saw her when I went to line up my putt, and my little boy was over there, too. He was jumping up and down. He thought I'd won. I didn't even want to look over at him. It was not a good moment.

I'll tell you this, though, I learned a lesson that day. I stood over that putt, and my heart was just pounding. I could feel my head pounding. I could feel it all the way down in my toes. I could feel everything in my body just getting tighter. Well, the result of not stepping back is something I'll never let happen again. I knew from that moment on, if I were ever in that situation again, I'd walk away from the ball, realign, throw up some grass—anything at all to kill a little time and regain my composure. Now every time I get into that position, that's exactly what I do. I step back from the ball and get a grip. I step back from it and just think to myself, *Alright, just take you a couple of deep breaths. It's okay.*

So there we were, in a four-way tie. I shook hands with Mark, and he said nothing. Mark didn't say a word. I'm not sure if he was just super focused or what, but I thought it was a little strange that he was so quiet. I said, "Congratulations."

He finally said something. "I reckon we'll just see each other here in a second." Not exactly wishing me well, but at least words had come out of his mouth.

"Yeah, we'll just see each other in a second," I followed up. I should have just said, "Okay." Anyway, we went in and signed our scorecards. They have to check them and run them through the PGA process to make sure they all check out, which they did.

We came back out, and all I wanted to do was give my mamma a hug and tell her everything was okay, because she was crying. She was very excited when she thought I was going to win, and I think she just didn't handle the swing very well. Parker came over, and I picked him up and was holding him on my hip. A reporter asked, "Hey, can I get an interview with you real fast?"

"Yeah, sure, come on," I said, not really feeling up to it, but not really feeling opposed to it either.

"Well, would you mind putting him down?" the reporter asked, referring to Parker.

"No, I'm hanging on to him," I said. There was no way I was putting him down. No way. "If you want to talk to me, then talk to me."

The reporter was apparently okay with that, because he asked, "What was going through your mind on that putt?"

"I thought I was going to make it," I said. "What I was going to do was, I was going to turn around to the crowd, and I was going to throw my hands into the air, and I was going to start hollering, 'Well, I finally did it. I finally did it.' You know. But it didn't happen."

"Well, what do you think?" the reporter asked.

"I can tell you what I think. I choked. That's what I think. I choked. There was a guy standing up in the corner of the bleachers. He said it best, 'He choked.' And I did. I choked. My adrenaline, the pressure, everything got to me. I choked. It was my responsibility to win that tournament for these people down here and for myself and for my family who're standing right here, and I didn't do it. I lost. I choked."

"Well, what do you think?" he asked again in one of the dumbest follow-up questions I've ever heard.

"I just told you. I'm done. I'm done. I'm through talking to you. I'm done talking. I choked. Okay?"

So Parker and I started walking away, and Parker had his little arm around me and he innocently asked, "Daddy, what does choked mean? Does that mean like when you grab me around the neck, and we're playing wrestling and stuff?"

I smiled and said, "Yeah, son, that's exactly what that means, but in this situation, you're daddy choked in golf."

"Well, shoot, Daddy, it's okay," Parker said. "It's really alright. It don't matter. You're still my dawg." Those words from my little boy meant so much. They really brought me back to what's important. Love and family. Man, if you have that, you can make it through anything.

"I appreciate that, son." Then I carried him over to the others, and I hugged my mamma and the rest of my family like they deserved to be hugged. It was a very emotional time for me. To this day, I still get emotional about it, because it hurt. I mean it really hurt me inside. I talked to some buddies and other players. They said, "Alright, hold your head up." I try not to show emotion in front of them, nothing to nobody, but the emotion was definitely there. If not for family, I might've cracked.

I got back in the locker room after seeing everyone, sat down, and cried to myself. I was very disappointed in the opportunity that'd slipped through my fingers, but at the same time, when I got my wits about me, I thought, *You know, it's better to have that opportunity than not to have it at all*, and I was right. I'd never been there before, yet here I was all upset about something I'd never had the chance to do before. I took that little "seeing the bright side of things" moment, and that's where I was headed with it. I was going to put it behind me and move forward with the "bright side of things" foremost in mind.

Moving forward meant going to a four-man playoff with

those other guys. Though I was looking at the bright side of things, we played the 1st hole right before dark, and we all made par. Before we went to the next hole, the round was postponed until the next day (Monday) because of darkness.

So we came back the next morning. We started on hole 10. The plan was to play holes 10, 17, and 18. At the 10th hole, I made bogey right out of the gate. I thought I hit a good drive, but it just went too far through the fairway. It went into the thick rough. I chopped it out, hit it up on the green, and missed about an 11- to 12-footer. I was the first one eliminated from the four-man playoff. I had a chance to win it the other day, and here I was now the first to go from the four-man playoff.

Still, that was a very special moment for me, because I learned so much about myself with regard to how to handle the little bit of the pressure and adversity that I'd been dealing with over the years. Looking back, I think that was the point. It really wasn't for me to win; it was for me to learn.

In years past, I would've handled the loss differently. I would've just gone out, gotten drunk as a skunk, and just said something like, "It's just not meant to be. I just pissed it away. I just can't do this." In a nutshell, I would've thrown a pity party and felt sorry for my sad self. This time, however, I took it to the good. My thinking was, *I choked for a reason. It's because I'm just not ready. I'm not ready for the limelight. I'm not ready for that much pressure yet, I reckon.* I think that's what the Lord was telling me, that I wasn't ready yet. At the same time, He was telling me that, one day, I'd be ready. I could feel it in my bones. Or was it my stomach? Either way, I just knew the roller coaster couldn't go on forever.

11 SINGIN', DREAMIN', AND PUTTIN'

Some roller coaster rides are too short. You stand in line all day, with sweaty people rubbing up on you, bumping you, and so forth. Then you finally get on the ride after what seemed like a couple of days. One little hill and a few turns later, the darn thing's over, and you feel that that time you spent standing in line's time you'll never get back. Then there are the monster roller coasters. The ones that humans really shouldn't have thought up, let alone actually built. The line, as long as it is, goes way faster than you'd like it to, and before you know it, you're screaming, "MAKE IT STOP!" Yeah, that's the golf roller coaster I was on, and it just wouldn't end.

After I lost the four-man playoff at the Honda Classic, we played in the PODS Championship in Tampa, Florida, at the Westin Innisbrook Copperhead course, a short drive up from Palm Beach. I was worn out mentally, of course. Exhausted. Beaten down. I mean, though I'd learned a lesson, like I said, and I was seeing the bright side of things, it still felt like I'd let everybody down. My family. My caddy. Myself. Everybody. Shoot, I even felt like I'd let down Boo 2 from back home. Plus, you know, I'm human. I was just plain tired.

When I got to Tampa, I really wasn't mentally ready to be playin' no golf. That loss at the Honda Classic really took a heck of a lot out of me. Now, had I won, of course, I would've been flying high as a kite, ready to play golf again the following week, no problem. Whereas that loss wasn't just a little hill on the roller coaster; it was one of them big ol' loops, followed by a corkscrew, followed by another loop, followed by a 90-degree drop. Straight down. Probably 500 feet or so. I'd've lost my hat for sure. Probably my lunch, too.

I went through the motions nonetheless that following week and went ahead and teed it up in Tampa. I may as well have been a ghost out there, though. Boo, the ghost! BOO! Shoot, even that kid from the movie *The Sixth Sense* might've been able to see me by how I felt. He would've looked right at me (and my caddy, Joe) and said, "I see dead people." I'd probably have said something like, "Look, kid, I choked at the Honda Classic, okay? What happens to people when they choke? That's right, they die." Anyway, we definitely felt like dead people in Tampa, and it showed in a big way.

I ended up missing the cut, and there was really no way to keep that from happening. I needed more than a week to rejuvenate and get ready to play again, so it really wasn't a surprise that I didn't perform well. Still, even with my poor play, lack of focus, and general deadness out there, I missed the cut by only one stroke. There's that bright side of things again.

I knew the roller coaster had a few more twists and turns for me before I was ready to step off it, look back, and say,

Yeah, I conquered that bad boy! I also knew that when it was my time to step off, I'd step off. When it was my time to win, I'd win. After all, like I said, the roller coaster couldn't go on forever. Right?

Maybe.

After missing the cut in Tampa, we drove over to Orlando to play in the Arnold Palmer Invitational. I was still feeling down but a little less dead than the previous week. I played pretty well, made the cut, and finished tied for 14th. Now, that wasn't quite enough to make me jump for joy, find the nearest podium, and announce to the world my return to championship form, but I was ready to press on to greater achievements and get over the Honda Classic choking incident. So I kept moving.

The Shell Houston Open was next up, and after a pretty good first round, I turned in a dismal second-round 77 and didn't make the cut. Hey, that's golf. That's what all the people say. You're flying high on one course, shot down the next day. Okay, I guess my attempt at rewriting that classic song doesn't have the same ring to it, but you get my point. Seriously, during the Shell Houston Open, I truly had no hangover from the Honda Classic. As much as I wanted to, I couldn't blame my poor performance on that. I just didn't play very well in Houston and was rewarded for it with a pink slip. Whether you're down about a loss or not, if you don't play well, you don't make the cut. That's it, and that's all. No excuses, and I was ready at that point to stop making 'em.

Though I was done making excuses, I was ready to make an exception the following week when it came to watching TV. I'm not much of a TV watcher, and when I do watch, I usually like tuning in to one of those huntin' shows on one of them outdoor channels. I never watch golf, but that week after the Shell Houston Open was when the exception came in. That was the week of the Masters Tournament, and I just had to tune in. I hadn't qualified for the Masters, of course, so this would be a week of TV watching for my eyes and a week of rest for the rest of me. I mean, how could I not watch the most prestigious golf tournament in the world? It's the only major to be played on the same course every year—and, oh, what a course it is!

Now, a course is a course, of course, of course, unless the course of our discourse is the great Augusta National! Alright, no more song rewrites, I promise! Still, Augusta National is worthy of a song. A serenade, to be exact. Azaleas are planted all over the place and around each green. The azaleas and dogwoods seem to be programmed to bloom only at tournament time. I wouldn't be surprised at all if one of them big ol' computer companies was behind the whole thing. Plus, those century-and-a-half-year-old magnolias, as only the South can grow 'em, overhang and line the driveway to the clubhouse. I'm telling you, you can't even reach your arms around some of them. They're just straight up and look like something out of a Halloween movie. You know how when you look down an old hallway you can kind of see something at the end, but you just can't seem to quite make it out? You're like, "What the heck is that?" Well, that's what those magnolias are like.

It's a shame that not everyone has the pleasure of walking the stately rooms of that clubhouse, which was built in 1854. It made me wonder, *Who lived here and what did they do? How did they live their lives?* If you have a chance, you really need to do it. Just walk through that clubhouse and let your mind go.

The live oaks and loblolly pines scattered everywhere read like history books. You know they've been through a lot and could tell some stories if they had mouths—or brains, for that matter. Still, they are good-looking visions of strength and time. Heck, I could climb up one of those old trees and bow-hunt all day. Wouldn't even have to see a deer. I could just sit up there, look out at nothing at all, and just wait with my bow. I imagine that's a little what Heaven's like. If a deer decided to come join my Heaven so I could attempt to send that deer to its own, well, that'd be just fine. Still, I'd be happy either way.

Oh, and there's water. Tranquil water, but the kind of tranquil that can go nuts in a moment. I mean, there're a couple of ponds on Augusta that cry for a popping bug to be gently laid on that calm water only to have a big bluegill erupt and shock that little bug's world, sending ripples through the liquidy stillness in the process.

The grass at Augusta looks like it was bought in a store and placed there. It's manicured to perfection—and talk about clean. Man, you can drop a ham sandwich on the ground there, and you don't even have to give it the 5-second rule. You just gotta beat the ants, that's all. Listen, I know a thing or two about grass, having studied turfgrass and all, so you can believe me when I say, that there's some nice grass.

There I was, that week after the Shell Houston Open, watching it all on my TV. Not quite the same as seeing it in person, or so I imagined at the time. I remember watching it and looking at the perfect landscaping and some of the stuff that was happening on the course. I kinda just sat there and thought to myself, *Man, it sure would be fun to go to that place, just to go see it. Just to go look at it and just to walk around there. Boy, if I ever got the chance to play there! I'd like to have that opportunity to go play it one time before I'm done with golf. Just one time.*

Now, I'm not one to linger on the prettiness of a place, so don't get me wrong, but Augusta National is just so dang pretty. I mean, it's pretty, pretty. If you put a wig on that golf course back when I was single, I might have been tempted to ask it out. I'd've said, "Hey, Augusta National, you're so pretty. Do you want to go get something to eat?" It'd probably have just said nothing because, well, it's a golf course and it can't think or talk. Then the people around me who might've witnessed my asking out the golf course would've gone right to the media to say, "Boo's done gone nuts!" Hey, it would've been true. I'm nuts about that course! It's the oldest traditional kind of golf course around, and people who've never had the opportunity to walk on it are missing something. It's really gorgeous. Agorgeous National. That's what they should've called it.

I wasn't hitting the ball all that great in the tournaments leading up to that Masters, so I decided to practice that week in addition to watching the Masters on TV. I was sort of in dreaming mode as I watched the events unfold on my TV and heard that beautiful course calling my name. The problem was, the announcers and analysts on TV didn't call my name once, and that really got to me. So I practiced. I practiced hard on driving the ball. While I wished I was at Augusta, and while I watched Zach Johnson win the Masters on my TV, I practiced. After all, I had a tournament to get ready for, in South Carolina. It would be my 35th career professional start on the PGA Tour at the age of thirty-three. After all the practicing and golf watching on my TV, I was ready to roll.

My sports agent, Jimmy Johnston, lives at Sea Island, Georgia, which is only an hour-and-a-half drive to Hilton Head, South Carolina, home of the Verizon Heritage at the Harbour Town Golf Links course. Jimmy called me up and said, "Hey, look, I have a place where you're going to stay. You, Johnson Wagner, and Brandt Snedeker are going to room in one house; me and Brian Bateman, Joe Durant, and Mac Barnhardt are staying in another place."

Mac Barnhardt works with Jimmy at Crown Sports, in case you were wondering. My casa was square on the Atlantic Ocean, which was perfectly okay with me. It put me in a good mood, and I was ready to go, especially with my mind energized by all the Masters dreamin'.

Joe and I got to the golf course on Monday, and I started hitting some balls and putts. Just getting loose. Joe said, "Hey, let's go play a practice round."

I said, "Alright, let's go."

As we were playing a practice round on a course we'd never seen, somewhere around the 2nd or 3rd hole, I told Joe, "Wow, this's our kind of golf course right here, dude. This thang's tight! It's got trees that overhang. I mean, it sets up pretty good for us, don't it?"

"Man, this's where it's at," Joe said excitedly. "This's just like playing at home, dawg. This's our golf course right here."

"Man, I feel good about this week," I carried on. "This's pretty awesome."

"Yeah, this's pretty awesome, but let's just play golf," Joe responded, always wanting to bring me back to reality.

"That's all we got to take care of is golf. The rest of it'll take care of itself."

I knew he was right. "You got it," I said.

When I was done playing the practice round on Monday, Joe took off somewhere, and I was sitting there by my lonesome on the putting green about to work on some putting. As I was sitting there, I happened to overhear Lucas Glover, Charles Warren, and Brian Bateman talking with some guy about putting. He was a putting instructor, as it turned out. He was going through some drills with them.

I thought, *Okay, I'm gonna take me in some of this right here.* I was sitting on the back of my bag, only five or six feet from them, drinking a Gatorade and listening to what their coach was saying, what he had to tell these guys about what was going to make them better players.

What the coach was saying was something very interesting to me about the lines you pick when you're putting. It really struck me and stuck with me. The coach said, "You know the hole is round, and there's not just one way this ball can go in that hole. There're a hundred eighty degrees right there. So if you give it that chance, it has a possibility to go in at any one of those angles." While I was sipping on my Gatorade, I thought, *Wow, I never thought about it like that. I never actually broke it down like that and looked at it like that.* Guess that's why he's a coach and I'm just a golfer.

I've always tried to find a spot where I wanted the ball to go in right in the center of the hole every time, but that coach was basically saying, "Nah, you've got a number of angles." He continued to go through a bunch of drills with those guys (and me, though he didn't know he was going through them with me). One of the guys was having problems with his head moving when he'd putt it. So the coach took a dime and set it down and rolled a ball on top of the dime. He got the player to keep his head down, watch for the dime, and tell him if it was heads or tails.

This was really profound to me, because I had the same problem. I moved my head a lot when I putted. I wondered if that little trick would work for me, too. So I got up and started practicing what he was saying from 3 feet away (where I struggled the most). Immediately, I noticed an improvement. It started feeling good, and I was making my putts. It was like a switch had been there the whole time, but no one had ever switched it on. Once a guy came along who could, though, he switched it on without even knowing it.

I thought, *Wow, okay, this makes a lot of sense*—and it didn't cost me no cents, so that was cool. I started doing it over and over. I'd try it on one hole, and it'd work. Then I'd go to another hole, just trying to make sure it wasn't a fluke or anything. It wasn't.

Then those guys started hitting some long putts with that coach, and I started paying attention to them again. I was hooked, so I got in there behind them, stood, and just listened. The coach got to talking about long putts and speed. He said, "I want you to look out there at the hole, and I want you to hit the ball. I want you to watch that ball roll. When it rolls out, I want you to take your putter, look down, put it right behind the ball, look back at that ball, and putt it again. Try to get them to group together. All it is is some muscle and memory. You ain't got to look at the ball to hit it. All you've got to do is look down and get it on the club, then you can putt it."

Once again, I was smacked upside the head by what he

was saying. I was like, *Wow, that makes sense, too, you know?* So when all those guys went off to the side, I did just that. I guess I was kinda following them like a little puppy dog trying to get some scraps. I was listening and trying to learn more about what was going on, just trying to grow as a golfer.

Well, time really got away from me that evening, and it got late before I knew it. I was so enthralled with what that coach was teaching them that I didn't even think about where I was or what I was doing. I called my agent and said, "Jimmy, where in the world are we staying at?" He gave me directions, and I was on my way, trying to remember everything that coach had said out there.

On my way to where I was staying, Jimmie called me back and said, "Hey, look, a guy named MT is going to stay with you, okay?"

I'm pretty flexible, as you should know by now, so I just said, "That's fine, dude. Sure, he can stay with me."

I got to the house first. I went upstairs and went to the farthest side of the house, away from the sun where it rises in the morning. I went up there and picked me out a bed. The bedroom was like a small loft bedroom, with three queen-sized beds, and they all looked soft enough, so I laid my stuff on one of the beds. Jimmy called back yet again, saying, "Hey, look, Mike Taylor's on his way. He shouldn't be long. He should be there in five or ten minutes."

I said, "Oh, okay."

As I was going back downstairs to get some stuff out of my truck, another truck pulled up that sported a big ol' buck sticker on the back of it. I was immediately interested and wondered, *Who in the world is this cat here? He's in a Z71.*

This guy must hunt around here or something. Wonder what he wants.

We were at the end of a cul-de-sac, on the road by ourselves. This guy jumped out, and I immediately recognized him as the guy who'd been giving all that good advice on the putting green. MT was the coach! The coach was MT! Aw, yeah!

I walked over to introduce myself, and he stuck his hand out right quick and said, "Hi, my name's Mike Taylor."

"Hi, I'm Boo Weekley."

"Yeah, I know who you are," he said with a smile. "Did you learn anything today?"

With a big ol' grin, I said, "I did indeed, sir. I did indeed. I'm glad you're staying with us. I want to pick your brain a bit, if that's okay. I want to learn a thing or two."

"Well, sure," he responded, "we'll do a little bit of that. But right now, let's get inside and have a cold beer, and we'll talk about it."

"Alright," I said. Cold beer and talking are two things I like, so no problem there. I looked at his truck and said, "Is there anything in there I can help you grab?"

"Yeah, you can grab all that stuff out of the back." He didn't even blink an eye when he said that. Guess he was thinking I owed him for the free advice I'd gotten earlier. Little did I know, he was simply asking me to grab the two cases of beer and another cooler he had in the back of his truck. He had a case of water, too, and some Cokes and Pepsis and stuff like that. My kinda guy.

So we went inside, had a few beers, sat, talked, and joked around. Then he started telling me different things to work on with my putting. My grip pressure. Where I got the ball at my stance. How I needed to widen my stance, and so on. He definitely knew a thing or two about what I needed to do.

As I said earlier in this book, my downfall has always been my putting. It seems like that's always where I struggle the most. It always let's me down. Heck, when I choked at the Honda Classic, it was on a putt. When I started talking and later working with Mike Taylor, though, I built the confidence I'd need to avoid choking like that again.

To this day, Mike's my putting instructor. I can call him up and tell him where I am, and he'll tell me exactly what I need to be doing. I'll call him up, hand the phone to Joe, and I'll stand there as I'm practicing putting. Joe'll say something like, "Yep, that's exactly what he's doing." Mike'll say, "Alright, this is what you need to do, Joe. Put a plug on his head. Make his head lean against it and make him putt it." Crazy stuff like that. Really, it only sounds crazy. It's not actually crazy. It always works, and nothing crazy works like that. Perhaps there's just a fine line between crazy and genius. I don't know. Fine line or not, though, Mike's definitely a genius. I knew it right from the start.

So there I was, staying with him in that house, and he had me willingly adjusting my putting on short notice heading into an important tournament. That's how much of an impact this guy had on me.

That following Tuesday, Brandt Snedeker, Johnson Wagner, their caddies, Scottie and Pepsi, and I teed it up for a practice round. Yes, I said Pepsi. And no, we weren't teeing it off with a bottle of cola. Johnson Wagner's caddy's name's Pepsi. That's the nickname my caddy, Joe, hung on him. Joe has a nickname for everybody. As you know, he calls me all sorts of things, and some of what he calls me doesn't even fit or make sense. But Pepsi's nickname is well earned. He goes out on the golf course and hides Pepsi colas everywhere. If you ever play a course and find an unopened Pepsi, then our boy Pepsi's been there and forgotten about the Pepsi he hid in the azalea bush (or wherever you found it). That guy simply won't drink nothing but Pepsi. He don't drink Gatorade or water. He drinks only Pepsi. It's like he has himself a nice little contract with Pepsi or something. Kind of crazy, really. It's funny as all get out to see Pepsi standing there on the fairway after Johnson's tee shot, and then reaching over in a bush to pull out a Pepsi. Looks like magic.

You might be wondering, *So, how do those Pepsis stay cold? Is that magic, too?* Nah. You see, most tee boxes will have drinks for us like water and Gatorade, and there's ice in there, too. So Pepsi'll get him a big ol' cup of ice and put it in Johnson's bag so his Pepsis in the bush'll be on ice and cold when he gets to 'em.

Then there's Scottie. His nickname is Pippen (obviously after Scottie Pippen, the famous former Chicago Bull). I seriously can't remember Scottie's real last name; we've been calling him Pippen for so long. We call him Pippen because his name is Scottie, of course, but also just 'cause he's bald (he shaves his head), which makes him look like the real Scottie Pippen. I guess you could say he plays the role of Pippen to Brandt's Michael Jordan.

Anyway, enough fun with nicknames and back to that Tuesday's practice round . . . We were done with hole 17 and had walked the fairway through the grove of fine-looking live oak trees. We got to hole 18, the famous finishing hole at Harbour Town. As you approach the green, Calibogue Sound flanks the hole on the left, and the lighthouse is the backdrop.

We were standing on the tee box, and all of us paused for a minute to soak it in, because it is truly a beautiful site to see.

The fairway comes out and makes a big ol' turn toward the water. At about 260 yards, it starts coming back to the right side of the fairway, away from the water. It comes in and makes a little inland sort of thing. It has some more swamp, too, like a mini-wetland down there. The roar of ocean waves slapping the rocky beach adds some racket to what's usually a very quiet final hole on any other course.

I mean, it's just a pretty sight, no two ways about it. No one can look at that and say, "Dang, that's ugly!" Nope, it's beautiful. So there we were, walking off the green, and ol' Johnson Wagner, in his best girly speak, said, "Man, ain't this purty?" We were all thinking it, but you just don't say it out loud.

"Dude, would you shut up?" one of us commanded, even though there's a question mark at the end of that there sentence. "You're sounding *purty* gay. You shouldn't be saying that kind of stuff. You just don't sound right saying that."

"Man, it's gorgeous!" Johnson kept it coming. "This here is beautiful!" So we all started making fun of him, which quickly turned into us all making fun of each other, until we were just a heap of laughing fools. Johnson was right, of course. None of us other guys would admit it, but, like I said, we were all thinking the same thing about how pretty it was out there. Now I'm not sure if any of us thought it in the same girly speak that Johnson said it, but we all definitely thought it was pretty.

After that Tuesday, there was the Pro-Am on Wednesday. I didn't play in it, instead choosing to hit more balls on the driving range and work on my putting. That's really where my mind was at the time. You know, working on my putting game. Thanks to Mike Taylor, of course.

Thursday morning came quickly, and we teed it up and got after it, forgetting the beauty and history surrounding us. All of that was gone, and golf was out front as the tournament started. For me, it was finally time to erase what had happened a few weeks prior at the Honda Classic and play some good golf.

I got off to a good start by making par on the 1st hole and got a huge boost by making eagle on the 2nd hole. I finished out round one with four birdies and two bogeys for a 4-under score of 67 on the par-71 course. I didn't really pay attention at the time, but I was four shots off the lead.

My play on Friday wasn't as good as the day before. I just couldn't pick up the birdies, though I did make eagle on hole 2 for the second consecutive day. I ended the day at a 2 under, 69. Ernie Els had back-to-back 65s and was sitting comfortably in the lead. Six shots back was fine with me, though, because I really liked this course and felt my best golf was still ahead of me.

I think I was in about 9th or 10th place going into the third round (Saturday). Well, in the third round, we had a bad storm come in, with blowing winds of 40–50 miles per hour. It was so bad that it was blowing the sand out of the bunkers and the flags out of the holes, and tree limbs were falling all over the course like it was the Texas Chainsaw Massacre. Pinecones were flying around all over the place, too. It was as if the squirrels were out there trying to compete on the golf course, hitting them pinecones with some serious oomph!

My group was about the fourth to the last group to tee off, so there were guys ahead of us already playing in the storm. The players who got to hole 16 couldn't even keep their balls on the ground. The wind was blowing so hard that the balls kept rolling off the green. I'm not sure why or how, but they ended up finishing that hole anyway and moved on to the next hole, the par-3, 17th hole, which requires a 185-yard shot over water. You'd have had to hit it dead into a 50-mile-per-hour wall of whirling air on that day. How exactly do you do that, you ask? Well, to put it quite simply (which is what I like to do), you just can't.

Finally, one of the PGA officials figured that out and came over to say, "Hey, look, you can't hit it from right here." He was pointing to the tee box.

"You can move us to the very front of this tee box and give us a chance to hit this shot," I suggested. That was the only way I thought it would work.

"Well, we can't do that!" they said, so they went back to blow the horn, which would stop play. When they blow the horn, that means you have to mark your ball, pick up your ball, and you're done until they start it up again. At that point, I'd done played the 1st hole and picked up a birdie. I'd also hit my tee shot on the par-5 2nd hole (which I'd eagled twice already), and I was halfway down on the fairway getting ready to hit my second shot to the green when the horn went off. I marked my ball, got all my stuff, and headed to the clubhouse.

We waited and waited and waited. Waiting on them PGA guys to make a decision is like watching somebody fly-fishing. It takes forever for the PGA to make a decision, because they try to make the right decision for the whole Tour. I understood that, but at the time, it was aggravating having to wait when I was ready to go play. Just like it's aggravating to watch someone fly-fishing when you're ready to head to the woods and hunt.

Finally, the decision came. Play was suspended for that Saturday. After back-to-back 65s, Ernie Els held a three-shot lead.

We came back Sunday and picked up play where the horn had sounded the day before. So I started up on hole 2, where I left off. I was like, *Okay, bam, here we go.* Not sure whether it was the time off or what, but I parred the 2nd hole. Still, I played very well from there. Bogey-free along with five birdies gave me a 66 on that Sunday for my best score of the tournament. When I finished, I was in 6th or 7th place. So I'd moved up like four spots. There were still other scores to come in, of course, so I knew I was likely fixin' to move some more. I felt thankful that Mike Taylor had been there, and I really think he helped me play better in that tournament.

Mike had to go home that Saturday, so he wasn't there with me on Sunday. On Thursday and Friday, he'd followed me around, just checking on me and watching my putting, so he was definitely missed on that Saturday and Sunday. Still, I really appreciated the fact that, when the players Mike was officially coaching had finished for the day, he was willing to tag along with me while I hit practice balls and worked on my putting a little. He was a huge help to me, that's for sure. So much so, in fact, that at the end of the day, when all scores were in, I'd moved into 3rd place. Ernie had shot a 71 and had fallen way back of the leaders. Just shows how things can change on a dime (no pun intended) out there on the course. Thanks, Mike!

Glen Day, Steve Elkington, two other guys, and I went down to someplace just inside the gate, ate there, hung out a while, went back to the house, ate a handful of jelly beans (don't ask me how or why I remember that), and then called it a night. The next morning (Monday), I went out on the course with no expectations at all. Just went out there to play golf. I was looking just to putt the ball the way Mike had been teaching me. I wanted to just hit the ball well. "Let's go play golf" was my simple, matter-of-fact attitude. Of course, just going out there to "play golf" is easier said than done.

I was grouped with Stephen Ames and Zach Johnson (whom I'd seen win the Masters on my TV the week before, remember). Both Stephen and Zach were friends of mine from the Nationwide Tour, so I was relaxed around them. I had a little bit of nerves going again, because I got to thinking way, way ahead of what was fixin' to happen in front of me instead of just staying right where I was and playing each hole.

Of course, when my nerves start acting up, I don't play so well. You already know that (unless you skipped ahead and are reading this chapter first or something), so you should be able to figure that I didn't play well to start that day. I struggled a little bit the first 4 holes (three pars and one birdie), and then all of a sudden, on hole 5 (which I'd handled very well up to that point), I made a long putt for eagle, and I felt like it all turned right then. I thought, *Alright, that's it. Now let's just focus on what we're doing here, Boo! Let's just stay right here in the moment.*

I started playing better, no doubt. I shot a 3 under on the front 9. I headed into the back 9 and birdied hole 10. Then I parred the next five holes. I was at 4 under for the day at that point, carrying a -15 for the tournament.

I looked up and saw that Stephen Leaney was in a group in front of me. I also saw that he and I were tied up top at -15.

Ernie and a couple of other guys were behind us, and the pressure was beginning to build.

I couldn't hit my third shot on hole 15, because it's par 5. The pin was tucked right on the front, and it has a false front on it where the green kinda runs away from the pin. It's sitting on a little ol' plateau, probably 12-feet wide and about 10-feet deep. If the ball lands past the hole about 10 feet, it's going to roll off down into the bottom of the green, which has a little tier in it. I told Joe, "If I make birdie right here, I can go ahead of these guys a little bit." No argument from him.

The wind was still blowing, but not as hard as it was the first three days, so I was okay. I hit my shot up there and spun it off the green. Right away I thought, *Oh no, here we go. Can't do this. Don't do this!* I got myself together, though, and went on up there and hit a nice chip to about 3–4 feet. I knocked it down for par. Not great, but not terrible.

As I walked the 80-yard distance from the back of the green to the next tee box at 16, I could see Stephen Leaney was on the tee box. As soon as he hit his shot, he banged his club on the ground. That's always a good sign if you're the opposing golfer. He'd hit a little pop-up hook. He didn't quite hit it far enough to get it to the corner (a little dog leg left). He left himself about a 175–180-yard shot, which is a pretty tough shot when you're hitting it into a 20-mile-per-hour wind.

I watched as he hit his shot up into that wind, hit a tree, and went out of bounds. I thought, *My oh my, did that just go out of bounds? I reckon it did.* I kept watching, and Stephen hit the next one way right. He ended up making a triple bogey. For the moment, that moved me three shots ahead of him for the lead.

Ernie was still back there behind us plugging away, but I had no idea what he was doing. The last I'd seen, he was at 13 under. I felt pretty good going to the 16th tee box at 15 under. It started to hit me that I was in a position to win this thing. I tried to keep my nerves back and just told myself, *Alright, now let's start focusing on tighter positions where we want the ball to come down.*

I got up there and drove it good off the tee, right down the middle of the fairway. My next shot fell just short of the green. I thought I hit a good chip shot after that, and it rolled about 4 feet beyond the hole. I was thinking, *Alright, now you can make this!* I started thinking about all the help Mike Taylor had given me, and I started feeling confident about my putting.

I hit a solid putt that I thought was the perfect line, and it was going and going . . . and then all of a sudden that wind hit it and just knocked it dead left about six inches from the hole. It hit the lower lip of the hole and spun out. I was like, *Gosh doggit!* So I tapped it in and made bogey.

Now at 14 under, I started to fear that Ernie, Stephen, and a few others could catch me. Stephen was in front of me, and I watched him par hole 17. So I maintained a two-shot lead over him, but I just wasn't sure what was going to happen with Ernie golfing behind me.

I went to hole 17 (which is one I'd parred the first three rounds) and using a 6-iron off the tee, I hit it over the green. I had the perfect line, though. The ball was sitting high. Now, flops ain't my favorite (I mean, that's just not a shot I've really gotten good at; I like to bump and run it around the golf course), and I had an easy chip, but the wind was hollering right behind me. I thought about my strategy a little, saying to myself, *All I've got to do is just lob this thing in there. I ain't got to hit it ten feet in the air. I've got fifteen feet, twenty feet of room to work with. All I've got to do is get this ball on the green, and I can make par.*

It was one of those shots that if the ball didn't go up on the green and end up close to the hole, I was screwed. I knew it. So I hit it, trying to land the ball just barely on the fringe and let the wind push it to the hole, but I flubbed it about 4 feet in front of me. I was pretty pissed. Pretty aggravated, too. Or are pissed and aggravated pretty much the same thing? Anyway, the point is, I wasn't a happy camper. I thought, *You've got to be kidding. I cannot believe you just did that, you stupid son of a gun! I just cannot believe you did that! You stupid . . .*

Then I stopped the stinkin' thinkin' I had going on and simply walked back there just as if I were fixing to hit my first chip. I picked a spot on the green that I felt, if I landed it right, would be close. I took a couple of practice strokes. Then I chipped it.

I landed it right on. I mean, if it'd been a tee, it probably would've landed right on that tee and stopped. It wasn't a tee, though, so when it landed there, it just took off rolling, rolling, and rolling. The wind was pushing it, like I wanted. I mean it just pushed it right along. It came down, took control of that ball, and helped it find its way. I watched it as it just went, plop! Right into the hole.

Joe and I immediately high-fived and hugged. I wasn't sure what else to do, though I felt like hollering. Instead of hollering, though, I went and got the ball. Zach Johnson came over and gave me a high five and said, "How 'bout that, dawg?" I got a bit caught up in the moment, actually, but there really wasn't much time to celebrate (or at least show it). All of a sudden, it was time to go to the next hole. Hole 18. The final hole.

Now, keep in mind that this whole time I didn't know what Ernie was doing behind me. I didn't have a clue. I tried not to think about it too much, but it was just sort of lingering there in the back of my mind.

Well, I got up there on the 18th tee box and turned to Joe and I asked, "Joe, what do we need to do here?"

He was calm. "I want you to hit a five-wood, but I want you to really hit it," he answered without wavering. The wind was just off our left side. "Just hit that five-wood," he said again. "We know it won't get in the water. We know it won't go out of bounds." Out of bounds ran all the way down the right side, so he was right. "So just hit it," he said.

Joe was trying to get me the right club so I could get where I could use a 6-iron on the next shot. The 5-wood was the right club. I went with it and laid it back a little bit farther, just in case the wind switched and pushed it a little more down.

Then I sent it.

It started right at the lighthouse and cut. The wind was pushing it and it pushed it right. It cut just a little more than I wanted. The ball went just into the rough, but it was still sitting fine. So we got there for my second shot, and Joe handed me my 6-iron. I was fixing to get ready to hit it, and I asked Joe, "Where do you want to start this one?"

Joe answered, "Man, we've got plenty of room on the right side to make this chip back onto the green and get us par."

"Well, where do we stand right now?" I asked, not really wanting to know, but needing to know. I was holding my breath.

"You're up by two."

I exhaled and said, "How in the world am I up by two?"

"Let's just focus on this right here, Boo, please!" Joe said, trying to keep everything on track.

"You got it, dawg."

Joe wasn't really in a "dawg" kind of mood. "Just shut up, and let's go," he said, growing tired of the chatter.

"I'll tell you what, we can make par," I said as I took my practice swings. "I can hit this green."

"I don't want you to hit this green, because if you aim at that flag and the wind . . ." The wind was howling in dead off our left and then swirling into us. I was about 190 yards to the pin. "Don't . . . Just listen. Just hit it to the right edge of the pin. Just aim it right about ten or fifteen feet and let the wind push it over here."

"Nah, I think I can get it right of the flag," I responded. So I took a couple of practice strokes and I said, "Well, if I pull this just that little bit, it's going to come up short and in that hazard." I stepped back away from it for a second and took another practice stroke.

"What are you doing?" Joe abruptly asked.

"Man, I just had a bad thought." I told myself before that if I ever had a bad thought, I'd step back.

"The good thought is, hit it right to the right of that pin," Joe said.

I agreed and welcomed that good thought into my head. Hitting it right to the right of that pin's exactly what I did. I hit it up there and let the wind push it over to the right. It was an easy chip. I had about a 15-yard pitch onto the green. I had all the room in the world. Well, not literally all the room in the world, but I had 30–40 feet of green to work with. So all I had to do was pitch it on the green and just let it roll close to the hole and tap it in for par. That was it.

I had a certain spot where I wanted to land it. There was a little ridge right in front of us, and if I landed it on my side of the ridge, it would catch the slope and kind of feed back to the left. I laid out the strategy quickly in my mind. It went something like this: *If I get it to the left side, it just goes straight down grain. It's going to haul butt. I'm going to aim it over here about ten feet right of the pin. Just chip it up. Let it catch that slope, and let it run on down there.*

Then the wind shifted and was blowing into my face, but off to my right a smidgen. I chipped the ball and it got up a little too high. When it got up in the air, the wind hit it, and it knocked it over on the opposite side of where I wanted to land that ball. Well, when it got on that downslope, it just took off, and it ran all the way through the green. The people up there behind me are saying, "Get down. Whoa, whoa, whoa. Ahh, it's done gone in the water!"

I was only about ten feet from the bleachers, and there were people standing up behind me going, "Ahhh, I can't believe that! I can't believe he just chipped it in the water from right here!"

"No, I didn't," I said in denial, looking at Joe. "I didn't just piss this tournament away, too, did I?"

Joe wasn't having it. "Man, you don't know what you've pissed away until we get over there. Now, shut up."

"Dude, I can't believe I just gave it away. Again."

"You shut up, man. You didn't give it away. We ain't done." Joe was defiant.

"Man, it's in the water," I said, in a bit of a pity-party kind of voice. "If it ain't in the water, it's in them rocks."

"Man, the tide's out, and there ain't no water over there, so if it's going to be anywhere down there, it's going to be on the beach."

"Dude, I can't believe I just gave this tournament away," I said again.

"You ain't given it away yet. Shut up!" Joe said, with anger growing. I mean Joe was getting fired up in a way I rarely saw.

We got to walking around there with me nay-saying and Joe telling me to shut up. Sure enough, though, there it was. I saw my ball right there. It was about 6 feet off the fringe, just in the rough, sitting absolutely perfect.

I mean, we'd practiced that shot. That's how perfect it was. That week we'd practiced that same shot on the chipping green. I couldn't believe it. All I had to do was bounce it up and let it hit in a certain spot and roll into the hole.

My negativity was gone. I looked at Joe with a sort of "sorry, man, you were right" kind of look. I said, "Man, this feels good right here." Then I got on up there and chipped it just a little bit. Suddenly the ball's on the green. I'm telling you, it was 2 feet left of the hole. Two whole feet. Then out of nowhere, that wind just started howling again. It was pushing the ball, pushing the ball, pushing the ball, and abruptly the ball turned toward the hole.

Now, when I chipped the ball, I landed it right in that perfect spot. It was going up, and it was about 2 feet just left of the hole, like I said. There's a little break there, but not that much break. It was the wind. The wind just took that ball as if to say, "No, no, not good enough, my man. Here, let me help you out a little bit." You could see the ball slowly starting to turn more and more as it was slowing down. Really, it was like everything was in slow motion. I was just watching it getting closer and closer to the hole. I was in disbelief, thinking, *Oh my gosh,* over and over. Then it happened. The ball got to the hole. It seemed to look down into the hole, maybe checking out how far the drop was going to be. Then it just fell right in.

Boo-yah!

I threw my club into the air. Joe and I hugged (he says I kissed him, but he's lying). It was unbelievable! Even the scant Monday crowd in the bleachers was hollering as loud as the crowd at an Alabama/Auburn football game. It was unreal. I heard chants of "Ahhh, Booooooo!"

We gathered up our stuff and walked to the scoring table. Zach Johnson, Stephen Ames, and their caddies were patting me on the back and congratulating me on my first win. I couldn't believe it. My first freakin' PGA win! A win! A real-life, honest-to-goodness PGA victory!

Then I realized Ernie was still on the course and thought, *Uh-oh.* My negativity started to show its ugly face again. In fairness to me, though, that negativity was well grounded in reality. Ernie is a good golfer. I started asking what Ernie had done on hole 17. Turned out he had been one stroke behind me and then made bogey on 17, which put him two strokes behind me going to 18. He'd have to eagle just to force a playoff.

I was sitting there, and I think it was Steve Sands who said something to me like "Congratulations on your first win." Another guy came up and said, "Don't jinx him. Come on, dude, Ernie's still got a chance to hit this shot." With the roller coaster I'd been on up to that point, I knew better than to think it was over.

Then, all of a sudden, I heard the crowd go, "Ahhh, ahh,

ahhh, ahh!" It was like another big hill on the roller coaster was coming up, just when I thought the ride was ending. I thought to myself, *Okay, what in the world's this? What's going on?* So I had to step out there and look. Ernie had hit it like a foot from the hole. Then I realized it was also about a foot from an eagle. They said it lipped out from going in for the eagle, which would have forced the playoff I so wanted to avoid. That stinkin' close! But, hey, horseshoes and hand grenades. I'd won. It was official.

I hardly had a chance to fully realize what had happened before a reporter came up and asked me, "How does it feel?" I just stared. I couldn't answer. I didn't have a funny comment to throw back. I didn't have anything at all. I didn't know what to feel. I'd never been there before.

Then I just started speaking. "I don't know what to feel," I think I answered. "I've never actually won a big event. It's an awesome feeling from what I'm feeling right now. It ain't sank in yet 'cause I just got done."

I know, I know. Pure eloquence!

Looking back, I'm just amazed to have won the way I did. Chipping in twice back-to-back to win—that's just unheard of. Never happens. Or so I'm told. In fact, I remember a reporter said this about it, "Well, yeah, that is unheard of. I can't remember the last time anybody has ever done it." My immediate retort at the time was, "Well, I can't remember either, but I don't keep up with golf."

After a bit, it started sinking in, and I started having fun with the win. I got on the TV and I was saying hi to Mom and Dad, Karyn and Parker. It was unbelievable. I mean, it was one of the greatest moments in my golfing career. From there on, I kinda just felt like, *Ok, it's on!* Every time I teed it up after that, I felt like, *Man, I can win.* Not that I did win every time, of course, but that attitude helped me play good solid golf the rest of the year. It helped me realize that I belonged.

After that, everything went into a sort of blur again, because I was recognized more. That was a whole new world for me. People phoned me, wanting me to do this, that, and the other. Fans wanted autographs everywhere I went. I started getting stuff in the mail from people for me to sign and return. I was shocked at how much recognition I was getting, because, I mean, dude, it's just a PGA Tour event (that's the way I see it), and I'm just Boo Weekley from Milton.

At the time, it felt great to finally win and get off that roller coaster, of course, but I have to say, it's just golf. It really ain't no different than anyone else going to work and doing the job they're paid to do. I ain't no better than you, and you ain't no better than me. We're all just people trying to get through life. Maybe trying to win or be the best at something a time or two along the way. We all have dreams, and those dreams were meant to be realized—or at least they were meant for us to try to realize them. That's the important part. Trying.

After trying hard, I just happened to realize a dream of mine on that day of my first PGA win. However, I ain't talking about my first PGA win. No, sir. The dream I realized is what the first PGA win got me. You see, with my first PGA victory came an invitation to the 2008 Masters Tournament. I was the first player eligible for the newly reinstated rule that awards all PGA Tour winners during the regular FedEx Cup season an invitation to the next Masters Tournament. Getting to the Masters was the dream I'd had while watching Zach Johnson win it in 2007 on my TV. Getting off my butt and practicing so I could win my first PGA event was how I realized my dream of getting to the Masters. Now that I'd made it, I realized something else. I realized that some other golfer (probably an everyday guy like me) would be out there sitting down in front of his TV set watching me, Boo Weekley, play at Augusta National, and dreaming of one day getting there himself. Well, if that someone was you, I hope you didn't stop there. You have a dream to realize, so I hope you've been practicing. If you haven't been, well, it's never too late. Augusta National truly is a beautiful place. Get off that roller coaster you're on, turn off your TV, and come see for yourself. Trust me, the grass is greener on the other side of your TV set. Literally.

12 OUTTAKES AND SUCH

There're lots of stories from my years as a pro golfer that didn't make it into this book, and I'm including some of them here—which means they made it into this book. Go figure. Anyway, let me jump right into it. I'll start with 2007.

What a great year 2007 was for me as a professional golfer. You've already read a lot about this in previous pages, but there are some things I just can't leave out. Like the World Cup in China.

In 2007 I was selected to go to the World Cup to represent the United States, and I was proud to do it. Still, I'd never been to China. I'd been to Canada and I'd been to Mexico, but that's not exactly world travelin' (though I thought it was at the time). China was a whole 'nuther story. In fact, someone once asked me, "What do you think of China, Boo?" and I answered, "China? I'd just as soon use paper plates."

It was an honor to be able to represent my country for sure. We weren't just playing for ourselves or the money. We were playing for the good ol' U.S. of A. We were playing for our country against twenty-seven other countries, and to me, that meant everything. There was a lot to be proud of as an American. It'd been a long year for our armed forces overseas, fighting the wars in Iraq and Afghanistan. So it was an honor for me to be able to go to China to represent this great land (where so many of us are free to do things such as play golf, thanks to the sacrifices of our men and women in uniform).

In putting together the team to go, the PGA started by asking the number one player in the United States (according to the money list), Tiger Woods. When he declined, they went down the list to Phil, and asked him, "Do you want to go to China to represent the U.S.A. in the World Cup?" Phil declined, too, as did some others on down the line. So they kept going until they reached me.

I was somewhere around the ninth man in line, and they were a little late getting to me, calling me only the week before! Talk about last minute. I was actually deer hunting in the woods when I got the call. The caller ID read PGA, and I declined the call and let it go to my voice mail. (I hate being interrupted while deer hunting, unless it's an emergency.) Later, while I was up in my stand, I listened to my messages. I listened to the message from the PGA. The man said, "Boo Weekley, this is the PGA Tour, and we want to know if you'd be interested in representing your country in the World Cup."

I hung up the phone and dialed that number back right away. My country needed me, and I'd say that qualified as an emergency. They took my call, and I told them, "Yes, sir, I would."

"Great, you get to choose your partner," the man on the

other end of the line revealed. "Do you know whom you'd like to pick?"

Did I know? Heck, yeah, I knew! "Heath Slocum," I answered, without hesitation.

Now, when they said I could pick anyone as my partner, they really meant anyone ranked in the top 100 in the world. Heath was somewhere around 70, so he was my man. I called him up to ask if he'd go. "Man, yeah, I'll go with you in a heartbeat," he said. "This is like our Olympics in golf, to be able to go over to China and represent the United States and play for our country, now that's very special!"

Heath's game and my game match up pretty well. As a team, we each bring a little something. I get a little more distance off the tee than he does. I'd say that, on average, I hit maybe a couple more greens than he does, with my longer irons. Still, Heath's much better at putting. He hits the ball real solid and has a real good short game around the greens. Plus, he drives the ball pretty dang good, too. He hits it in the fairway, which means I'll be able to go ahead, swing a little harder, and try to get the distance.

I was excited I'd be playing for my country, but to play for my country with Heath as my partner? Man, that's where it's at! We knew each other's game very well, and like I said, we complement each other. So I was pretty dang excited. The only problem: It'd been a while since we'd played together, so we were going to need to practice. A lot. The only other problem: We had only a week, and I'd already set up a hunting trip in Illinois, and I wasn't about to back out of that, so practicing a lot was not really in the cards.

I'd been dreaming about going to Illinois to hunt those huge whitetail bucks with those high-scoring racks, more points than you can shake a stick at. Golf is golf, but huntin' is life. My ol' huntin' buddy Ronnie "Cuz" Strickland and one of my right-hand guys and longtime friend Toggy Pace had been planning on going out there, and this was an opportunity not only to hunt, but to hang out with those crazy guys. Plus, the Illinois hunt had been planned way before this World Cup stuff came up. Still, I knew I'd have to try to explain this to Heath.

"Listen dude, seriously, I'm going to be hunting," I attempted to explain. I know, I know, some explanation, huh? "I ain't going to be doing a lot of practicing, a lot of playing golf, and I'll be gone for exactly a week."

Heath totally understood, which I should've figured he'd do, since he's totally cool. "That's fine," he said. "Man, I don't care, dude. It'll just be an honor to be there—and the worse we can make is twenty thousand dollars each. That's last place."

"Okay. Sweet," I said, with a mixture of relief and gratitude. "Thanks, man!"

Though I was going to be huntin' and not playing no golf in Illinois, I wasn't going to completely ignore golf before the World Cup. I played a little prior to leaving for the hunt, just hitting the ball a little. It was hard to do much else with my mind on the hunting trip, but I figured I had to do something.

Then I started packing. I packed all my cold-weather camo clothes, because I knew it'd be cold up there. My two rifles went snuggly in my gun case. Then I stuck a Medic, a heavy club, in my duffel bag so I could swing it while I was up there, just goofing off. I figured when we finished hunting in the mornings and came out of the woods, I could take that golf club and swing it to sort of keep my form up.

I did just that. When we were done hunting and I'd put my rifle back in the gun case, I took that golf club out and stood behind the camp house and hit white oak acorns. I bet those squirrels had a heck of a time finding all them acorns. Must've been hundreds scattered around out there. I just hope I didn't hit any of those little guys in the head. Not that I was really concerned about the squirrels, 'cause they can run so darn fast. Maybe I was just concerned about the camera.

You see, we weren't just hunting up there. We were also shooting the hunt for a Mossy Oak TV series. Cuz Strickland is a horrible one to hunt with while filming, because everything has to be "just right" on camera before I'm allowed to pull the trigger. So that's my excuse for not bringing home any venison (and there's always an excuse for that). Still, we had a good time, and that's the important thing. I have a great relationship with Mossy Oak, so it was real nice to be up there with Toxey Haas (founder of Mossy Oak) shooting (no pun intended) that TV series.

Before I knew it, the trip was over and it was time to head home and get my mind on golf and representing my country in the World Cup. I called up Heath and told him, "I'm flying home. When are you leaving?"

"I'm leaving right now from Atlanta," he said. "I'm fixing to board the airplane right now."

"Well, alright, man, I'm going home now, and JoJo and I'll be on a plane early tomorrow morning." I was getting pumped. "When we get there we'll call you."

"Alright. I don't know if we'll have good cell service over there, but whatever you say."

I got back to Pensacola around nine o'clock Sunday morning and hardly had time to think about how good the hunting trip was. I rearranged and freshened up my bags and went to sleep. I got up at three thirty the next morning and headed out. The plane took off at around six o'clock, and it was a long, long flight, let me tell you. I had plenty of time to think about the hunting trip on that flight. Too much time. We arrived in Hong Kong at 6:00 P.M. the next day.

I don't know what you think about it, but for me, it's pretty remarkable when you take a flight and arrive on another continent the next day without getting off the plane during the trip. That's a *Twilight Zone* experience for guys like me. No monsters on the wings or nothing like that, of course, but it definitely blew my mind.

Now, back before I left for my hunting trip, I had to go get a passport, and with only a week before the World Cup, I had to get one in a hurry. Mind you, I ain't never had a passport and didn't intend on ever getting one, really. After that nightmare in Canada, I told myself, "I ain't never leaving America again." Based on my experience in Canada, I figured any other trip outside the U.S.A. would only turn into a major clusterfuck. However, I just *had* to go for the World Cup.

Joe already had a passport, because he was in the military. My agent, Jimmy Johnston, said he'd talked to a guy in Hong Kong who'd said that all Joe had to have was his visa, but not a working visa. I needed a working visa along with my regular visa, however, because I'd be over there "working." Well, turns out Joe was supposed to have a working visa, too. Uh-oh.

When we got to the Hong Kong airport . . . Oh, wait a second. A sidebar: That airport is the biggest damn airport I've ever been in. It has a mall in it. It literally has a mall up in there. That mother's forever big. It's cool, because you can eat over here, you can go shopping a little bit over there, and you can do something else cool over in another spot. I mean, you can do all kinds of stuff. Okay, back to the story . . .

When we got to the Hong Kong airport, we went to Baggage Claim and picked up our stuff. We were then met by a taxi guy who worked with the golf tournament. He escorted us outside to his car. As we settled into the car, he said, "Let me see your passports." So we showed him the passports, and everything seemed to be in order.

In China they have these little checkpoints where you pull up in your car, and they shoot you with a red laser beam of some sort that takes your temperature to see if you've got a fever. I don't know what they're checking for, but they're checking some stuff, and it felt a little weird. It was like we were in some sci-fi, end-of-days movie or something. The laser shoots the driver, the person in the front, and the person in the backseat.

I reckon we passed the check because they then asked us for our paperwork. So we handed our visas and passports to the cab driver, and he passed them to the attendant at the window, like you do when you pull up with a carload of guys at a McDonald's, with everyone ponying up cash separately. The checker waved us on, and we continued our journey toward Shenzhen, for the OMEGA Mission Hills World Cup.

As we got closer to the town of Shenzhen, however, we came to another freakin' checkpoint. It was kind of like we were crossing over into the rural part of China. This time we had to get out, leaving our bags in the cab, go inside the small shabby building and show our passports and visas, and they were stamped again. The one-room building was crowded with travelers anxious to continue their journeys. Though I'm sure they were as innocent as I was, everyone looked guilty of some horrible crime. We all stood in line awaiting our turns with the steely faced customs agent in the glass booth. While our paperwork was being examined, our driver started walking back to the car, saying he'd pick us up on the backside of the check station. I looked at Joe and said, "Man, I ain't leaving this dude with my bag. He must be crazy." I then turned my attention to the driver and said, "Hold up, I'm going with you."

"You can't go with me," the driver said.

"Well, you ain't taking my bags by yourself." I was thinking, *With my luck, what he's going to do is do a U-turn and haul butt back to Hong Kong to sell my stuff.*

Joe tried to calm me down before I needed too much calming down. "Nah, dude, he's alright, really," Joe assured me of the driver. "He works with the Tour."

"Look, dawg," I said, "we're in a foreign country, and I ain't going to trust nobody." I trusted Joe, though, so I added, "But if you think it's okay—"

"Come on," Joe said, cutting me off. We went inside, got in line, and waited, and waited, and waited some more. As we got to the front of the line, Joe said, "Listen, you go first, so if something happens I'll be on this side with you, okay?" He knows me well.

"Alright, but I don't think anything's going to happen to me, Joe. I'll be fine."

We finally made it to the booth and I handed this guy my documents. He started talking, and of course I couldn't understand a word he said. Suddenly, he barked out something and another guy came over and *bam,* stamped my papers. A guard then walked with me to the other side of the room. I was in! I started thinking, *Alright! We're almost done*—that was, until Joe handed his documents to the dude.

It was around nine o'clock at night, China time—that's about two in the morning back home, and we were tired and ready to get settled in our hotel rooms. I guess that just wasn't meant to be, though. Shortly after Joe handed over his documents, the guy started hollering and hand waving while saying something. "This is all I got, this is all I got," Joe snapped. I wanted to go see what was up and help him, but I had a guard standing right there in front of me making sure I wasn't going nowhere. Then the hollering turned up a few notches, and the guy said something to Joe and then turned and started yelling in my direction. Then all these security cops came running over and got in front of Joe to block him from crossing over to the walkway leading to the street where our car was parked.

Now, you have to understand that my caddie, Joe, is like 6'4". He's a big ol' tall son of a gun, and we're in China, where big ol' tall sons of guns aren't the norm. Joe can put a mean look on you, too, and he was looking down at those dudes like he could just bop 'em on the head. You know, like in Whac-a-Mole.

The Chinese officials were all yelling at once, and I couldn't understand a word of it. Meanwhile, we were trying to find someone who could speak a little bit of English. Just one guy. Finally, some dude came over and told Joe, "You don't have a working visa."

"Well, I've got a visa," Joe replied angrily, "and I'm not working here. I'm coming in here to watch my buddy play golf. I'm not working." They weren't buying that.

Well, none of this sat well with me at all. I done got hotter than a two-dollar pistol. I was ready to pack my stuff up and get on back home. "I'm fixin' to just get on a plane and go on back home," I yelled over at Joe. Seriously, I can't handle that kind of stuff, especially being in another country, 'cause any minute they can lock you up, and then you don't know what's fixin' to happen. Have you ever seen the show *Locked Up Abroad*? Pretty dang scary when you're faced with that possibility, and my mind loves running with possibilities. Well, it went a little beyond mere possibilities when the guards suddenly started shoving me around, and then it was on.

"What are you doing?" I asked repeatedly. "Look. Hold on. Me and that guy right there"—pointing at Joe—"are fixing to get on the phone and make some calls." They just stared at us. So we started pounding the keys on our phones. While Joe tried to get Jimmy on the phone, I dialed the World Cup rules official. We couldn't get anybody, though. Nothing but voice mail.

After some more hand waving and motioning of my intentions, the guards let me walk out to the cab to talk to the driver. "Listen, we've got an issue in here," I told him. "My boy can't get in." I might as well have been talking to the Great Wall of China, because I got nothing from that guy. Zippo. Nada. Uh, I mean, *méi shénme*. I gave up. He couldn't understand a single thing I was saying or gesturing. A guy who spoke English heard me trying to explain, though, and he came up to me and said, "Can I help you?"

"Yeah, you can help me. Damn, you speak English?"

"Yes, I speak English."

"Aw, man, can you come inside with us and explain something to these guys for me?"

The cab driver was yelling, "Hurry up, hurry up, hurry up, we've got to go, we've got to go!" I told my new interpreter friend to tell the cabby to hang on, 'cause we had ourselves a crisis in there.

So, this new English-speaking friend of mine agreed to go inside, and we found out that Joe had to have a working visa to come into this part of China as an American. Somehow, I'd got one (I guess because Jimmy knew I'd be "working" and would need one), but Joe hadn't, as you know.

Finally, Jimmy phoned me back. I answered the call, and he blurted out, "What's going on, dude?"

"We've got a crisis in here," I said, and then explained our situation to him.

"Well, that's what they told me," Jimmy said. "They said Joe just had to have a regular visa."

"Man, I'm telling you they ain't letting us in. They're going to take one of us to jail before this is all said and done."

"Y'all calm down, y'all calm down. Hang on," Jimmy responded, ready to get things back on track. "I'll get a hold of some more people."

"Yeah, that's just what we need, more damn people," I said, pretty irritated at that point by the whole mess.

Somebody else who was part of the Tour finally pulled up, and I could sort of understand his broken English. With his help, the officials worked it out. All Joe had to do was go back to Hong Kong, stay the night, get up the next morning, go to a passport place downstairs in the lobby of the airport, and get a special stamp on his passport that would get him in. The stamp would mean that he was officially there to watch and not work, which was a bit of a fudge. Joe'd say it was a helluva fudge.

Well, I was really crossed up. I figured I'd done gone

down the rabbit hole too far to turn around. I couldn't go back with Joe, 'cause I had a thirty-day working visa. I had to stay in Shenzhen. I got to thinking that the thirty-day working visa meant I had to stay there for thirty damn days.

"Joe, call me later," I said to him as I headed for the cab. "Make sure your phone's charged and call me later."

Joe nodded and then headed back to Hong Kong, and I jumped in the cab and headed to Mission Hills and the hotel where the players were staying. When I got there, I called Heath and told him what was going on.

"Boo, how does this stuff happen only to you?" he asked. I didn't have an answer. "That's alright, dawg," he said. "It'll all work out."

I went to sleep that night imagining how I was going to break Joe out of jail, *Mission: Impossible* style. I finally got some sleep, and the next day Joe called. He said he wouldn't make it until probably three o'clock. He'd run into a little EFP (Everything's a Fuckin' Problem), but he was coming nonetheless.

Sure enough, Joe got to the hotel at three. I wasn't going to let him get out of my sight again. I said, "Man, you're going to stay with me from here on out. Period."

I went up to the desk to check him in and get him a room key. The desk clerk said caddies weren't allowed to stay at that hotel. EFP.

"Well, unbook me out of that room if my caddie can't stay with me," I said, with some disgust in my voice, no doubt. "He's staying with me; he ain't leaving me again."

"Well, we're sorry, but you can't do that," the clerk said, and another argument started. The tournament director came over and got involved at one point.

"Mr. Weekley," she said, "we have another place for the caddies to stay."

"Then I'll stay with the caddies, 'cause I'm not staying here."

"You have to stay here."

"No, I don't. I don't have to stay nowhere. I don't want to stay."

"Well, you're here," she countered.

"Well, then my caddie's staying here. Why does this have to be a big ordeal?" I sometimes don't understand why people do things the way they do.

Finally, after much back-and-forth, we wore them down and they allowed Joe to stay in my room. Like I said when he got to the hotel, he was going to stay with me, period.

Then we were finally off to the golf course. I was never so glad to see a golf course in my life. Heath had seen it the first day. We didn't have a whole lot of daylight left after the argument, but we still played 18 practice holes. We were playing in the tournament the next day, so it was good to get the practice in.

The tournament was set up for two-man teams. Heath and I were Team U.S.A. The first day was a "best ball," where you played your own ball and you took the best score of the two. The second day was "alternate shot," which means if I hit the drive, Heath would hit the second shot, and if it was on the green, I'd putt it, and if I didn't make it, Heath'd finish it out. If I finished the hole, Heath'd tee off the next shot. The third day went back to best-ball play. The fourth day went back to alternate shot.

Heath and I played very well the first round and finished with a 61. That was 11 under, and we led by one stroke over Germany. We tag-teamed 'em pretty well in that first round, playing very solid, both of us. We both hit some squirrelly shots, of course, but we leaned on each other, and that's what team play's all about. I think we both hit the ball fairly straight off the tee, and that's a plus for the two of us. Gravy, if you will.

We played alternate shot the second round and continued our good play, finishing with a 69, which was 3 under. We maintained our lead by one stroke over Scotland and England. As for the strategy for the second day, we sort of had one and we sort of didn't. Back in the practice round, we'd said that I'd play the par 3s and 5s, I'd tee it off on the odd numbers, and Heath'd take the evens. The night before, however, we didn't even talk about the strategy. We had dinner, went and listened to some music, and then returned to the room and slept. We had breakfast together the next morning, but we still didn't discuss our strategy. When we got to the 1st hole, a par 5, I said, "Heath, what do you think?," and he said, "Dawg, you've got it." So, basically, we planned it out, then forgot about the plan, and then acted according to plan anyway. I love it when a plan comes together.

We birdied four of the par 5s, and we should have birdied the other one; I just hit a bad chip. It worked out in our favor, though. We couldn't get our putters in a rhythm. We both hit a bunch of good shots, but we just couldn't putt. I missed one from about three and a half feet. Then Heath missed a couple of decent putts, and I missed another par putt from about 10 feet, but Heath picked us back up with another birdie putt on the following hole.

The crowds and the people were great all week. I actually heard a few in the crowd holler my name. It didn't sound the way it did back home of course, being in Chinese, but they hollered their version of "Boo" nonetheless. I heard it, but I can't pronounce it or spell it out for you here, so you'll just have to trust me.

Saturday wasn't a good day for Team U.S.A. The third round was pretty dang aggravating, to say the least. It seemed that we just couldn't get anything going. Heath hit a lot of good putts, but I really didn't hit so well, at least not to my standards. The greens were tough. The pins were tucked, and it was hard to get it close. I struggled. Heath struggled, too, except for some of the putts. He kind of got down on himself, and then I got down on myself. We both got a little aggravated out there and a little impatient, and that kept feeding itself.

I'd leave Heath stranded or he'd leave me stranded. I'd pull the ball left or push it right. I think Heath said it best when he said we "survived the day." He hit a lot of good putts, true. Unfortunately, hitting a lot of good putts doesn't always mean they go in—and they didn't. The good news, however, is that after Saturday, we were still in first place on the leaderboard. We finished with a 66, which was nowhere near the 61 we'd shot on Thursday's best ball. Still, we led France and Scotland by one stroke. We "survived the day" and still led. So, all in all, we could live with it.

The key to our game was that Heath and I complement each other so well, whether we're hitting it bad or hitting it good. We'll still pick each other up and try to stay focused and positive. Lord knows we wanted to win.

On the last day of the tournament, we were playing well, but we just weren't making our putts. We couldn't even make the putts we were making the first three days. If we'd made the putts we made the first three days, we'd have won by six strokes. As it was, we had a hole where Heath had about a 3-footer to put us up by 2. Well, he missed it. I was like, "Well, that's alright, dawg." Sometimes that's just the way it goes. You go out there and you try, and sometimes it just doesn't fall for ya. My boy just didn't putt well that day.

Heath's one of the best putters on the PGA Tour. For me, he's in the top 10 among the players I've watched putting the ball under pressure on tour. Well, he missed that putt, and it was kind of like watching Reggie Miller miss a free throw. If that guy was missing free throws back in the day, you knew it was just an off day and probably not a good one for the Pacers.

Our strategy for the final round on Sunday was the same as it was during the second round on Friday. I was going to tee off on the par 5s and give Heath a good shot to the green. I wanted to be able to give him an iron or at least a 3-iron to the greens. We knew we had to make some birdies if we were going to have a chance to win.

The problem was, in the alternate-shot format, it all comes down to putting. You have to hit the shots, but at the same time you have to make the putts. I left Heath some tough putts. He was all around the cup all week, but he just couldn't get them to drop in.

In that final Sunday round, the Scottish team of Colin Montgomerie and Marc Warren birdied two of the last three holes to go up by 1. They shot a 6-under 66, which with alternate shot is excellent. So we got down to the last hole, and Heath hit the drive down there, and he looked at me and said, "All you've got to do, Boo, is just put it on the green, and I'll make it, I'll make it."

It felt like a movie. It was like *Hoosiers* or something, with that one guy saying, "I'll make it."

I responded with my customary "Alright, dawg, you got it."

Well, I hit a pretty little 8-iron about 5 feet from the hole. Heath got there, lined it up, and we looked at it together. He said, "I like it right here."

"Pour it in there, baby," I implored. "Pour it on in there just like you're pouring water in a cup. Just pour it in there."

Heath nailed it. Watching him putt was nerve-wracking, because I knew I would've felt that last putt and probably missed it. Sure, it was a short 5-foot putt, but under the kind of pressure that was on Heath, it was a clutch putt. It tied Scotland at 25 under and put us into a playoff. It was like hitting the 3-pointer in basketball to go into overtime. You just gotta get into overtime.

We went inside and signed our scorecards. Now we had to play a playoff with the Scots. We should've won that sucker in regulation, but we'd had our chances and missed. We'd got into overtime, so we were good. Now it was time to focus on the sudden-death playoff.

We started at 18 and would play until one team won. We were still playing alternate-shot format. I hit my first shot right down the middle. Colin hit his way right off the tee and into a bunker. Marc hit his shot into another bunker, short of the green but near the flag. Heath hit it onto the green. Colin hit a fat bunker shot, leaving it about 12 feet to the hole for par, and we thought we had them on the ropes. A miss by Marc would've given us the win, but he got up there and poured it right in. It was unreal. It was a great putt. Just poured it in. Heath missed his 7-foot birdie attempt for the win. Then we made par, forcing another hole. Double overtime.

On the 2nd playoff hole, I barely missed a 20-foot birdie putt, and Marc missed his from 12 feet. We both parred. Triple overtime.

On the 3rd playoff hole, I hit my approach fat and didn't reach the green. Heath's pitch left about a 15-footer. Scotland had a long putt for birdie and left it just short, and Colin tapped it in for par. I faced a 15-foot putt to save par and force another extra hole. Now, that's a long putt.

I sent the ball on its way. It was going, going, going . . . it was not going in. Seriously, I thought I'd made it. I'd given it one of them fist hooks from the bottom of the dirt, I was so sure, but that dang ball turned and just missed. The buzzer sounded. Game over.

We felt disappointed with the way we finished up, but overall it was a great week. We weren't even supposed to have been in the tournament, so that was a bonus. Plus, to finish second (and a close second, one that really could've gone either way) was huge. Besides that, it'd been a good time, a real good time. Something special. Even with Joe's visa issue, it'd been a wonderful experience. Heath had said the worst we could do would be to come in last place and split $40,000, so splitting $800,000 for second place made a great trip even better.

The best part was representing my country. I mean, for real, to be able to do that far outweighed any prize money I could bring home. It was my first time to play for the United States in any event, and it felt good. It felt right. It felt bigger than golf.

The World Cup was the end of 2007 for me and, man,

what a great way to end the season. Not a bad carryover to 2008. Not bad at all.

Now, when I got my Tour card in 2002, I'd had no expectations of what could happen in my life because of the game of golf. Overall, it's been a helluva ride. It's been a crazy ride, one of the craziest, and I'm not even superfamous like Dale Jr., Brett Favre, Tiger, Peyton, and guys like that. I don't know how they deal with it all, I really don't. I mean, they must have zero freedom. They can't go nowhere without getting bombarded. Now I've gotten a taste of what they go through, but I'm nowhere near their level of fame or recognition. Really, I can't even imagine it. In fact, I don't even like trying to imagine it. Fame just ain't my thing.

I think the reason people can come up to me is, in a way, because I don't care. It doesn't bother me or infringe on my privacy at all. I'll talk to just about anybody, because I'm no different from anybody. You know, if I don't want to talk to you, I'll just keep on walking, and if I don't want to talk to you, it won't be because I think I'm better than you or nothing like that. It ain't that I'm trying to be rude; it's just I ain't in the mood to talk or I'm in a hurry to get somewhere. Regardless, I still don't understand why people want my autograph. For whatever reason, my success in 2007 spawned that level of notoriety.

In the past, I used hunting as an escape and used the deer woods as a refuge. After the 2007 golf season, though, I went hunting to cool my heels, I reckon. I hunted a lot, but I didn't retreat to it this time. I'd say I didn't have to go there for sanctuary anymore. In the past, I'd go into the woods and sit high in a tree with nature's beauty all around me, but I'd sit there feeling all sorry for myself, frettin' and worryin'. I think every athlete has experienced that feeling. How many of you've had a coach or even a parent yell at you, "Quit sittin' there feeling sorry for yourself"? Now you know they were right.

Anyway, after the 2007 season, I went hunting more to enjoy the mind-set the woods put me in. The splendor of the woods and its critters, with all of God's creation surrounding me. The good stuff. That environment makes me feel peaceful and alone, which are two things I really like feeling. Hunting is freedom for me. It's discovery of nature and one's self, myself, through my thoughts. I'd go hunting and look back on what happened during 2007 and reflect on my blessings. You can't feel both blessed and sorry for yourself at the same time. The two feelings don't compatabate, so I started focusing on my blessings. No more *woe is me*. Instead, I'd think stuff like, *I had a helluva year. It was awesome. Now what can I do to make it even better?*

Up there in them trees I kinda realized that I did belong as a pro golfer. I realized I was a winner, and no one could take that from me. I knew that I'd worked my ass off to get what I had, and all I had to do was look forward to good times ahead, as long as I believed in what I was doing and what my main focus was. That's my goal: to stay in that moment and focus on what I've got to focus on, whether it's golf, my family, or hunting. Wherever I'm at, I've got to focus on that one thing. If I get to thinking about other things, I'm not really putting my heart and soul in what I'm doing.

Or maybe it was just the money that was putting me in a more "focused" mind-set. I'm just kidding, of course, but there's no avoiding the fact that after the 2007 season, I had a lot more money than I could ever have imagined. I had to think about where I was going to put it all. I spent a lot of time talking with my uncle Jim Young and my banker, Dewayne Bond. We tried to figure out where to put the money so I could retire (which, for me, means hunting and fishing all the time). I set for myself a retirement date. I'll keep that to myself right now, but I'll tell you that the date I have in mind is when I want to be done with golf. We have a plan in place to take care of my family and me, and golf is just a way to get there.

Of course, if I wanted to hit that date and get where I wanted to be in terms of taking care of my family and myself, well, I had to keep playing good golf at least for a time—and as good as 2007 was for me as a golfer, 2008 was even better.

We started the year out in Hawaii. I didn't play any golf at all before I went to Hawaii for the very first tournament of the year, the Mercedes-Benz Championship. That's where all the players who won a PGA Tour event the previous year come together for a tournament. Also, if you've won the Mercedes-Benz Championship in any year in the past, you automatically get to come back.

I knew that this tournament would be a lot more fun than most, because I was taking Karyn and my little boy, Parker. They hadn't come to a lot of my tournaments in the past; it was kinda hard to get Parker out of school, and we usually didn't even try messin' with that. I can't wait until he gets a little older so he can come with me and really be a part of it. He'll be able to walk the golf course with me instead of having to go to day care while I play. Don't get me wrong, he has fun with the other kids in day care, but I'd much rather have him out there with me on the course. I want him outside enjoying the outdoors, and I want to spend time with him, plain and simple.

I knew if I could get him and Karyn over there to Hawaii with me, we'd have a good time. So I told Parker, "Look, we're going to miss a little bit of school. The first couple of days after Christmas break, you're going to miss, but you're going to come with me, to Hawaii. You ain't never been to Hawaii, boy."

I also took Karyn's mom and dad, my mamma, and my cousins Tyler and Curvy. Well, doggies, it was like *The Clampetts Take on Hawaii*. It was more like a family trip for me than a golf tournament, and I didn't even pretend I was there to win. I told Joe, "My goal is not to finish dead last." Well, I didn't. I finished 23rd.

I shot 80 the first day. Then I shot like 74 or something. I was falling about six numbers every time I teed it up, so I started steadily getting better just by playing. The next day I shot 68. Then I shot 66 the last day. It was nice to improve day by day, heading into the next tournament.

The next tournament was the Sony Open in Waikiki. Unfortunately, my improvement did not continue, and I missed the cut. I played next in the Bob Hope Chrysler Classic and played well there, finishing 8th. Then I went to Torrey Pines for the Buick Invitational. I played well there, too. I love that course. It's right on the Pacific Ocean—and I mean actually *on* it. One of the holes runs right out into the ocean, with a dropoff of over 100 feet straight down to the water. The cliff is high enough that people jump off and hang glide there. The course sets up the way I like to hit it. It's pretty long. The greens are usually good, but they're a little beaten up. The grass on them greens is awful.

I went through there and played decent. After the second round, I was in second place behind Tiger. But a 77 on the final round pushed me down to 19th. It was as if my solid play had decided to grab a hang glider and jump off that cliff.

The really good thing about 2008, though, was that it came after 2006 and 2007. You see, I'd done grown up and learned a lot from all my gallivanting in 2006, followed by my divorce in early '07. So I didn't do a whole lot of off-the-course ramblin' in '08. I hardly left my hotel room, in fact. I went to bed early. My caddie, Joe, would go out and party a little, and I lived vicariously through him. What he was doing, I was kind of wishing I was doing, but I wasn't doing it because I was all grown up and remembered my responsibilities back home, and I always tried to keep my mind on them. I'd think, *My wife isn't out partying back home, so why should I be out partying here?*

It's hard not to get caught up in that lifestyle, though, because we pro golfers have the perfect opportunity to go out every night and party. It can be easy to justify, too. You know what, though? You can have a good time without doing anything wrong. You can go out and visit with other players and the caddies, have a couple of beers, eat dinner, have a couple more beers, and go to bed.

In 2008 (and beyond), I was usually "home" by nine or ten if I had a late tee time. If I had an early tee time, I was usually home by eight thirty or nine. I'd try to be asleep, shutting everything off by ten, the time at which I know I can get me a good eight hours of sleep.

The rest of 2008 was good. I got to play in the Masters that year, which, as you know, was a dream come true for this country boy. It's a neat place with its history and all. I mean, it ain't my favorite golf course, because some of the holes just aren't built right, in my opinion. They keep adding to it, too, making it longer. I think they're trying to Tiger-proof the dang thing. It's being converted for him and all those other superstar long hitters.

I'm not saying I'm a short hitter or a long hitter. That's not the point. The point is, no matter what type of hitter I am, it just isn't fair that they're building these golf courses now where the greens aren't built for us to hit a 5-iron or a 6-iron. They're built to hit 7-irons, 8-irons, and 9-irons. The longer your iron, the lower the ball flies. The shorter your iron—going from your sand wedge, the shortest side putter in your bag, to your 3-iron or 4-iron—the harder it is to get the ball in the air, whether it's me or other guys.

That said, I really enjoyed participating in the Masters. The best part was having my family and friends there to watch and support me. Family and friends are always the best part these days.

I also got to play in the World Golf Championships in 2008. This is where the top 50 ranked golfers in the world have their own separate tournament. They have four of them a year, and I got to play in all four in 2008, which was a huge honor for me.

You see, when I got my Tour card in '02, I was ranked like 798th in the world. By the end of '07, I was ranked 47th in the world. During '08, I was ranked as high as 37th in the world. I feel I've done pretty well in my short time.

One of the WGCs was like a match play: You went out and played another player. It'd been so long since I'd played in a match play event that I'd forgotten the rules. We were seeded like an NCAA basketball tourney. Number one played the last ranked player and so on. I was ranked 47th, and I played a European player named Martin Kaymer.

We were playing the 1st hole, a par 5. I hit it down there in 2. He hit it just short of the bunker. He banked it up on the green. I was on the green, too. I put it up there and had a putt from about 3 feet. Martin had a putt for birdie, a little bit farther than mine. Well, he missed it. He left it a little farther than a gimme tap-in. I stood there looking at him like, *Well, are you going to putt that or what?* He looked at me, and I'm kinda thinking, *What are you doing?* I didn't say it, but I was looking at him and thinking, *Well, what* are *you doing? Are you going to finish that? I mean, I can't give it to you.* It was all in my eyes.

Joe came up to me and said, "Just tell him it's good. Pick it up."

"You can't do that," I said, looking at Joe as if he'd lost his mind. "He's got to putt it out."

"Not in match play, son," Joe reminded me. "Not in match play. You can tell him it's good, and he can pick it up."

"Oh," I said, embarrassed that I hadn't remembered.

It was too late, though. Martin finally went ahead and tapped it in.

I made my putt and then walked over to him. I said, "Man, I'm sorry. I apologize. I forgot. I didn't know the rules there. That won't happen again." It kinda pissed him off, of course, but at the same time, those foreigners can be just a wee bit touchy. Still, hey, I seriously didn't know. From there on, I didn't make that mistake again, so I hope I proved it to Martin.

In that same tournament, I was matched against Sergio Garcia. Sergio and I had already had a spill one time. In 2007, at the PGA Championship, we were paired on Saturday, in the third round of the tournament.

We had finished up on 18, as we always do, and were walking into the scoring trailer to sign our scorecards. Well, Sergio had missed three putts. He wasn't playing well, and I think he was mad 'cause I'd just beaten his brains in. I'd just given him an ass whooping on the golf course, his style. So he wasn't in a very good mood. In fact, he was steamed.

We were sitting there signing our scorecards, and I'd written the wrong number in the column on hole 17. I'd given him a 4 instead of a 5. Well, instead of noticing the error, he signed his scorecard and—like I said, he was aggravated—then stood up, tossed the card toward the official, turned, and walked out. My caddie, Joe, always comes in and reads the numbers out to me, and I check them with mine. Then I check mine again, and if I think they're right, I'll hand the card to the official.

Sergio was standing right outside the door putting some stuff in his bag, putting balls away or whatever he was doing. Well, the official who was reading Sergio's scorecard said, "Something isn't adding up right. His score is one stroke off—too low."

"Well, I must've messed up on a hole," I said.

"Well, where's Sergio?" the official asked.

"He's right out there," I answered. "Hold on. I'll grab him."

Well, Sergio wasn't out there, so I hollered, "Sergio!"

He was at the very top of the stairs. I'd say it's about a 40-foot walk up them stairs. I shouted, "Hey, come back down here. Your scorecard ain't right." He just kept right on walking. Maybe he couldn't hear me, I don't know.

I ran back in and told the official, "Hey, hang on and let me go get him. He's up there at the top of the stairs talking to some people. Let me go get him."

"It's too late," the official said.

"What do you mean it's too late?" I asked.

Joe was standing right there, so he took off up the stairs, grabbed Sergio, and brought him back down to the scoring trailer. When he came in I said, "Sergio, I put a four, but in fact you had a five on seventeen."

"That just puts the icing on the cake," he said to me.

He turned and started talking to the official and the official is like, "Well, it's too late. You left the signing area." Which is true; once you leave the area, it doesn't matter what happens. There's nothing you can do then. That's why I always double-check my scorecard.

I'm so caught up in my stuff, I really don't focus on another player's score. I'm caught up in mine and what I'm supposed to be doing. So that day, I hadn't kept up with Sergio's score. I just wrote in what I believed he'd gotten. It happens out there more than anybody will know. It happens all the time.

Well, Sergio got disqualified from the tournament because I'd written the wrong score in there. The media made it look bad, too, as if it were my fault. The truth of the matter is that it wasn't my fault, because it isn't my responsibility to check the card to make sure it's right. All I'm supposed to do is write numbers in. I could write 9 in all across the card. If that's not right, it's the other player's responsibility to make sure it's right.

Sergio was in a bad mood anyway because he'd just shot a 75. Well, he got even madder. He'd thrown his card down and walked out. It ain't my fault he did that. He should've been a little more responsible about what he had going on in front of him instead of being a tootie little baby and walking out in a big ol' huff.

Anyway, he went on his way and got DQ'd. Of course, here come the media. They were like a pack of hungry huntin' dogs; they made such a big deal out of it. They did that for the same reason they do most things: They wanted something sensational to report, to get attention. This was a major distraction for me, because at the time, I'd just played one of the best rounds of golf of my life. I almost broke the course record during a major. If I'd birdied the last hole, I would've broken the record: the lowest round ever in that major. I had a pretty tough putt. Still, I 3-putted it. Not good, but I finished with a 65. Of course, I had no idea during the round that my round could've been the lowest in the history of the PGA Championship.

So they called me into the media room, and then it happened. The press always start out real gentle, with the questions like "Did you know with that last putt you could've been the only man ever to shoot sixty-three in the PGA Championship?" (What they'd forgotten was that Tiger shot a 63 in round two the day before.)

"I sure didn't. I didn't know that."

"Really?"

"No, I didn't know that. Every one of y'all has asked me the same kind of question over the last two years. Y'all know I don't keep up with golf. Now, is there another question?"

"Well, what were you thinking on eighteen?" one reporter asked.

"Well, what I was thinking was trying to two-putt it, and what did I end up doing? I three-putted it. That's how much I was thinking, that all I want is to two-putt it instead of trying to make the putt for a record."

Another reporter shouted out a question: "Well, what do

you think about tomorrow's round? Do you think you've got a chance of being in contention?"

"Do I have a chance?" I asked rhetorically. "Am I in contention now?"

"Yeah," someone meekly answered.

"Well, I'm sitting here in fourth place, so yeah, I have a chance." Now they'd gotten under my skin with their questions. Then came the question that ripped my skin off.

"What do you think about what you did to Sergio?"

"What do you mean what I did to Sergio?"

"Well, you gave Sergio the incorrect score on his card."

"I did. I wrote the wrong number down on seventeen. You're right, I did."

"Well, how do you feel about that?"

"I don't feel no different than if it was Heath Slocum I did it to. Heath Slocum's got enough sense to stand there and make sure it's correct."

"Oh, so you don't like Sergio?"

"No, sir. I didn't say I didn't like Sergio." I really wasn't saying I didn't like Sergio. I was just saying I like Heath Slocum. He's my buddy, and I was just saying I wouldn't have felt bad about it even if I'd done it to Heath, because I hadn't done nothing wrong (and anyway, Heath would've caught the mistake). I continued, "What I'm saying is this is our job. We are supposed to take responsibility for checking our scorecard, making sure our scorecard's correct. You cannot rely on the other person to make sure it's correct. This is your score. This is what you turn in."

"Well, how did you do that?" one reporter pressed.

"It happens all the time, guys. If you go and ask every player out here how many times somebody has written the wrong score in, I guarantee you every player will say the same thing: 'I have at least once.' All Sergio had to do was erase the wrong number and write in the right number and put his initials by it. That's all he had to do."

Still, the questions kept coming: "Do you think Sergio is mad at you?"

"I hope he's not mad at me, because I hope he has enough sense to know that it ain't my responsibility for his card."

The next day the media had a field day with the whole thing. They wrote or said things like "Don't let Boo Weekley do your taxes," and "Boo isn't good at arithmetic," and something about my needing "a lesson in math."

Anyway, as soon as I was done with my interview, Sergio came into the media room. Then the press replayed everything I'd said about him. I went into the locker room. When Sergio finished his interview he caught me in the locker room, pulled me off to the side, and said, "Hey, listen, you don't need to speak for me. You need to speak for yourself. You don't need to be worried about what I need to be worried about. You need to be worried about you."

"That's all I'm worried about, Sergio," I said, thinking he should've been worried about his own dang scorecard. "Is there a problem here?"

"I just don't want you talking about me behind my back. If you're going to talk about me, you talk to me to my face."

"What did I say behind your back, Sergio? I told them what just happened. If you're not man enough to stand up and say, 'Hey, I made the mistake,' you don't need to blame me for it. If you do, then you're the biggest titty baby on this tour. Grow up a little bit and understand what's going on."

Sergio needed to hear that, but he didn't like it much. I

know he didn't like it because he responded by saying, "Fuck you, Boo!"

"Dude, there's no need for that," I said, more relaxed than I might've been a few years earlier.

"You don't need to be talking about me," he said one last time. Those were the last words said between us for a long while. Nowadays we'll say "hey" to one another and "hey, how you doing?" Stuff like that. We won't have a conversation or nothing, though. Fine by me, really. I don't have nothing to say to him. I think that to this day he blames me for his problems.

Now, granted, he was young at the time. Twenty-seven, I think. I mean, I understand. I've been in his shoes. I think he understands now that it's not that I don't care, because I'm going to say what I want, what's on my mind. That's just who I am. You make me mad, and I'm going to tell you I'm mad. Still, for me, all that is over. I can't speak for Sergio. He made that clear.

Notwithstanding that little incident, my cup overflowed, really, in 2008. I won the Verizon Heritage for the second straight year. On Sunday, as I approached the 18th fairway, the gallery started chanting, "Booooo! Booooo!" Still, as Yogi Berra (not Yogi Bear) once said, "It ain't over till it's over." I still had one more hole to play. I'd been there before and I lost it on that final hole. However, I knew it'd take a major meltdown for me to lose. I was as nervous as a teenager on his first date. My nerves showed as I bogeyed 18, but I still won by three strokes.

In 2007, I had to have back-to-back chip-ins on 17 and 18 to maintain my lead, but I didn't get to stand in front of the crowd and do the fist pump back then. As you know, there'd been more players behind me in '07, and I'd had to wait on them. In particular, I had to wait for Ernie Els to finish before I knew I'd won. I got to do the fist pump and more in '08, though. Anthony Kim and I were the last group, so when I completed hole 18, I knew I was the champion. I gave the thumbs-up, bowed to the crowd, and then threw both hands up in victory. Heck, I wanted to do the moonwalk and the belly roll, too. I just thought I'd cut the crowd a break and spare them the sight.

It was an awesome feeling to successfully defend my title at the Verizon Heritage, but I won something else during that tournament week. Steve Spurrier, head football coach at the University of South Carolina, was supposed to play in the Pro-Am tournament on Wednesday, but he backed out. So I called the tournament director and asked, "Is there any way my mom can play with me in the Pro-Am?" He said since Steve Spurrier had backed out, she could play.

Well, my mom and I won the Pro-Am, and we got to do it as a team. She won it with me. Then I got to turn around and defend my title. What a special week, and to be around all of those super nice people at the Verizon was like Heaven (a Heaven without any deer hunting, but a heaven nonetheless). The people who run the Verizon love that tournament, and it shows in the way it's run and organized.

What more can I say about the Ryder Cup? Maybe you should just go back and reread the Ryder Cup chapter of this book. I reckon my successes of 2007 and the first part of '08 were overshadowed somewhat by the Ryder Cup and what happened there. There's no question that tournament was my true breakout moment. Seems like I play my best golf when I'm playing for the good ol' U.S. of A. I mean, we had six rookies, including me, and we still went out there and skinned us some Euros.

Sometimes when it's quiet, when I first lie down at night, just before I fall asleep, I reflect on those enormous crowds at the Ryder Cup and the chants of "Boo-S-A, Boo-S-A, Boo-S-A," "Red, White, and Boo," "Boo's the man," "BOOOOOOO!" More important than those cheers for me, though, was my opportunity to represent my country. I think about that honor all the time and am very grateful for that and the opportunities I've been given.

I finished out 2008 by participating in the Shark Shoot-out and the Chevron World Challenge. J. B. Holmes and I teamed up at the Shark Shootout and finished 2nd. I finished 9th at the Chevron to close out a winning 2008. Then I went hunting. Let me tell you, that's even better than ending a year with the World Cup.

The start of the 2009 season was very promising. A top-20 finish in the Mercedes-Benz Championship followed by a top-10 in the Sony Open kick-started my season. Both tournaments were in Hawaii, and I was able to take my family to enjoy the beauty of the islands once again.

I won a nice chunk of change ($95,000) in the WGC-Accenture Match Play Championship, but I wasn't satisfied with my play. I began to think that something was about to change with my game. Well, my prognosticatin' turned out to be prophetic, I suppose.

The first signs that I was struggling with my game flashed like neon in the next five tournaments. I couldn't break the top 50, and what's worse, I missed the cut at the Masters. Finally, I arrived at the Verizon Heritage in one piece. Hilton Head was like going home. Having won it the past two years gave me the encouragement I needed—and buddy, I needed the confidence boost like a drunkard needs wine.

Boost or not, though, no one was going to catch Brian Gay. He blew everybody away with his -20, and won by 10 strokes. I finished at -5 for a tie for 13th. I played much better and took home a nice reward ($95,000). A couple more top-20 finishes followed, and I was feeling good about myself again.

So I was playing what I call steady golf, but not up to my own standards or potential. Still, there was a lot more golf ahead, and I was by no means panicking. I'd been gone from home thirteen straight weeks and really needed a break.

Then came the PLAYERS Championship at Sawgrass. "The fifth major," as some call it. This big, big tournament carries a lot of prestige and is one I enjoy playing for sure. I started out playing fairly well, although I shot a 73 the first round. I came back on Friday (the second round) and shot a 5 under 67 and moved into the top 10. My mojo was returning, and I was getting all motivized again.

With a top 10 clearly in my crosshairs, I entered the third round with high expectations. I started off pretty well, then started pressing and paying too much attention to what was going on in front of me. I know, it's easy to say, "Well, don't do that!" Kinda like telling the doctor, "Doc, it hurts when I do this," and the doctor says, "Well, don't do that, dumbass," but you're doing it for a while before you realize what's happening. I hit a shot way right on hole 4 and had an awkward lie-up on the hillside. I walked up, assessed the shot, and struck the ball. Immediately I felt a stinging pain in my left shoulder. I knew I was done, but the competitor in me pushed on. I double-bogeyed hole 4 as my shoulder continued to hurt.

I limped through the next five holes either bogeying or doubling three of those. I kept on keepin' on and fighting as hard as I could, and when I parred hole 10, I thought I could at least finish. When I got to hole 11 and topped it—which is unheard of for me—I knew it was over. I told Joe that was it. He tried to talk me into playing on and finishing the tourney, just to stay in the money. He and I got into an intense argument about it on the fairway, actually. Finally I told him, "If that's the way you feel, you can go find another player to caddy for." It was my decision, and I withdrew.

I understood Joe, though. He and I are both extremely competitive and want to play it out, play hard, and finish strong. There was just no way I could do it that day, though. Turned out I wasn't just done for that day. In essence my season was over. I'd torn the labrum (the cartilage that helps promote movement of the shoulder) in my left shoulder.

I'm not one to throw in the towel, of course, especially with my family and friends from all over Mississippi, Alabama, and Florida there to watch me. My coauthor on this book, Paul Brown, and our editor from St. Martin's, Marc Resnick, were on hand there with me, too. I was playing for all of them, really. I mean, that's how I saw it.

The doctor ordered rest and hit me with an injection of cortisone. Six weeks later, I attempted to come back at the St. Jude Classic in Memphis, but I didn't make the cut. Now, I missed it by only one stroke, but this was a tournament I'd played well in before. I tried it at the U.S. Open the next week, shot an 11 over in just two rounds, but missed the cut by a Jay, Florida, country mile. That's a long way, baby.

I suppose my injured shoulder affected me more mentally than physically. It's like a kid who hurts his leg and won't walk on it even when it doesn't hurt anymore because he thinks it will (or that it'll get worse). It didn't really hurt that bad; it was just aggravating. I have to be honest: I was a little afraid of hurting it worse and having to have season-ending surgery.

I worked on my shoulder with an at-home exercise program, trying to nurse it back to health so I could keep playing, but it never really healed properly. I don't think I actually gave it enough time to mend. I played in eight more events in 2009 and made every cut, but struggled in most. My best finish was a tie for 13th in the (British) Open Championship. I thought I had a real chance to win that thing, but a 3 putt on hole 17 on the last day did me in. If I'd parred it and then parred hole 18 (which I did), it would've given me a top-7 finish and an exemption for the 2010 Open. Instead, I missed the Open in 2010.

I hollered "calf rope" [I surrender] on September 7 after the Deutsche Bank Championship, where I finished tied for 54th. Then I hung up the spikes, grabbed my camouflage and tree stand, and headed for the healing powers of the woods. I took off four months to rest my shoulder and my mind, hunting at home, in Illinois, and in Texas. Didn't do much else, really, though I did participate in two off-season tournaments at the end of 2009. I won the ADT Skills Challenge in October at the Breakers in Palm Beach, Florida, with partner Brandt Snedeker, and finished 8th in the Shark Shootout in December at the Tiburón Golf Club at the Ritz-Carlton Golf Resort, Naples, Florida, with partner Graeme McDowell.

When I hurt my shoulder, I was something like 43rd in the world. Because I'd missed so many events or hadn't finished very well, when I started 2010 I was like 118th in the world, which knocked me out of all the majors, the match play, and the big tournaments. Many of those events were guaranteed money, so it hurt more than my shoulder, if you know what I mean. I got to play in only one of those big events in 2010, the Bridgestone Invitational at the Firestone Country Club in Akron, Ohio.

I was in contention a few times early in the season, but I just couldn't catch a break. Then I started struggling with over-par Sundays. I think it's a mental thing, where I put too much pressure on myself to play over my head—to make myself go out and shoot 66, 65, the last day, to jump back up in there where I feel I belong. When I do that, it puts more pressure on my shoulder to do something it ain't supposed to do or ain't ready to do—and the dominos fall.

I work out two to five times a week, so I'm in pretty good shape now. I've even lost 10 pounds. Granted, I need to work on this here gut for sure. Fatigue's not a factor, but the first three letters of "fatigue" could be from time to time. I mean, I get tired out there just like everybody else, but I usually have the energy to finish the round. I talk to a lot of guys out there who're having foot, knee, back, or shoulder issues, and they are taking pain meds—serious medication. I'm just not that type of person. I'll take the anti-inflammatory pills, but that's about it. I can't see going out there and playing golf all drugged up. Now, I'm not saying there are a lot of players walking around all doped up. Just saying I ain't one of 'em.

By the spring of 2010, I was playing pretty good golf, finishing 12th at the Verizon, 10th at the Zurich, and 9th at the Crowne Plaza. I also tied my career best Tour round of 63 twice at the Crowne Plaza and the John Deere. Then I hit a summer slump. Still, I'm feeling better now. I'm getting there—and I'm looking forward to what the future holds.

So what does the future hold for ol' Boo? More big events? More wins? More good huntin' and fishin'? Another book, perhaps? Who knows? I can tell you one thing for sure. The future for Boo Weekley will be worth following, so stay tuned. If you do, I promise I'll stay true.

ACKNOWLEDGMENTS
Boo Weekley

A special thanks to my agent, Jimmy Johnston of Crown Sports Management, for working with all concerned to make this book a reality.

Thanks to my editor, Marc Resnick, for meeting with me and having enthusiasm for my story.

Thanks to Ronnie "Cuz" Strickland for getting the ball rolling on this book, and for his companionship outdoors.

To my coauthor, Paul Brown, for chasing me all over the country to get my story and for his faith, support, and friendship.

Literary agent Craig Wiley hooked up the deal with St. Martin's, and I'm forever grateful for that. He worked closely with my agent, Jimmy Johnston, to handle all of the negotiations between my publisher, my writer, and me.

ACKNOWLEDGMENTS

Paul Brown

I have many people to acknowledge for their contributions to the writing of this book. It's been a genuine pleasure to work with each of them. To Boo Weekley for putting up with me and my microphones and tape recorders, which malfunctioned more often than not, and for answering my countless questions whether redundant, sensitive, or just plain stupid.

Thanks to my editor, Marc Resnick, and the extraordinary team at St. Martin's. Marc met with Boo and me at TPC Sawgrass and mapped out a plan of action for the writing of this book. Marc was a joy to work with from the start.

Many thanks to Ronnie "Cuz" Strickland for introducing me to Boo, and for his friendship over the years.

A special thanks to Boo's agent, Jimmy Johnston of Crown Sports Management, for working closely with my agent, Craig Wiley, and me on the contracts with Boo and St. Martin's.

Thanks to Boo's wonderful family and many friends I've

met along the way. There're too many to name without missing one or two, but each was helpful in his or her own way.

Accolades go out to Heath Slocum for writing the foreword and sharing Boo stories.

I'm grateful to Janet Watkins for her assistance transcribing many of the tapes.

I'd like to give special recognition to my agent and friend Craig Wiley of the Craig Wiley Agency. He was enthusiastic about this project from the beginning, and it found a home at such a great publisher because of him. Craig went well above and beyond the call of duty for this book. His feedback, ideas, and help during the writing were invaluable. We make a good team, and I look forward to working with him for years to come.